POSTCARD HISTORY SERIES

Eufaula and Barbour County in Vintage Postcards

POSTCARD HISTORY SERIES

Eufaula and Barbour County in Vintage Postcards

Eufaula/Barbour County Chamber of Commerce and the Eufaula Heritage Association

ARCADIA PUBLISHING

ISBN 978-0-7385-1595-3

Published by Arcadia Publishing
Charleston, South Carolina

Printed in the United States of America

Library of Congress Catalog Card Number: 2003111362

For all general information contact Arcadia Publishing at:
Telephone 843-853-2070
Fax 843-853-0044
E-mail sales@arcadiapublishing.com
For customer service and orders:
Toll-Free 1-888-313-2665

Visit us on the Internet at www.arcadiapublishing.com

Contents

ACKNOWLEDGMENTS

While putting this book together, the Heritage Committee relied heavily on the research of those before us. We would like to acknowledge the works used in creating this postcard book. They are as follows: *History of Eufaula, Alabama 1930*, Eugenia Persons Smartt; *Backtracking in Barbour County*, Anne Kendrick Walker; *Along Broad Street,* Robert Flewellan; *A Eufaula Album—A Pictorial History of Eufaula, AL,* Joel P. Smith; and *The Heritage of Barbour County, Alabama,* The Barbour County Heritage Book Committee.

Many of the postcards used in this work were published by only a few businesses. To J.H. Whitlock Jewelry Store, J.D. Schaub & Company, and Earl Roberts Studio we owe an enormous amount of gratitude for giving us the subjects we had to work with.

Last, but certainly not least, a special thank you to all those who shared their private collections with us. We were stewards of these precious reminders of the past, and we are forever grateful for your assistance and patience.

The Heritage Committee members who worked on this project were Paige Green, Beth Morton, Doug Purcell, Dawn Thomas, Sherri Walker, and Calvin Wingo.

INTRODUCTION

Eufaula was created about 1823 when the first white settlers began building on land then in Creek Indian Territory. In 1832 Barbour County was formed with Clayton as the county seat. By 1877, Eufaula, the largest city in the county, had a branch courthouse. Barbour County is in southeast Alabama and borders on the Chattahoochee River to the east, which is the boundary between Alabama and Georgia. Columbus, Georgia, is 45 miles north of Eufaula and Dothan, Alabama, is 55 miles south of Eufaula. Barbour County has a rich and distinguished history centered on, in its early decades, growing and cultivating cotton and, in more recent years, peanuts, soybeans, corn, and other row crops. Eufaula and other communities also have a small, but growing, industrial base.

A group called the Eufaula Regency helped lead Alabama out of the Union during the early days of the Civil War. At the close of the war, as Federal troops were advancing on Montgomery, the capital of the state and the cradle of the Confederacy, all constitutional officers of the state were ordered to move with haste to Eufaula where they were to reassemble to conduct state business. However, the war came to a swift conclusion and the state government resumed its work in Montgomery. One of Alabama's Civil War governors was John Gill Shorter of Eufaula. In fact, he was the first of eight governors produced by the county, which is by far more than any other county in the state.

With the formation of Lake Eufaula/George in the early 1960s, the City of Eufaula began to attract more light industry, and tourism became a major contributor to the local economy. In 1965 the Eufaula Heritage Association sponsored the first historic home tour (the Eufaula Pilgrimage) in the State of Alabama, which annually attracts thousands of visitors to the city each spring and throughout the year. Clayton has also hosted historic home tours to capitalize on the rich architectural treasures that remain in that town. The Seth Lore and Irwinton Historic Districts in Eufaula have over 700 buildings listed on the National Register of Historic Places. Other Alabama cities rely heavily on advice from Eufaula historians and preservationists to help with home tours and other similar events in their historic districts.

Eufaula and Barbour County in Vintage Postcards will hopefully be an introduction or reminder of what a unique and wonderful place this area is. Steeped in history, Barbour County continues to look to its future without forgetting its past. Enjoy!

One

Life Views

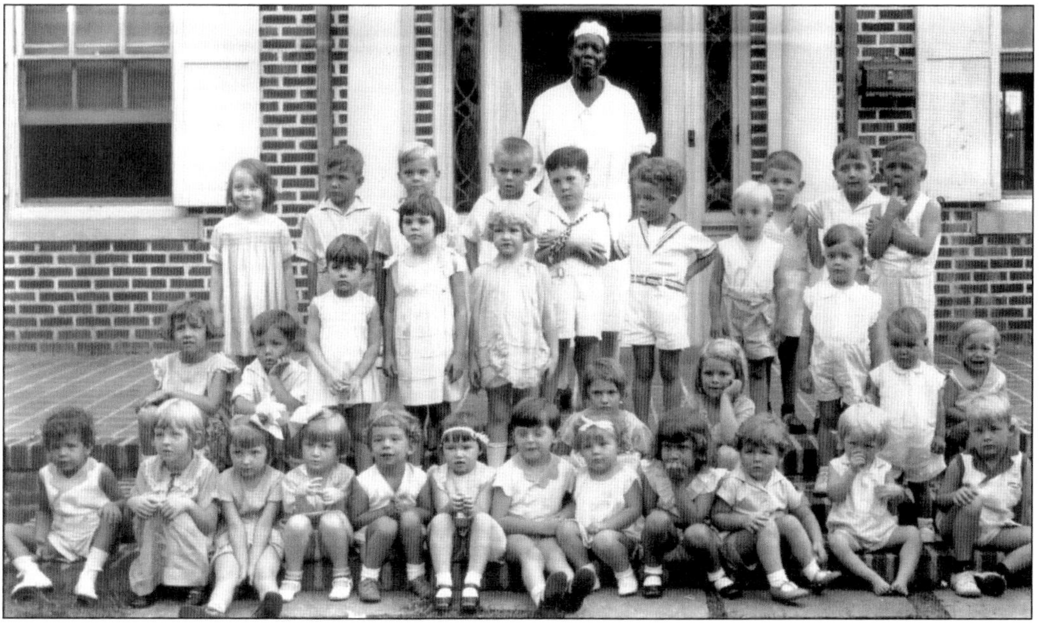

In 1929 children gather for the fourth birthday party of Terese Merrill at the home of Mr. W.H. Merrill on Eufaula Avenue. Mr. W.H. Merrill was on the first board of directors of the Eufaula Country Club and was an original stockholder of the Tribune Publishing Company. (Courtesy of Tade Lampley.)

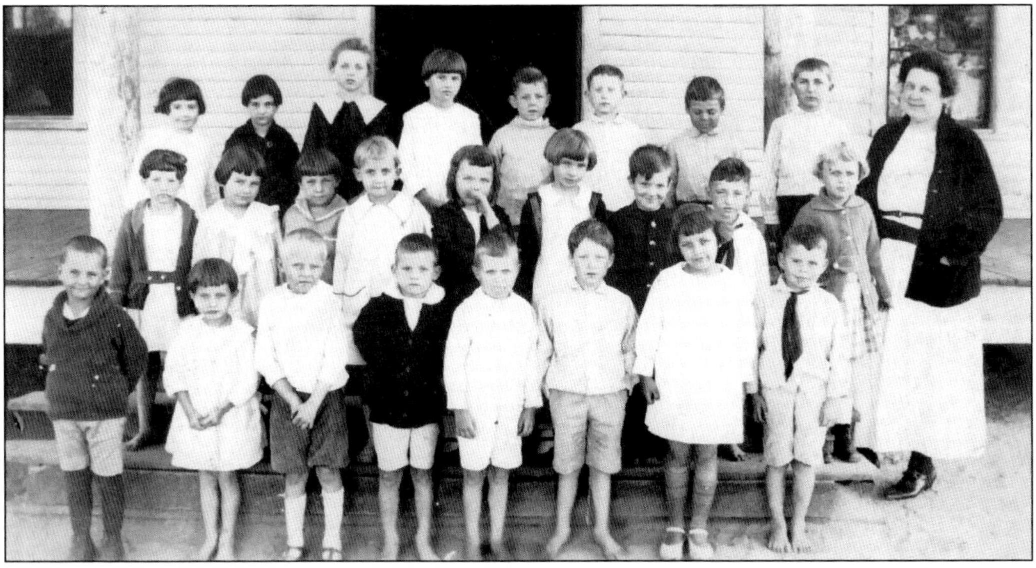

Mrs. Maude Wright's first and second grade in 1921, pictured from left to right, are (front row) Max ?, Emma Floyd, Edward Nix, James Johns, Huck Fenn, Huey Lee, Catherine Teal, and Milbourn Senad; (middle row) Louise Hulen, Alice Street Robertson, Jessie Mae Clark, Margaret Floyd, Janice Baker, Gladys Nix, Davie Napier, Harry Menkoff, and Bertie Gamell; (back row) Mary Neil Ventress, Sarah Stevens ?, Emma Boyd, ? Hagler, Charles West, Edgar Bowden, Jack Teal, Murray Seay, and Mrs S.J. Wright. (Courtesy of Rebecca Beasley.)

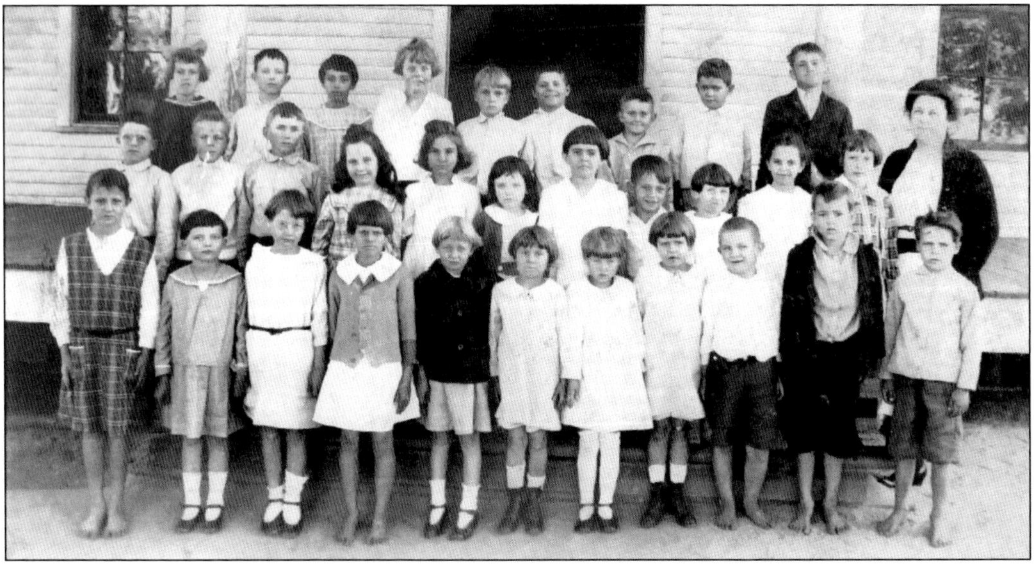

Pictured from left to right are (front row) Willie Mae Gann, Alice Bowden, Allie Mae Baker, Elizabeth Scheffer, Sara Stevens, Sara Ellen Martin, Alice White, Imogene Martin, Walter Bracewell, Knox Win, and Enoch Kennedy; (middle row) Quinn Laseter, Edgar Kennedy, unknown, Ethel Cox, unknown, Frances Jones, Lucile Warr, Page Floyd, Lillian Ventress, Stella Leigh White, Willie Pearle Gammell, and Mrs. Maude Wright (teacher); (back row) Audrey Kennedy, Edgar Bowden, Estelle Snead, Maggie Mae Hall, Thad Floyd Jr., Edgar Quillen, James Scroggins, Harmon Stevens, and Wyatt Maddox. (Courtesy of Rebecca Beasley.)

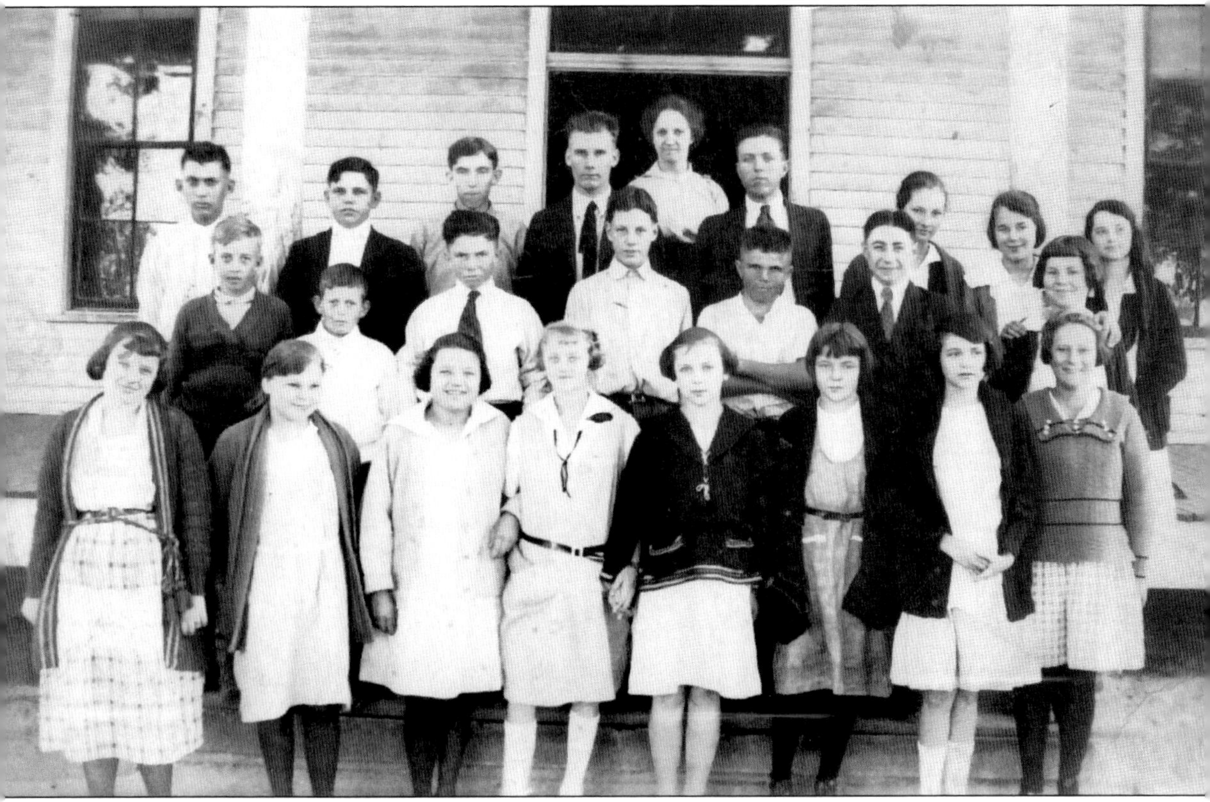

A building on South Midway Street in Clayton housed grades one through eleven. Though the date of this postcard is unknown, many in this group made up the graduating class of 1924. Pictured from left to right are (front row) Grace Brooks, Margaret (Maggie) Searcy, Emmie Lou Clark, Eugenia Fenn, Lucile West, Mary Winn, Mildred Martin, and Rosa Norton; (middle row) Tolbert White, William Kennedy, Jack Lasiter, Tom Parish, Welton (Tony) Lasiter, Clifton Feagin, and Lucy Quillen; (back row) Harvey Zorn, Frank Harrison, Levy Gann, Homer Walker ?, Edward Tew, Julia Hightower, Louise Hudson, and Nettie Bowden. Mrs. India McRae, the teacher, is standing in the doorway. (Courtesy of Rebecca Beasley.)

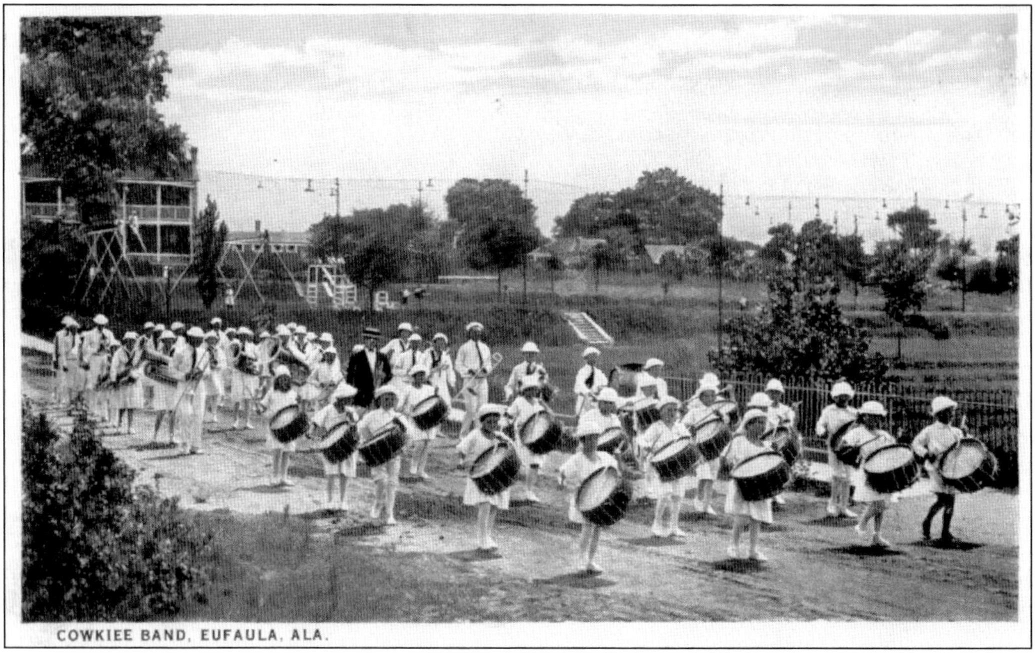

Cowikee Mills, in Eufaula, was owned and operated by several generations of the Comer family. As employers, the Comers not only sought to provide fair wages and good working conditions but also improved housing and the community for their workers. A Cowikee Mills Band—along with baseball teams, a camp, social clubs, and college scholarships—was among the many generous things the family made available to their workers. There was a mill-owned "Community House" on South Eufaula Street and a playground where social functions were held. Notice the band marching next to the "Community House" and playground. (Top postcard courtesy of Tade Lampley; bottom courtesy of Hank Johnson.)

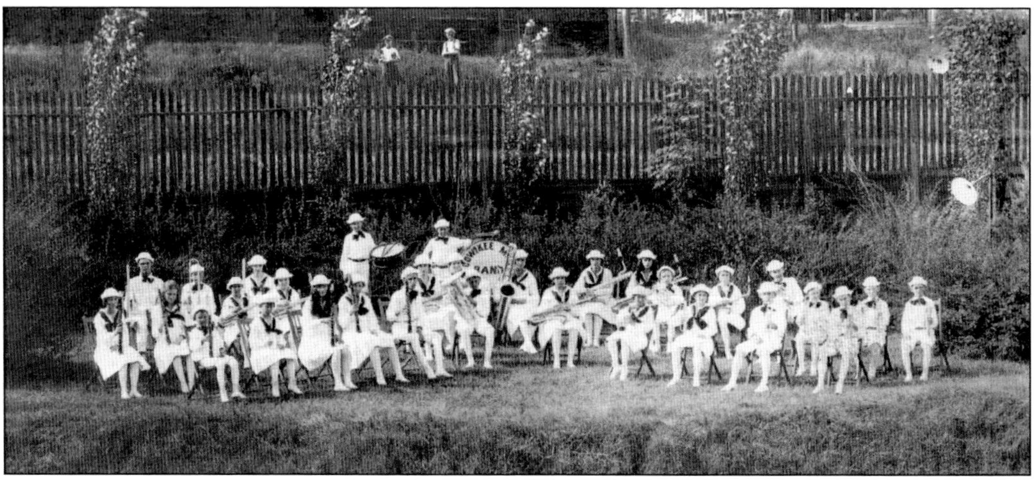

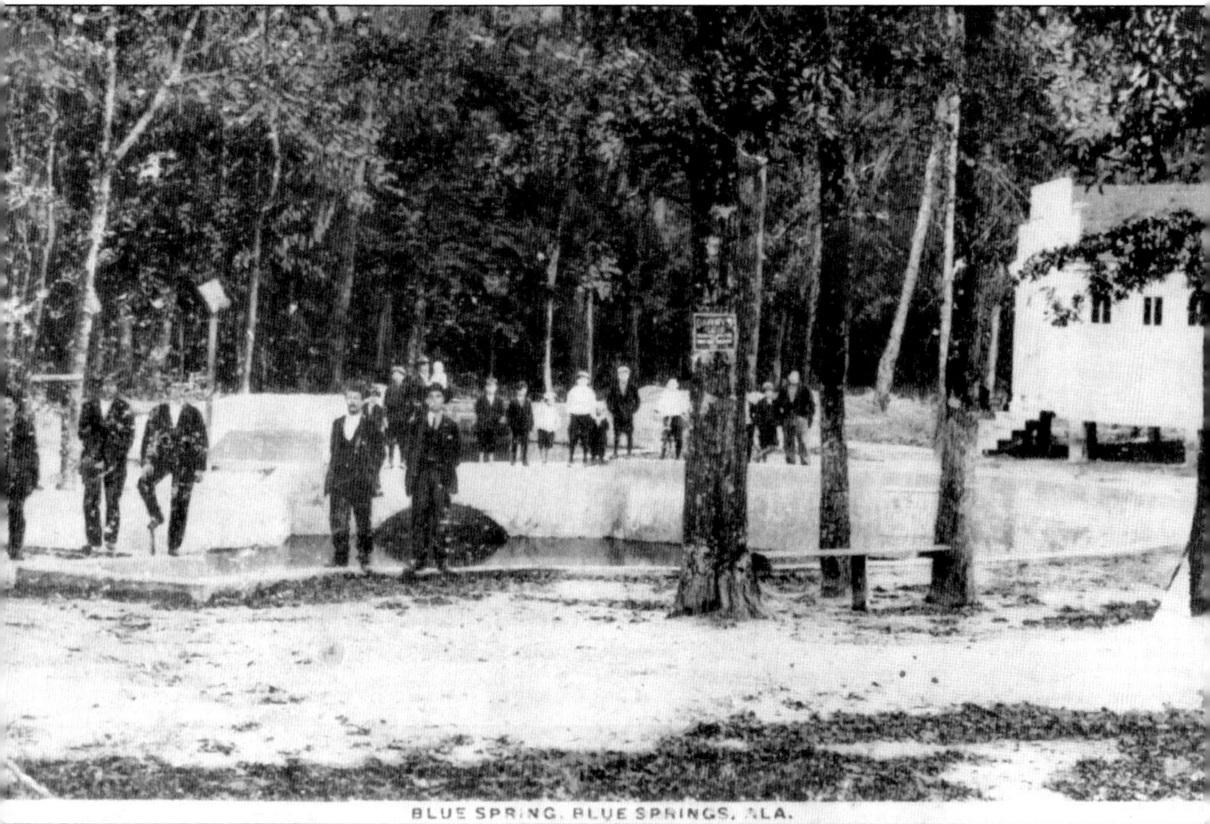

Discovered in 1845, Blue Springs was a popular, turn-of-the-century tourist destination. George W. Harrison built a hotel with a dining hall and dance pavilion at the resort area. Today, Blue Springs is one of Alabama's state parks. The main attraction is still the 58-degree, year-round natural spring. (Courtesy of Comer Hagler.)

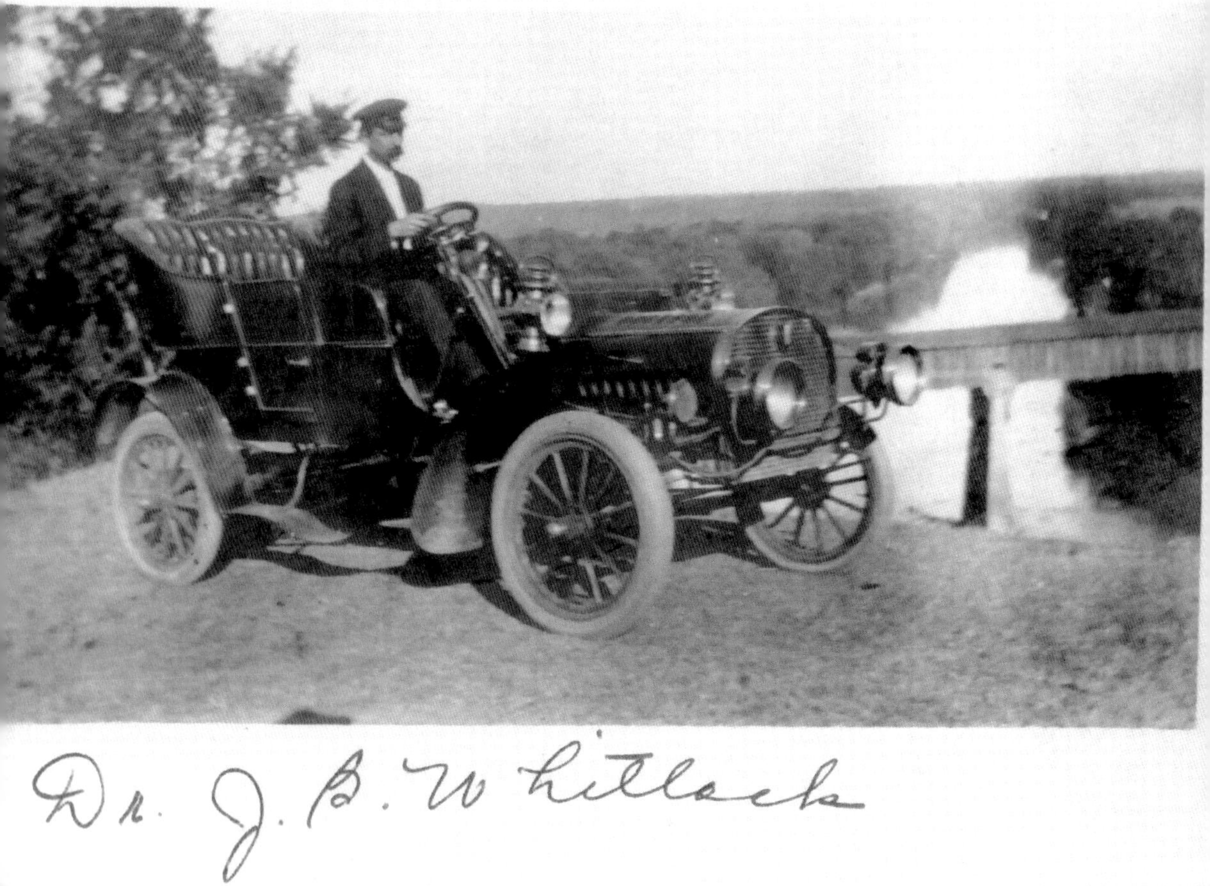

Born in Eufaula on February 5, 1867, Dr. John B. Whitlock, optometrist, was one of the community's leading citizens during his lifetime. He was president of the Carnegie Library Board of Trustees and an organizer of the chamber of commerce, the Bank of Eufaula, the Eufaula Bank and Trust Company, and the Kiwanis Club. He was a charter member of B.P.O. Elks, Commercial Club, and the Eufaula Country Club. (Courtesy of Rob Schaffeld.)

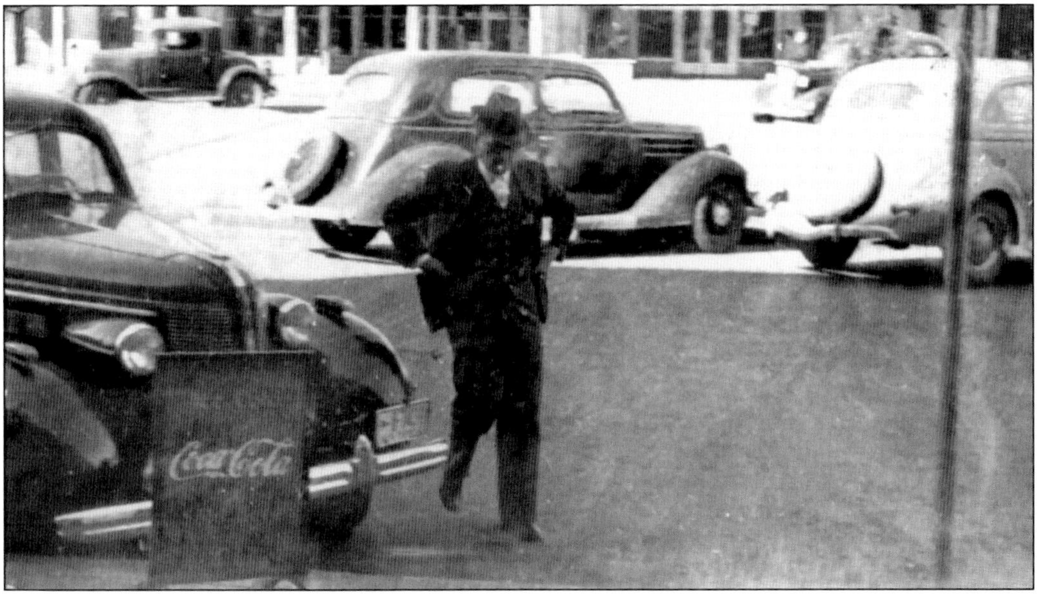

Nothing is known of the man featured on this postcard, but the automobiles date the card to the 1940s. The Coca-Cola sign gives the impression that he may be downtown entering a drug store or other place of business. (Courtesy of Rob Schaffeld.)

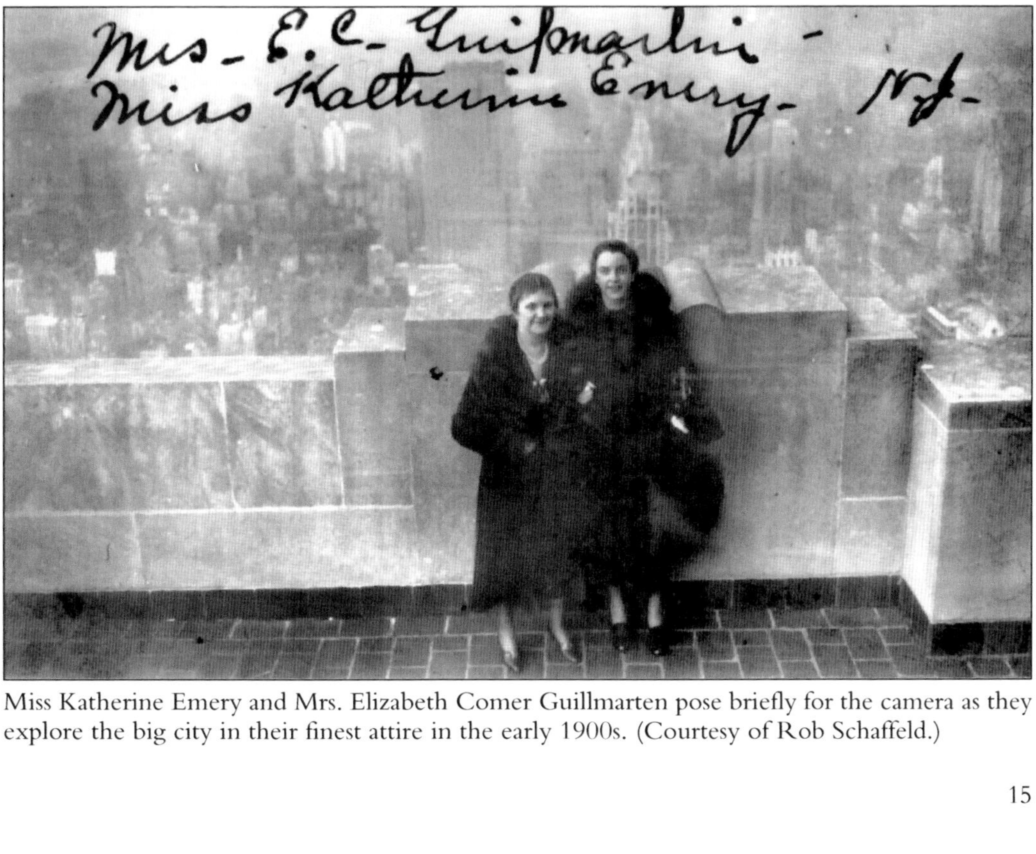

Miss Katherine Emery and Mrs. Elizabeth Comer Guillmarten pose briefly for the camera as they explore the big city in their finest attire in the early 1900s. (Courtesy of Rob Schaffeld.)

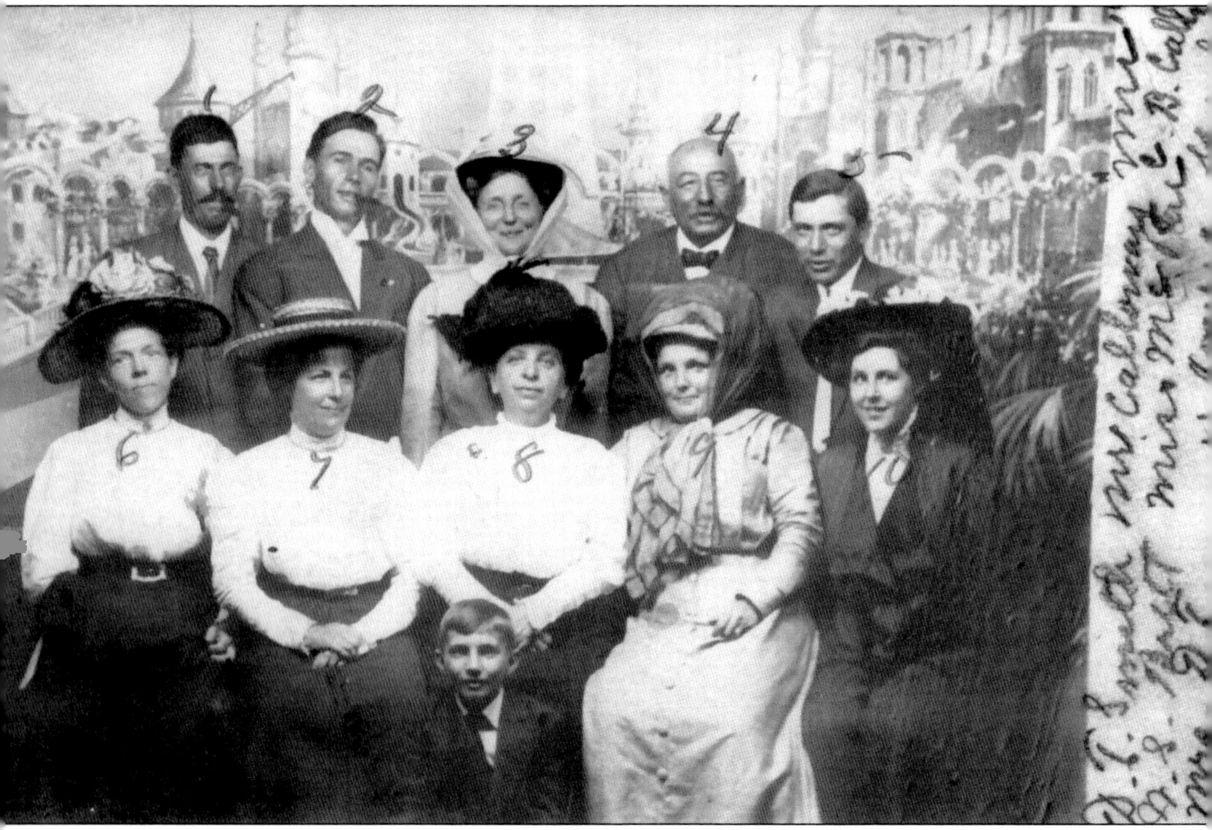

Ten local citizens and a young boy posed in their best clothing in this late 1800s portrait postcard. Notice the two men on the top left with cigars in their mouths. Many of the names listed for this postcard are illegible, but some of the last names include Smith, Callaway, Britt, McRae, and Couric. (Courtesy of Rob Schaffeld.)

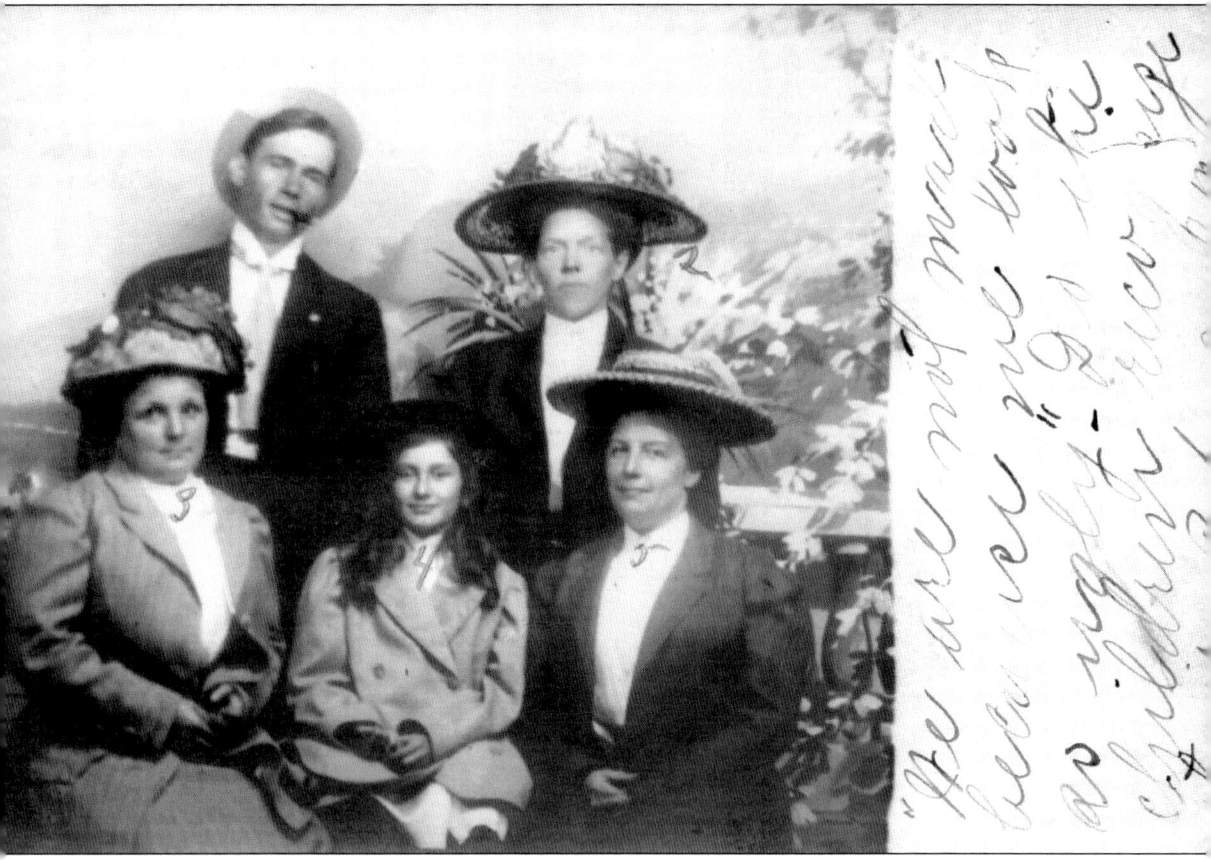

This formal portrait taken in the late 1880s shows five local citizens. The inscription reads, "We are not mad because we look so ugly. Do the children recognize their Papa and Mama?" (Courtesy of Rob Schaffeld.)

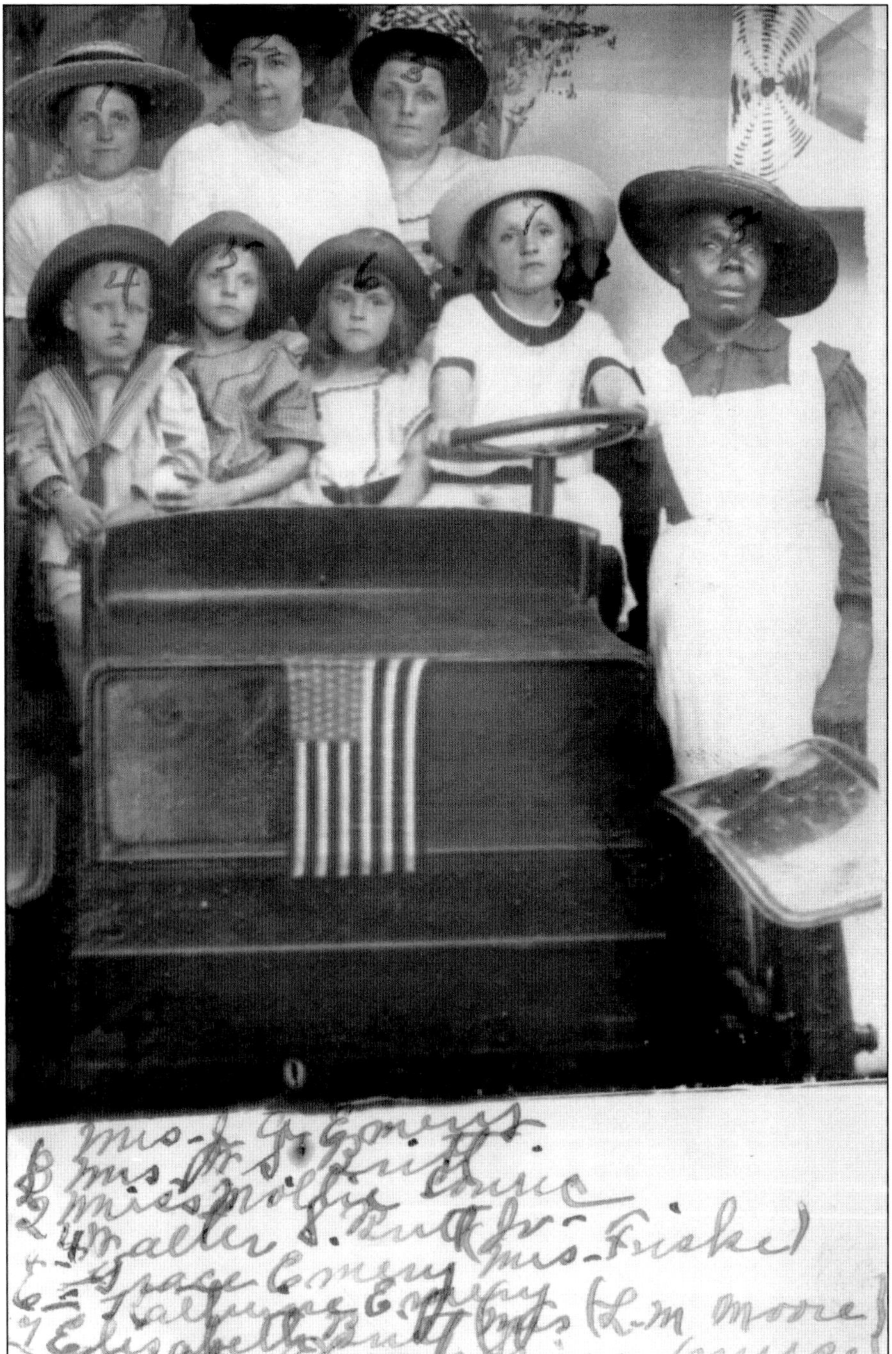

This early 1900s card portrays four youngsters, three young ladies, and a nursemaid dressed in their Sunday finest. Nursemaids were an important part of the social fabric and family household of the time. Though all the names listed on the postcard are not legible, some are as follows: Mrs. J.A. Emery, Miss Mollie Couric, Mrs. W.S. Britt, Walter S. Britt Jr., Miss Elizabeth Britt, and L.M. Moore, nurse. (Courtesy of Rob Schaffeld.)

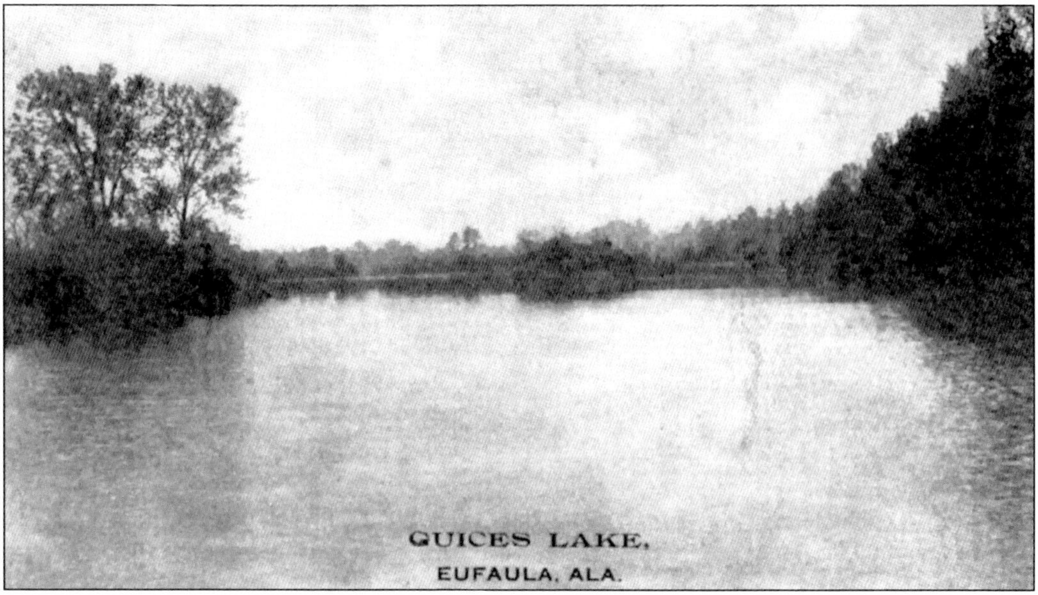

Very little is known or written about Guice's Lake; however, it was known to be in the area just southeast of downtown Eufaula near the Moulthrop property. There was a brickyard near the lake. Guice's Lake is no longer in existence. When the U.S. Corps of Engineers backed up the water of the Chattahoochee River to form Lake Eufaula/Walter F. George in the early 1960s, Guice's Lake was consumed. (Top postcard courtesy of Rob Schaffeld; bottom courtesy of Doug Purcell.)

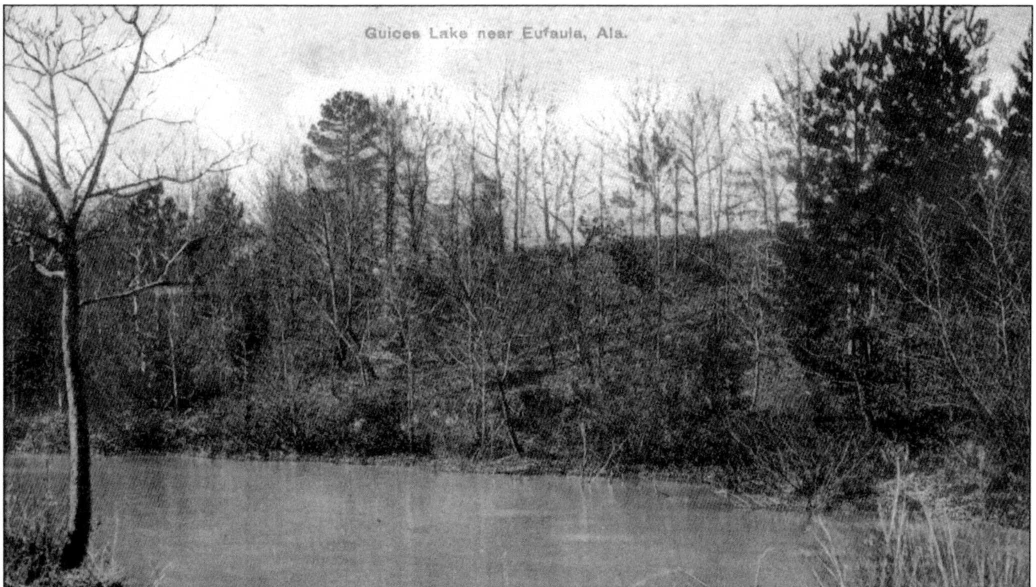

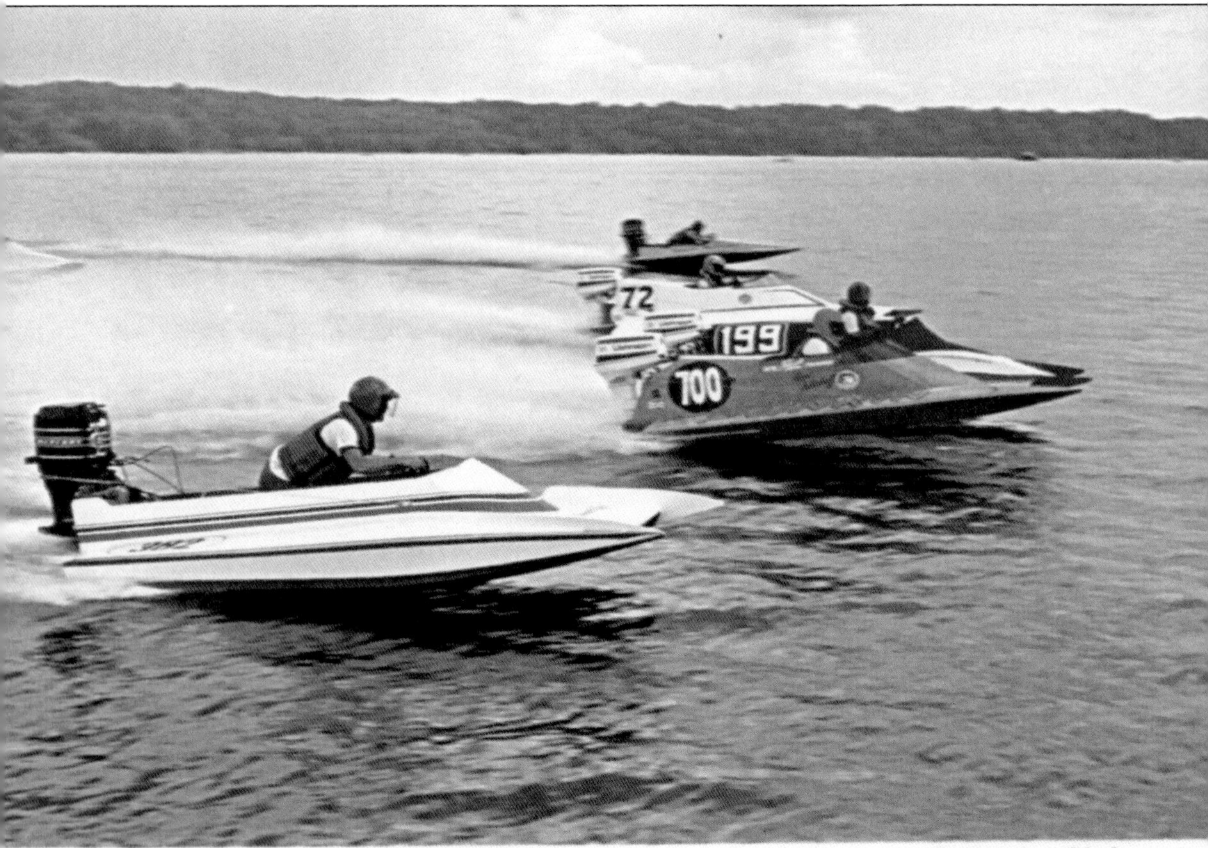

.ake Eufaula Summer Spectacular **Eufaula, Alabama**

The Lake Eufaula Summer Spectacular featured American Power Boat Association (APBA)-sanctioned, outboard performance-class, closed-course national championship boat races. Often called the "Daytona 500" of powerboat racing, this event attracted approximately 200 competitors racing before more than 25,000 spectators. The boat races were held throughout the 1970s and into the early 1980s. (Courtesy of Doug Purcell.)

Two

STREET SCENES

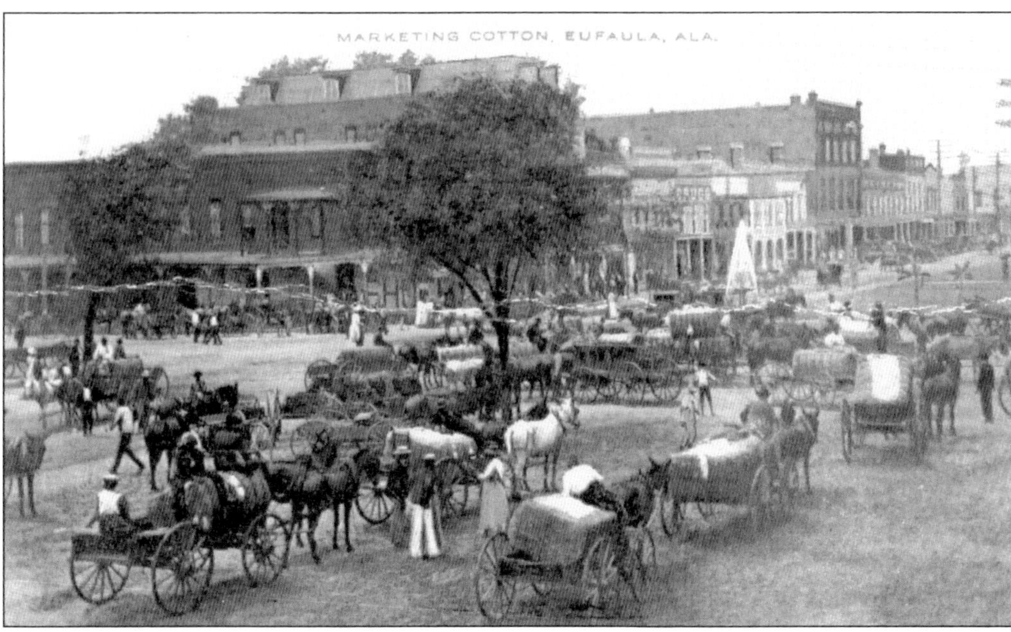

Published by J.D. Schaub & Co., this card depicts the importance of the area's cotton trade on the downtown businesses. In 1912, wagon traffic was heavy as farmers brought their goods to town and shopped with merchants. (Courtesy of Rob Schaffeld.)

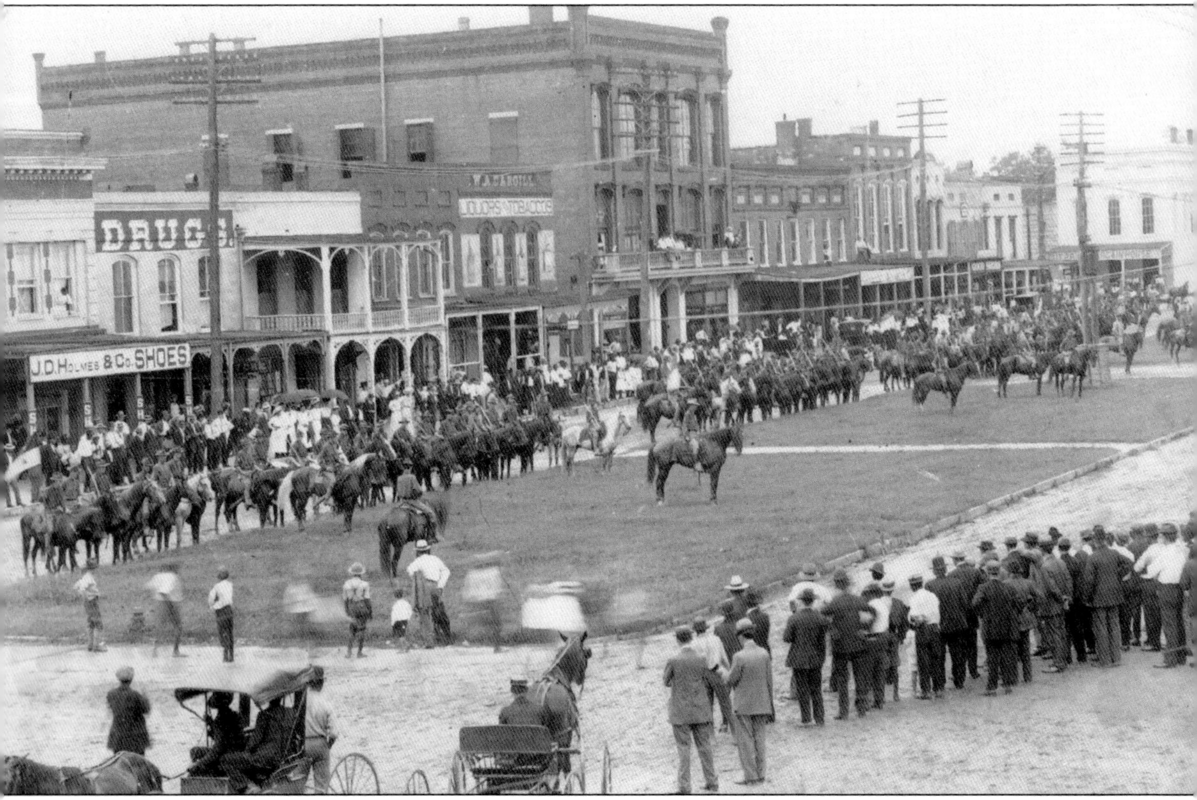

Citizens gather along Broad Street to watch a military reenactment. Dozens of men on horseback bearing swords enthrall the crowd. Prominent businesses of this time were the J.D. Homes & Co. shoe store and the St. Elmo Saloon, operated by W.A. Cargill, once proclaimed "a first class establishment, unsurpassed in the South." (Courtesy of Rob Schaffeld.)

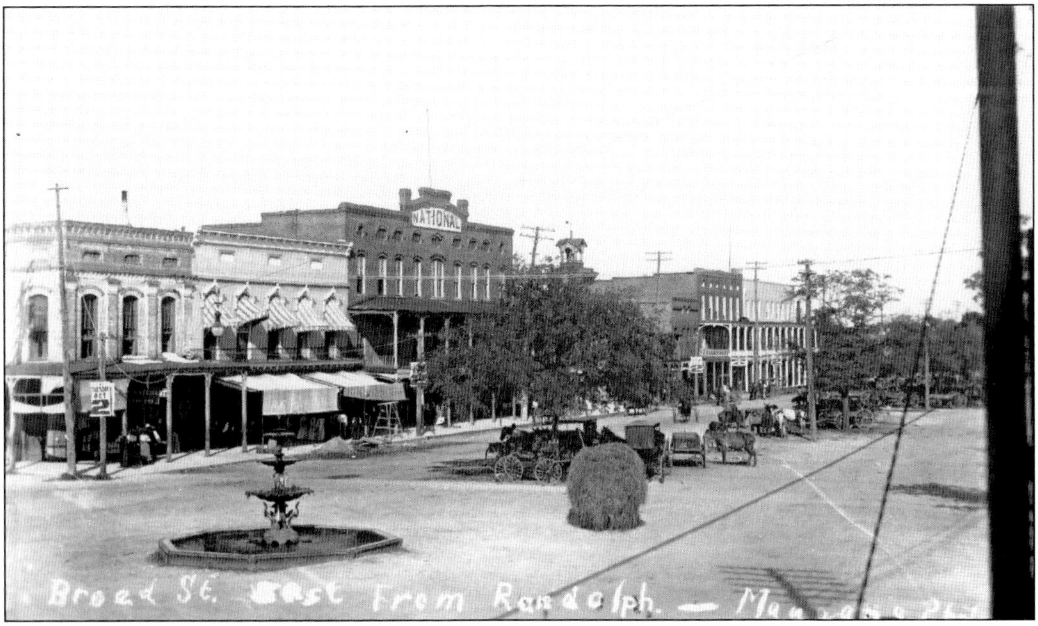

Maugan's photo of the corner of Broad Street looking from Randolph Avenue highlights the MacMonnie's Fountain that was purchased from the City of Dayton, Ohio, in the 1880s. The fountain is still a centerpiece of the downtown streetscape. (Courtesy of Mary Gray.)

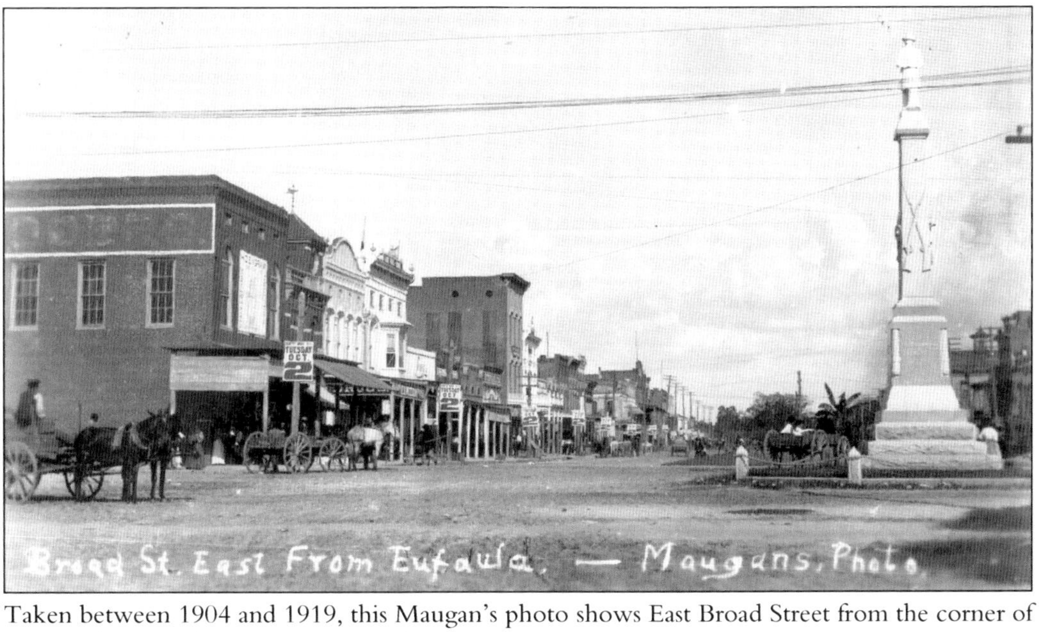

Taken between 1904 and 1919, this Maugan's photo shows East Broad Street from the corner of Eufaula Avenue. (Courtesy of Mary Gray.)

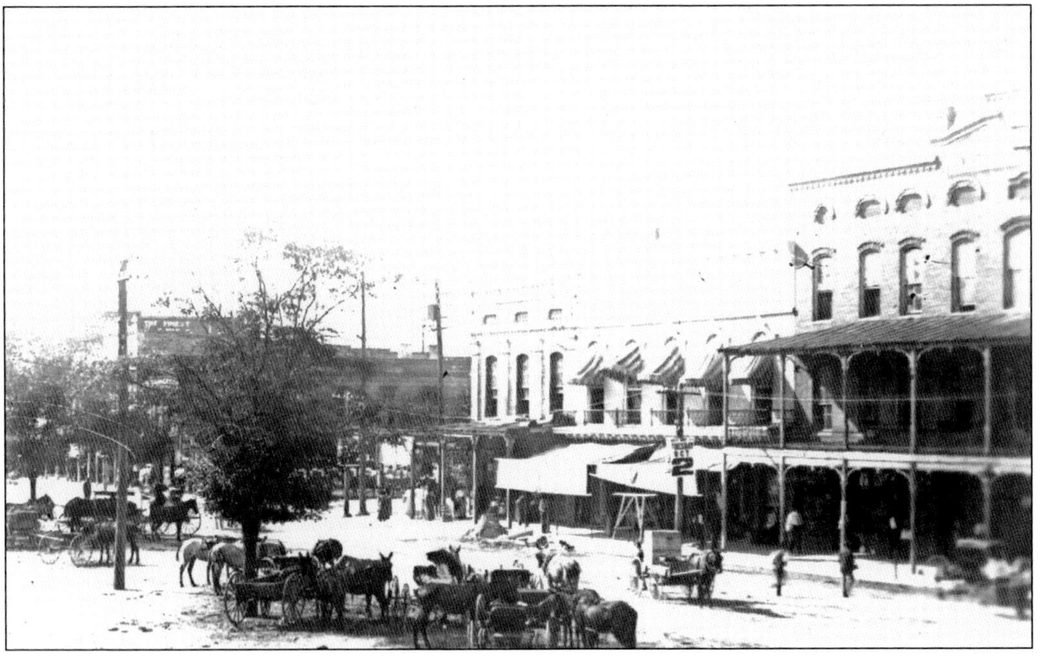

Horse- and mule-drawn wagons could be seen tied to trees along Broad Street. As in most small towns, downtown was the center of activity during the late 1800s and early 1900s. Downtown Eufaula has seen many changes, brought on by tragedies such as tornados and fire, yet it remains the heart of the community even today. (Courtesy of Mary Gray.)

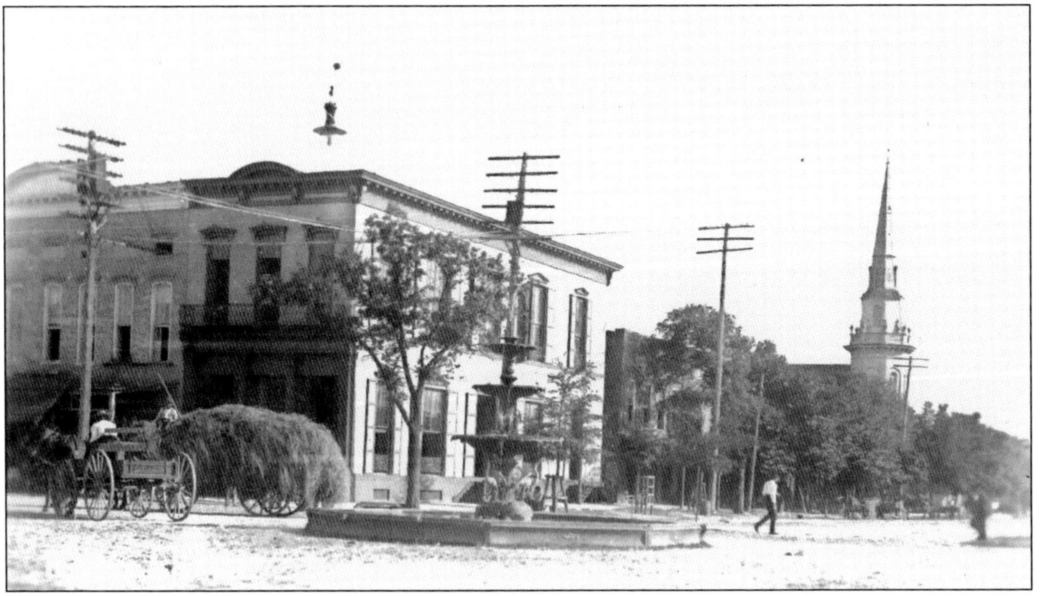

Changes in the streetscape of downtown Eufaula indicate this photo was taken between 1880 and 1907. The McNab Bank building, just behind the fountain left, is prominent in the scene. It was built between 1853 and 1859. The Eastern Bank of Alabama was chartered at this location in 1859. Mr. McNab's bank closed in 1891 under a black cloud of lawsuits and accusations. (Courtesy of Mary Gray.)

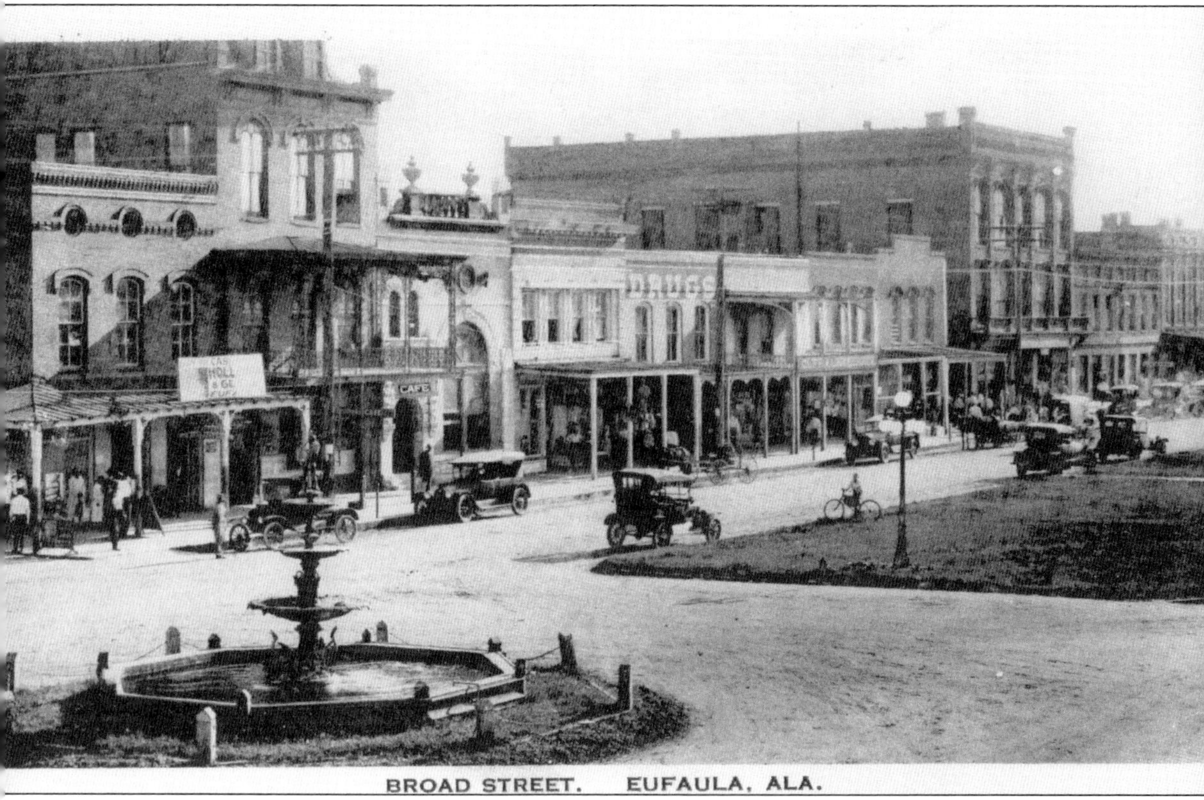

Again, the MacMonnie's Fountain is featured in this Broad Street scene. The fountain was considered too small for the City of Dayton, Ohio, and was purchased by the City of Eufaula in 1880. The graceful, three-tiered, wrought iron fountain originally had swans along the bottom and a cherub on top. (Courtesy of Rob Schaffeld.)

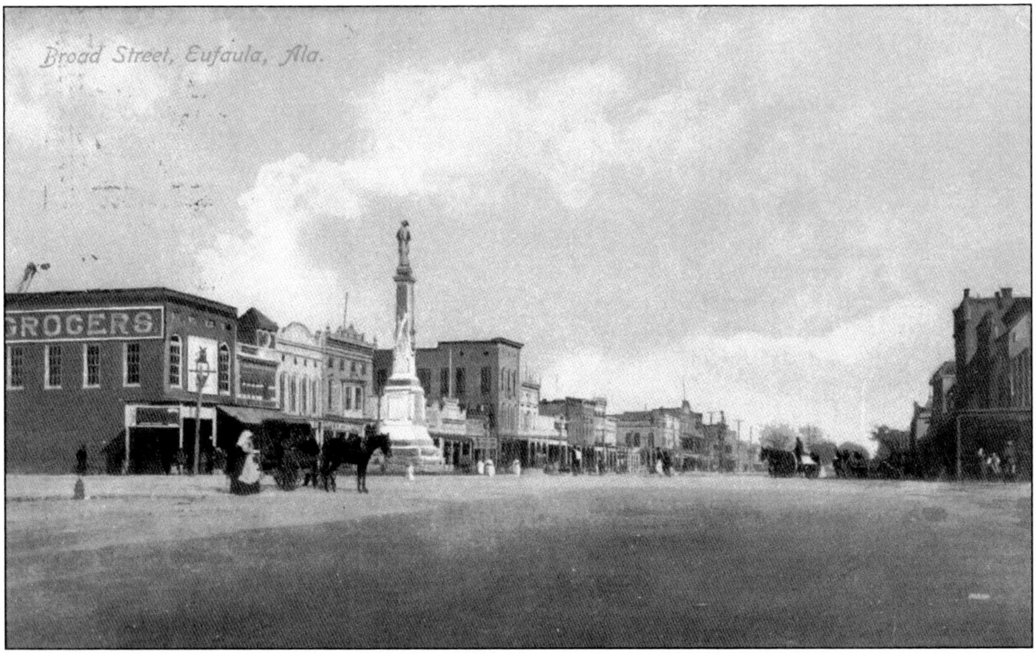

A horse-drawn carriage patiently awaits its passenger in downtown Eufaula. This card dates between 1904 and 1919. (Courtesy of Rob Schaffeld.)

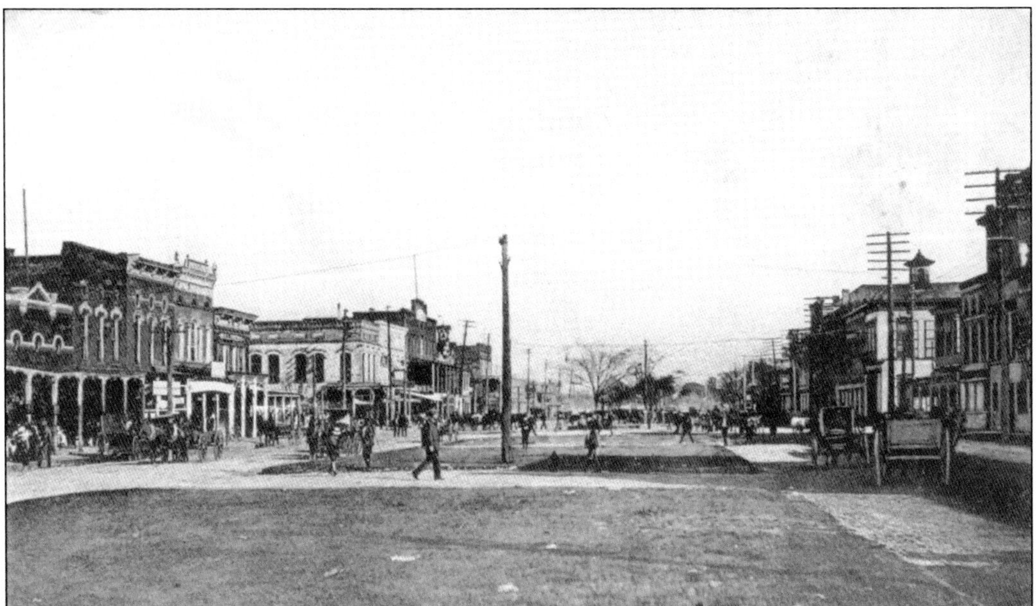

Citizens congregate on Broad Street, the business and social epicenter of Eufaula for over 100 years. The wide medians still exist today with live oaks lining the streets. (Courtesy of Hank Johnson.)

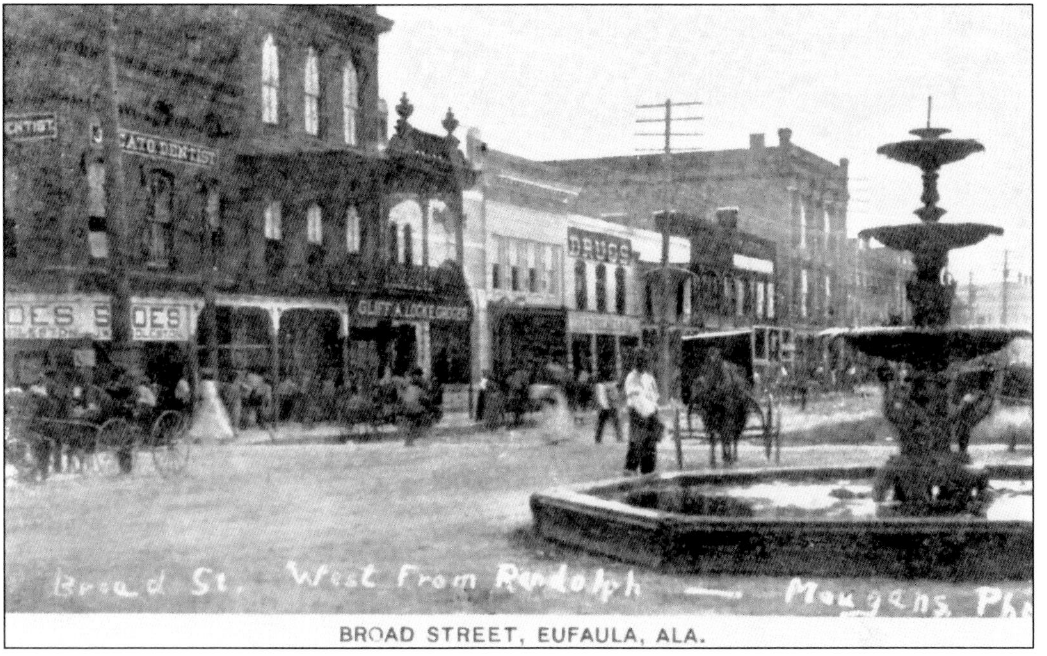

Prominent in this Maugan's photo are several turn-of-the-century businesses including the dentist office of Dr. J.C. Cato and the Cliff Locke Grocery. The Locke building was constructed in 1877. A local fraternal order was located on the upper floor. It was later used for the local phone company with offices on the second floor and the switchboard on the third floor. Today it houses Johnston Jewelry. (Courtesy of Rob Schaffeld.)

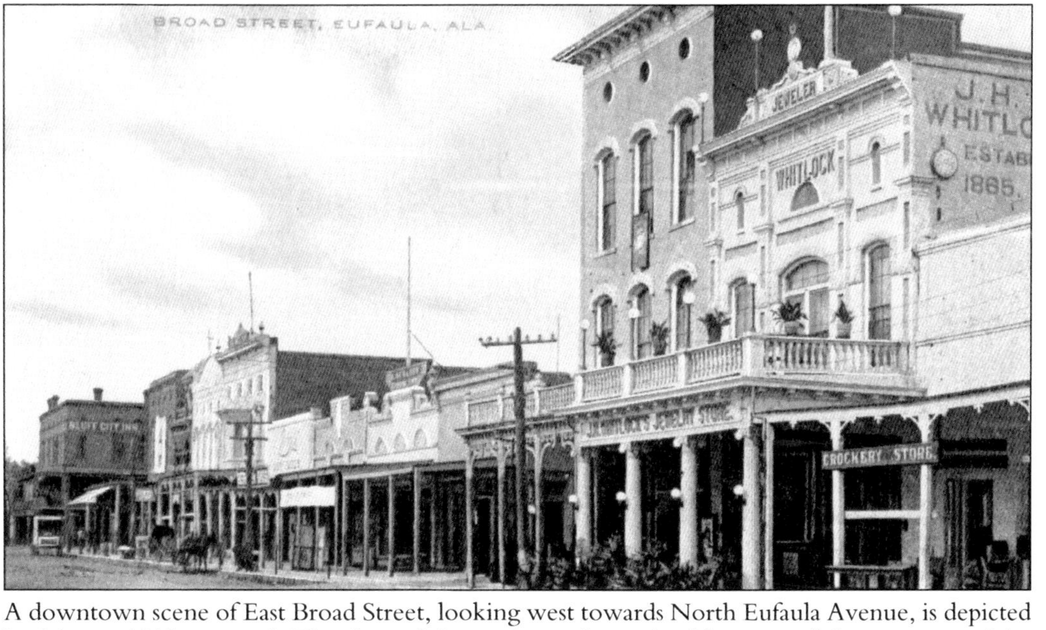

A downtown scene of East Broad Street, looking west towards North Eufaula Avenue, is depicted in this pre-1919 postcard. The date of the card was determined because of the presence of the prominent three-story brick building that was destroyed in a March 1919 tornado. (Courtesy of Eufaula Heritage Association.)

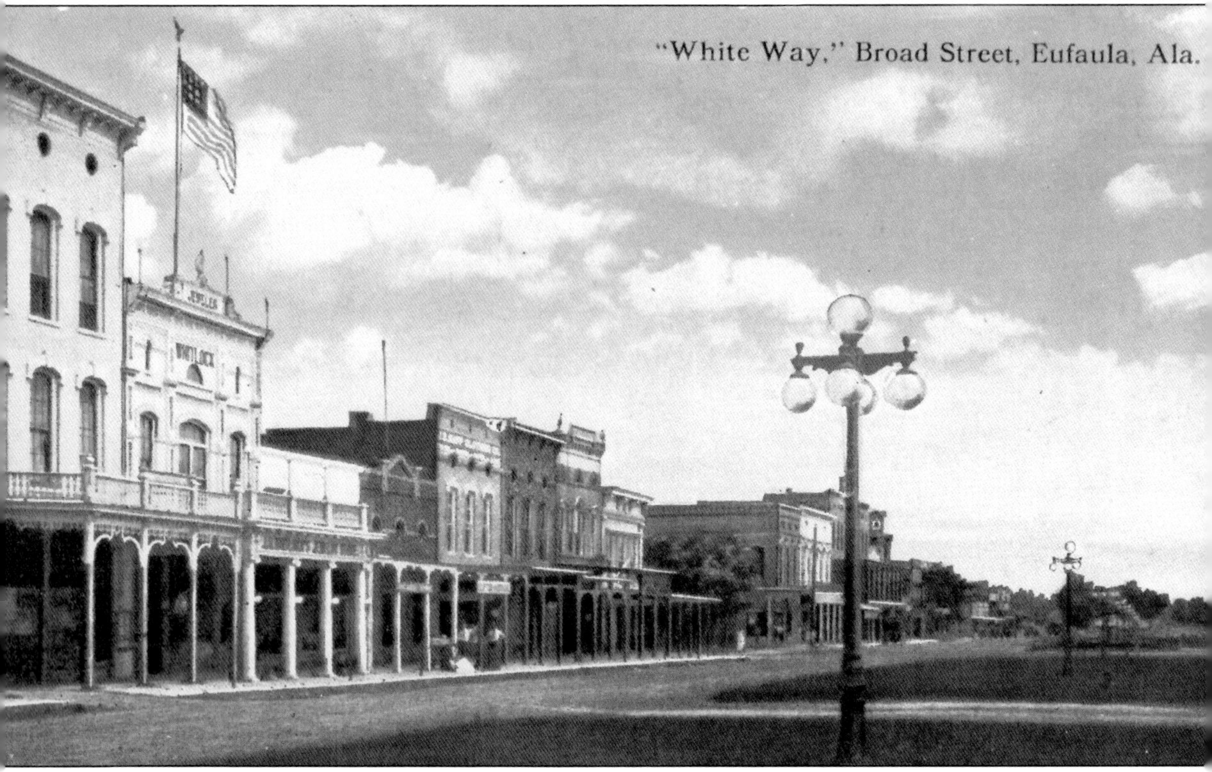

Another scene of East Broad Street declares the "White Way." Mrs. Eugenia Persons Smartt says, in her 1930 *History of Eufaula, AL*, "The Great White Way of electric lights is most beautiful and would do credit to a much larger city." (Courtesy of Frank Mixon.)

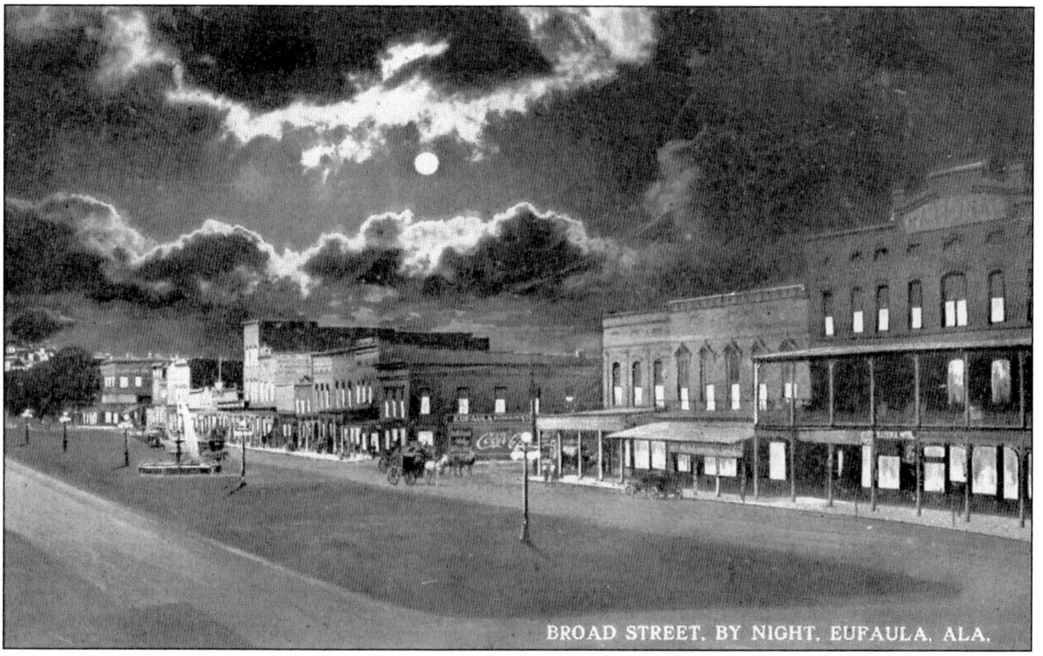

A peaceful night scene is depicted in this drawing of Broad Street. Businesses such as the National Hotel, Ross Furniture Company, J.H. Whitlock's Jewelry Store, and the Bluff City Inn are present in the drawing. (Courtesy of Hank Johnson.)

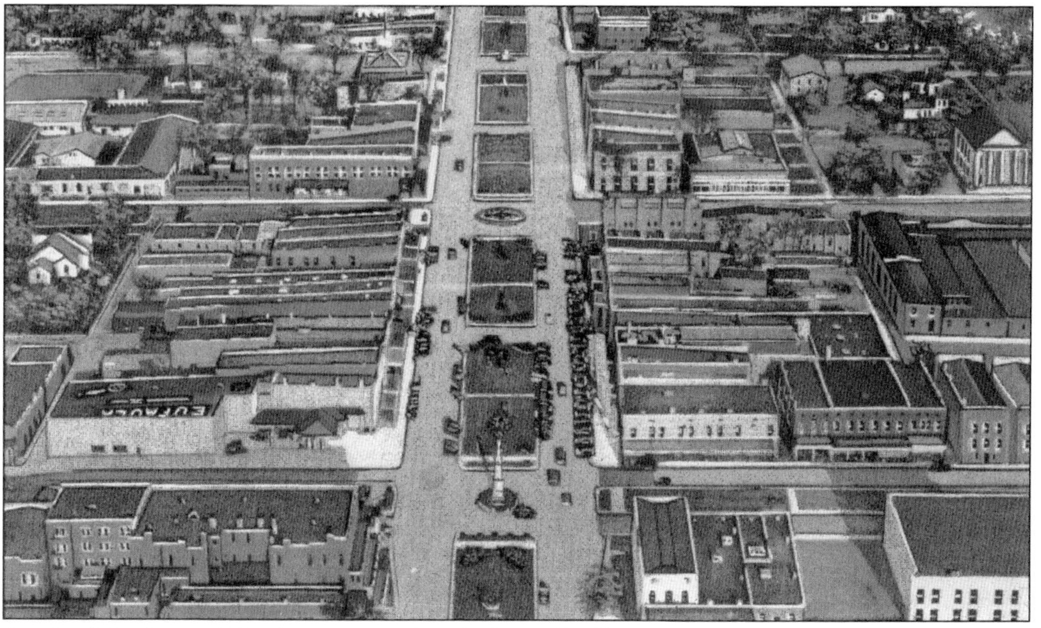

A colorfully drawn "Airplane View of Eufaula, AL" offers a unique perspective on downtown. The Confederate Monument and the MacMonnie's Fountain indicate where Broad Street is located. (Courtesy of Rob Schaffeld.)

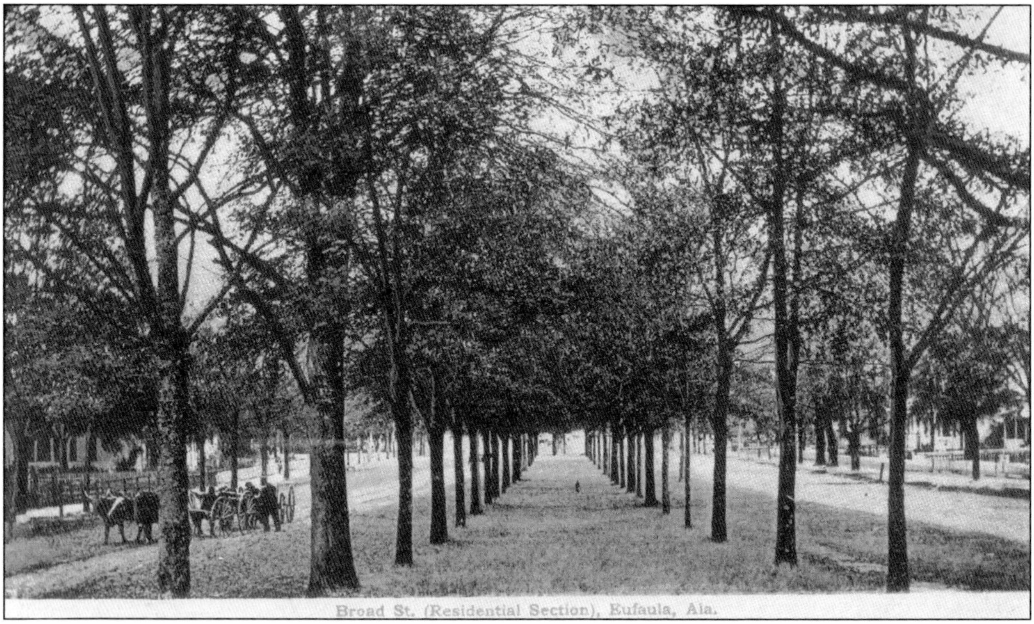

While East Broad Street comprises much of Eufaula's business district, West Broad Street is a beautiful, tree-lined, residential area. Note the ox-drawn cart on the left side of the postcard. (Courtesy of Rob Schaffeld.)

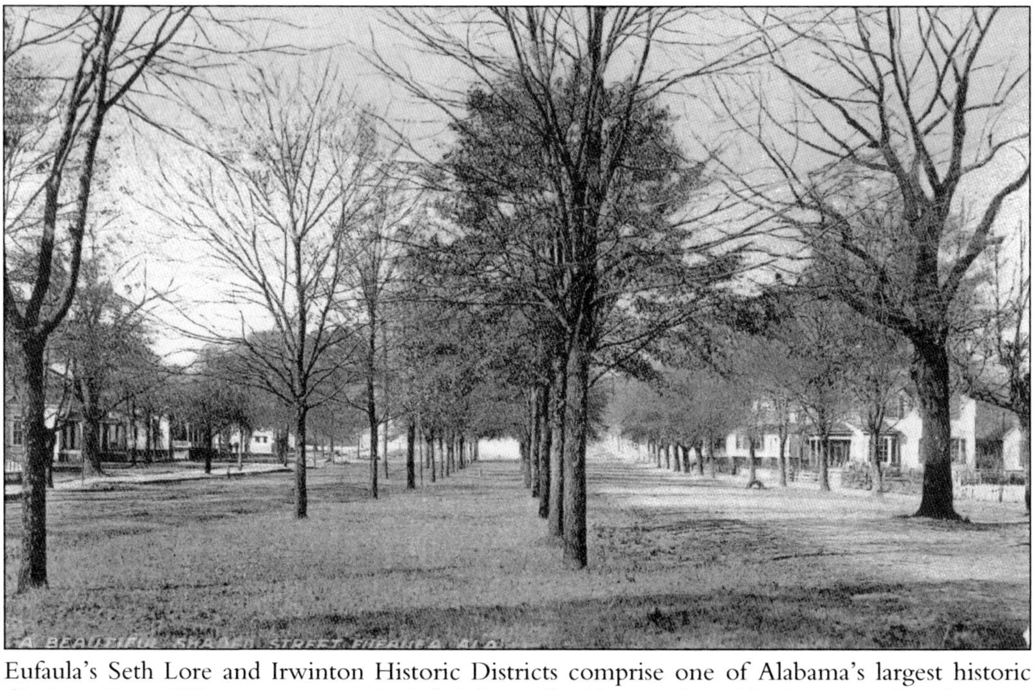

Eufaula's Seth Lore and Irwinton Historic Districts comprise one of Alabama's largest historic districts. Over 700 structures are included here. Residents take pride in preserving the past; therefore, much of the two districts remain unchanged today. (Courtesy of Hank Johnson.)

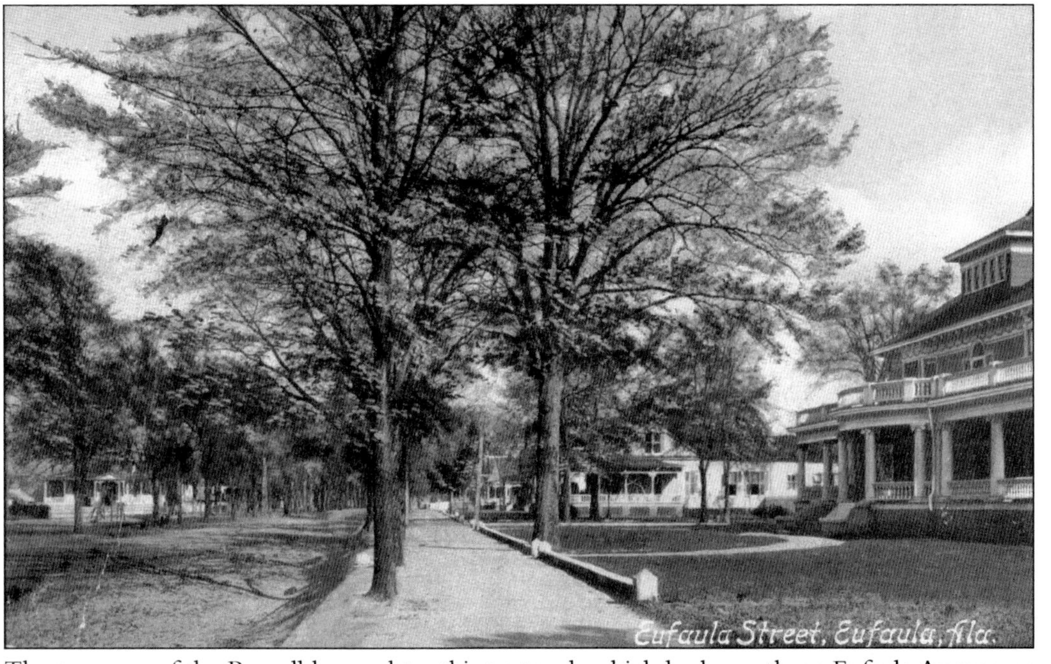

The presence of the Russell home dates this postcard, which looks north on Eufaula Avenue, as after 1905. Mrs. Thomas Smith and her daughter and son-in-law, Mr. and Mrs. Lore Russell, constructed the Neoclassical home. Mr. Lore Russell was a great-nephew of Seth Lore, who helped develop Eufaula. (Courtesy of Rob Schaffeld.)

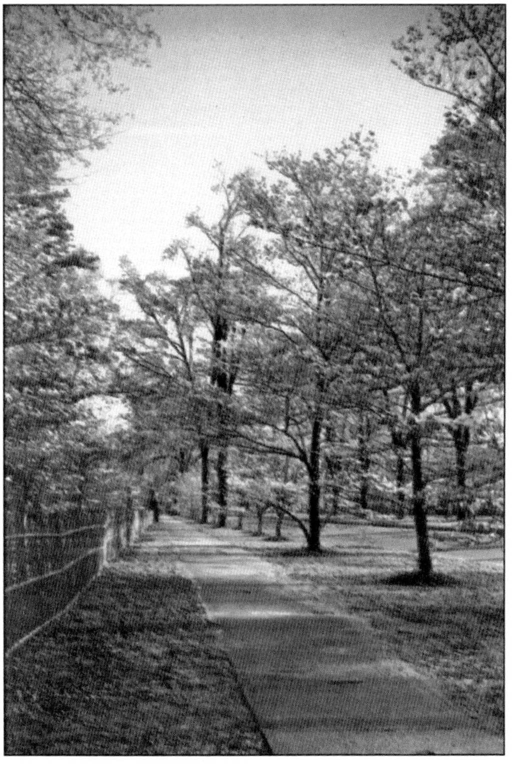

Dogwoods bloom on North Randolph Avenue near the entrance to Fairview Cemetery. Spring brings colorful azaleas, dogwoods, and more to this picturesque historic district. Area residents can often be seen walking the sidewalks, enjoying nature's beauty. (Courtesy of Eufaula Heritage Association.)

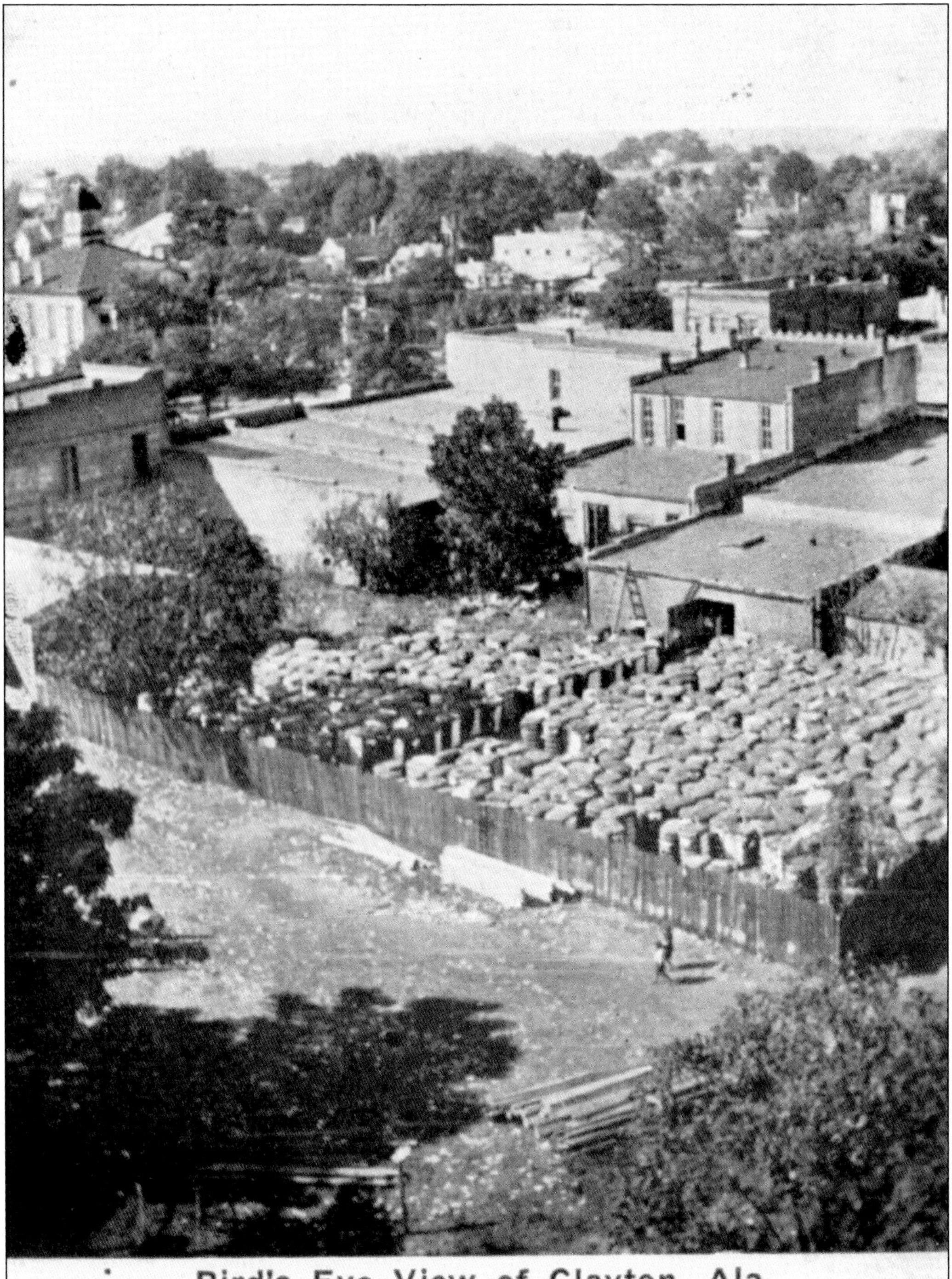

Taken from the water tower once located on Reed Avenue in Clayton, this bird's eye view obviously shows Barbour County during one of its big cotton seasons as evident by the many bales shown. From this view Barbour County's original courthouse, including the clock tower, can be seen to the left. Notice the many trees in downtown Clayton. (Courtesy of Betty Greene.)

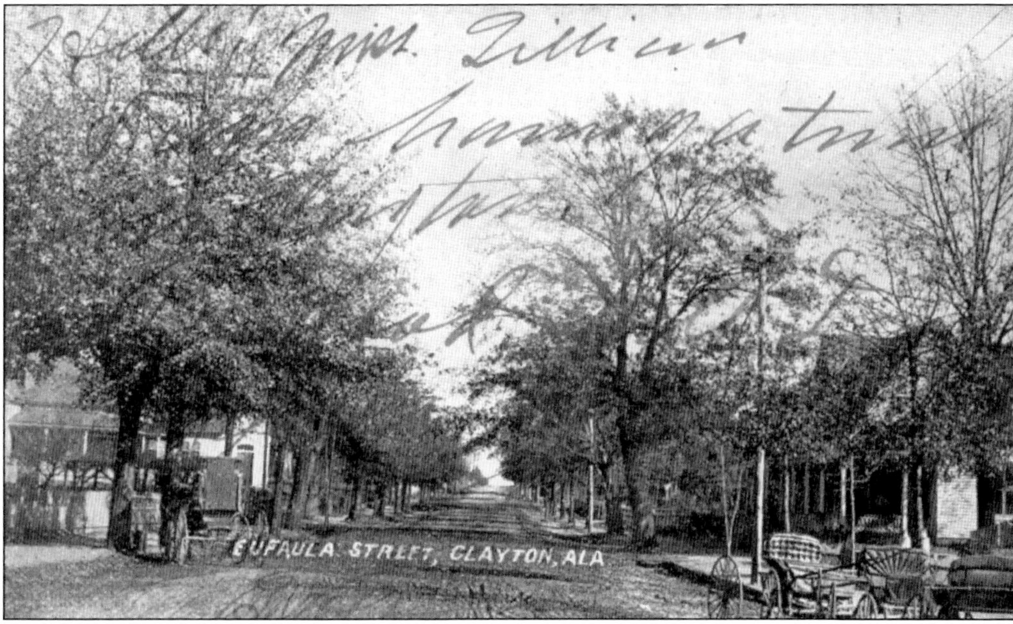

Though much of the inscription is illegible, it is known that this postcard was mailed to Miss Lillian Jordan of Dothan, Alabama, in June 1957. This scene is of the beautifully tree-lined Eufaula Street in Clayton. The white building to the left is the Clayton Presbyterian Church. (Courtesy of Ben Spurlock.)

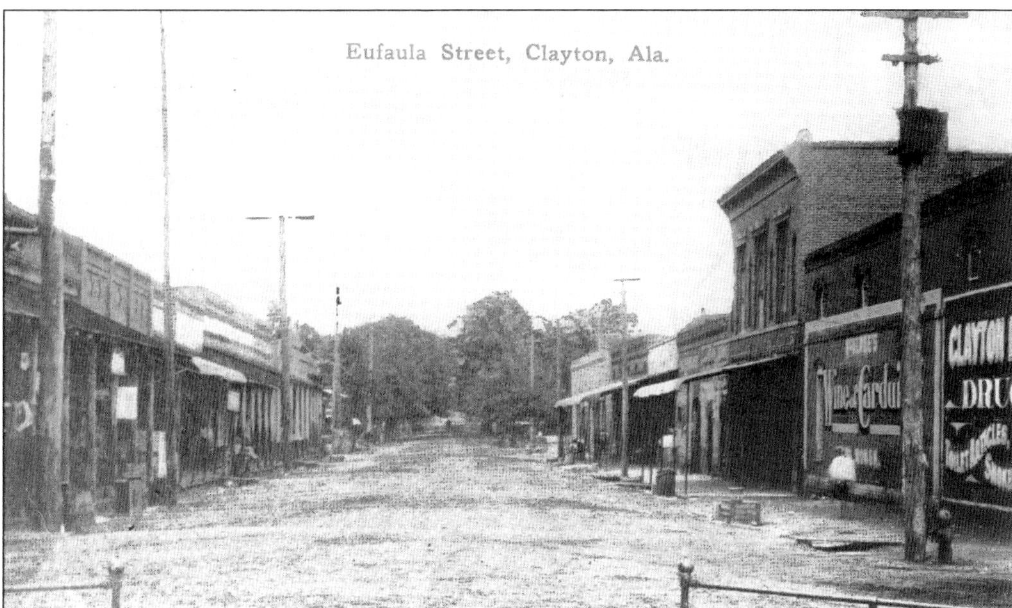

Postmarked 1914, this postcard was received by Ms. M.C? Smart of Dothan, Alabama. This scene of Eufaula Street, in Clayton, looks east from town square through the business district and on further to the tree-lined residential area. Clayton Drug Company, located in the forward right, remained at this site until 2003 when owner and Alabama State Representative William "Billy" Beasley relocated next door. (Courtesy of Doug Purcell.)

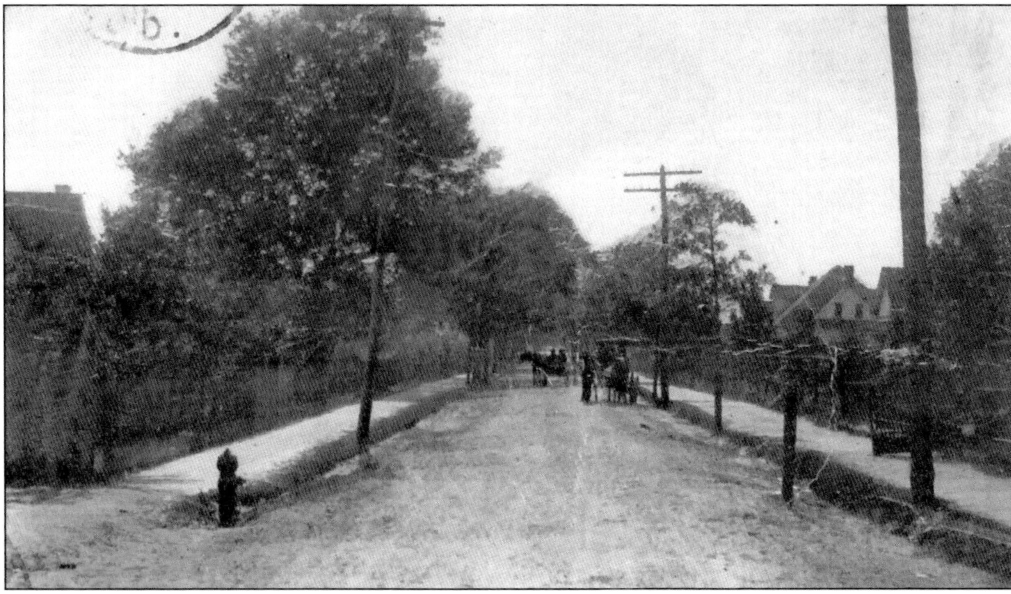

Postmarked February 2, 1909, Mr. Porter Hatfield Sr., received this after he moved from Batesville, Alabama, to Eufaula. The sender is unknown but obviously an admirer of Clayton's beautiful tree-lined neighborhood along Louisville Street, because the inscription asks "How would you like a stroll up this street?" Many of the same homes pictured still stand in Clayton today. (Courtesy of Janet Scroggins.)

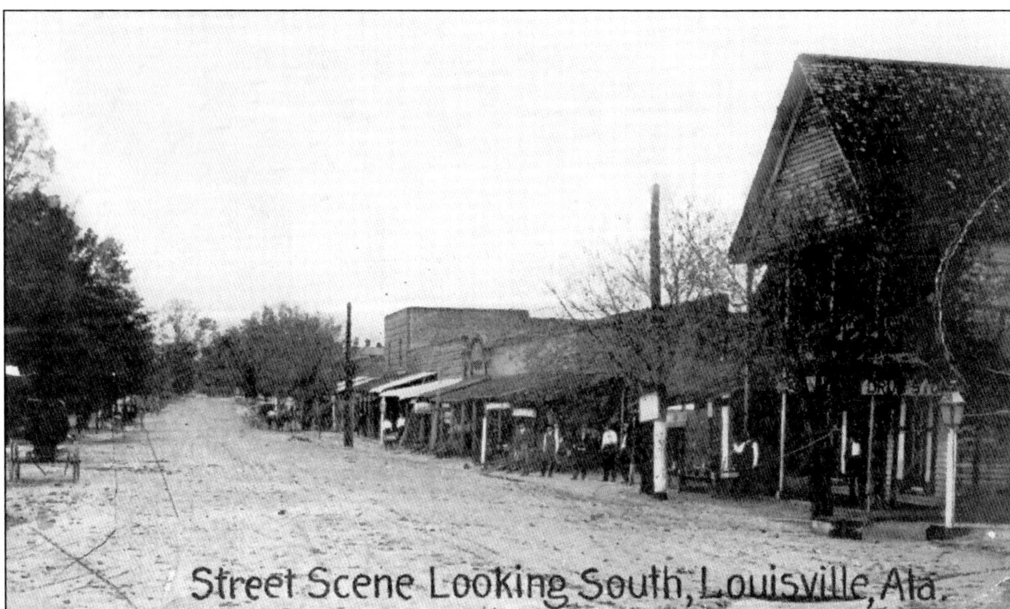

Miss India McRae of Clayton received this postcard postmarked December 17, 1909. Though the streets have since been paved, a travel through Louisville is much the same as when this photograph was taken. The two-story drug store to the right is no longer there, but the Louisville Drug Company still operates in downtown. Notice the proud storeowners and residents along the sidewalk. (Courtesy of Betty Greene.)

Three

Residences

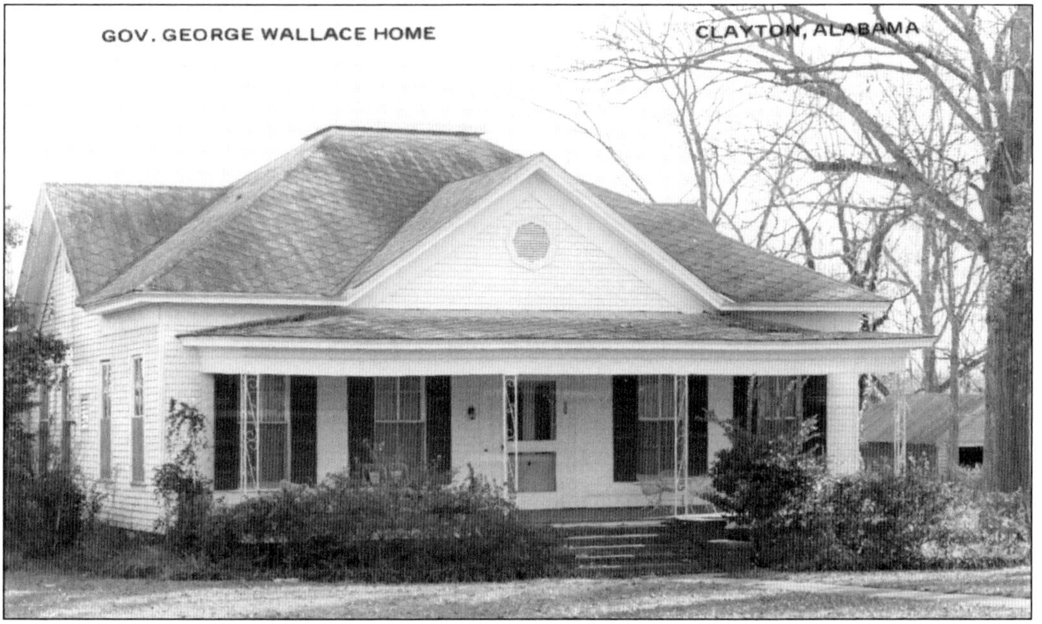

Though born in Clio, it was in Clayton that Gov. George C. Wallace and Gov. Lurleen B. Wallace lived and where he practiced law. This house on South Eufaula Avenue was only blocks from downtown where his law office was located near the courthouse. This house burned on January 15, 1990, and locals often comment, "It was the hottest fire they can ever remember." (Courtesy of Rebecca Beasley.)

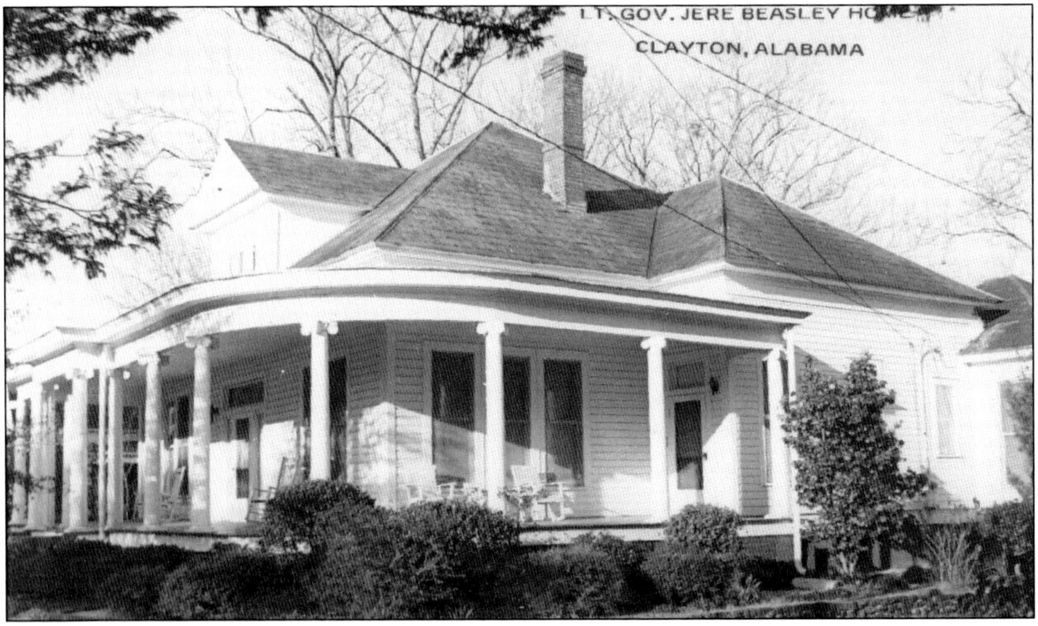

Jere and Sarah Beasley lived in this *c.* 1914 home until he was elected lieutenant governor of Alabama in 1970 and moved to Montgomery. Dr. and Mrs. H.E. Peach, a local dentist, built the home. Lieutenant Governor Beasley sold the home in 1974. The present owners are Bob and Malinda Ross. (Courtesy of Bob and Malinda Ross.)

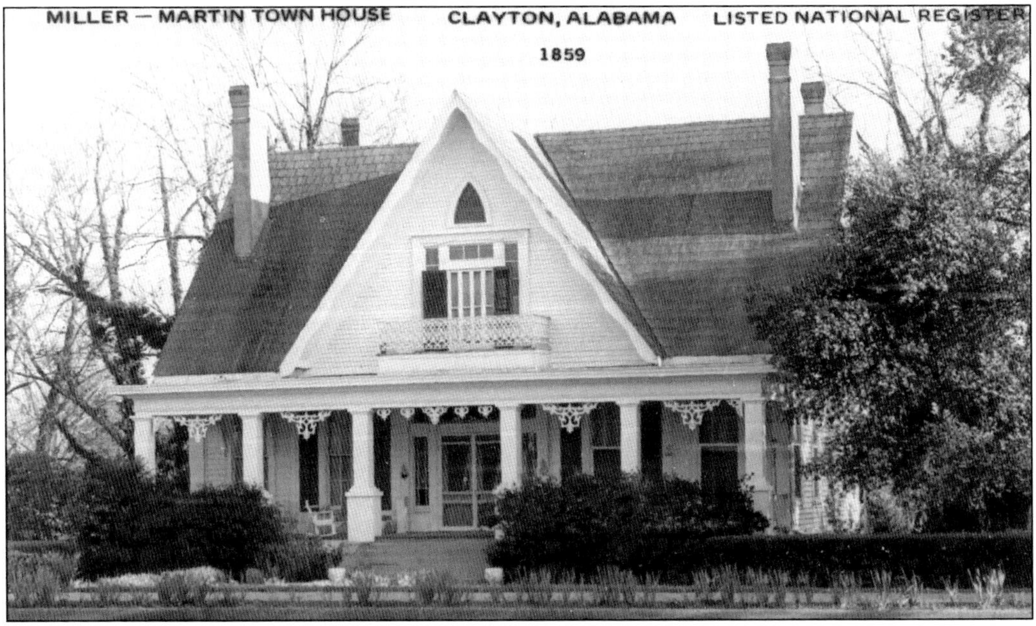

Constructed in 1859, the Miller-Martin Town House was built by John Hilland Miller. Mr. Miller owned a plantation five miles southwest of Clayton and built the home as a place to stay while in town on business. The opulent interior was the site of many galas and parties in the early years of the Civil War. Beautiful, hand-painted ceiling murals still greet visitors at the Four Seasons Bed and Breakfast that operates in the home today. (Courtesy of Rebecca Beasley.)

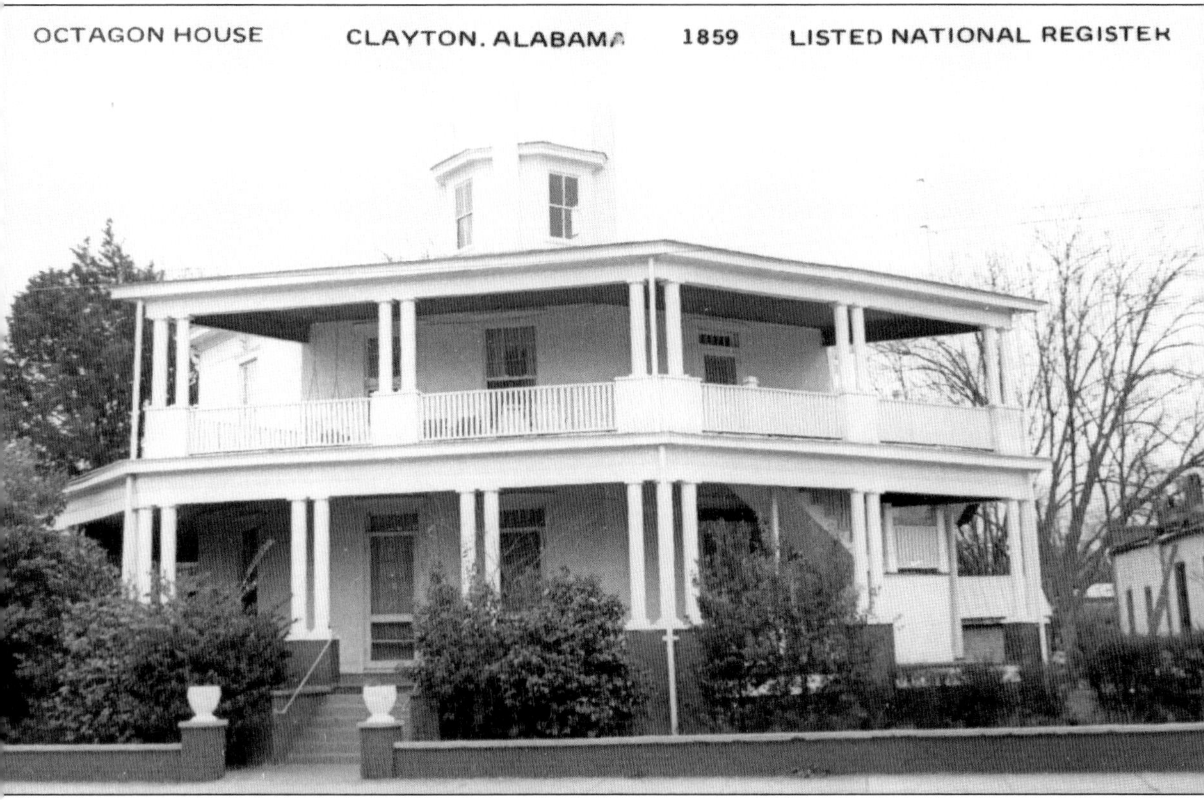

B.F. Petty built this architecturally unique home on Midway Street in Clayton in 1859. Octagon shaped homes appeared as early as 1815 in New England; however, it was not until the 1850s that they grew in popularity. Mr. Petty found the floor plans while visiting New York with his family. It is believed to be the only antebellum example of an octagon house remaining in the Southeast. There are eight large rooms, four upstairs, and four downstairs. Because of a center square stairwell, there are eight small corner rooms as well. There are four chimneys extending from the basement to the cupola. Modifications were done in 1900 and 1924 that changed the original small porch surrounding the home into its present look. Modernization also took place in the 1940s. In the 1970s Clayton mayor Ed Ventress arranged for purchase of the home. It is now owned by the Town of Clayton and open for tours, meetings, and receptions. (Courtesy of Rebecca Beasley.)

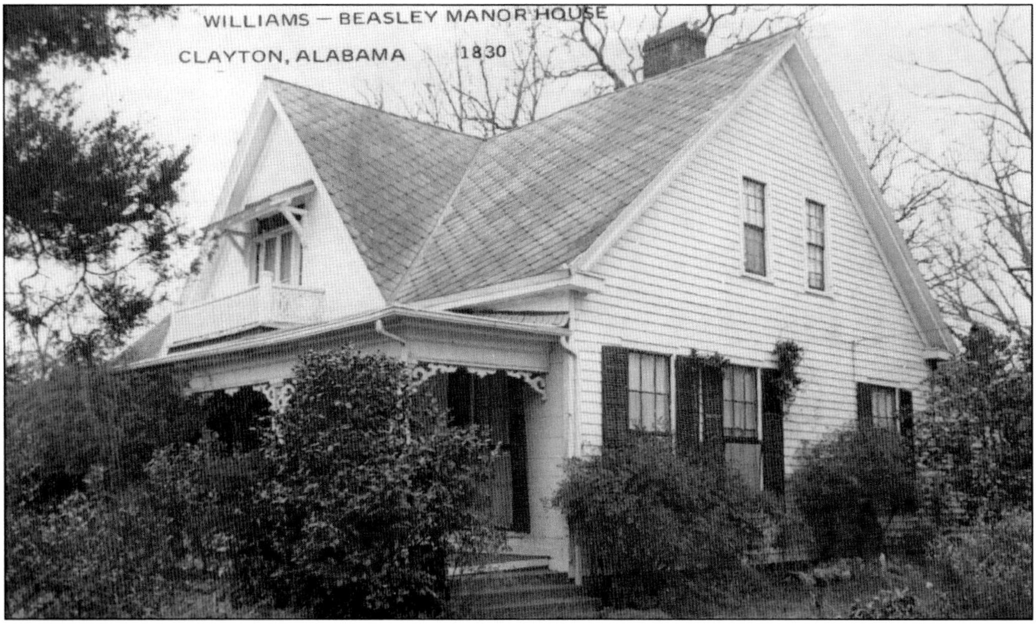

The Williams-Beasley Manor House, built *c.* 1840, is the ancestral home of Judge Sterling Williams located on Louisville Street in Clayton. In 1971, Walter Vernon Beasley purchased the property and installed the marble mantel in the dining room. He also made extensive repairs to the house, which then remained empty for a number of years. Dr. and Mrs. Danny L. Hartzog are the present owners. (Courtesy of Rebecca Beasley.)

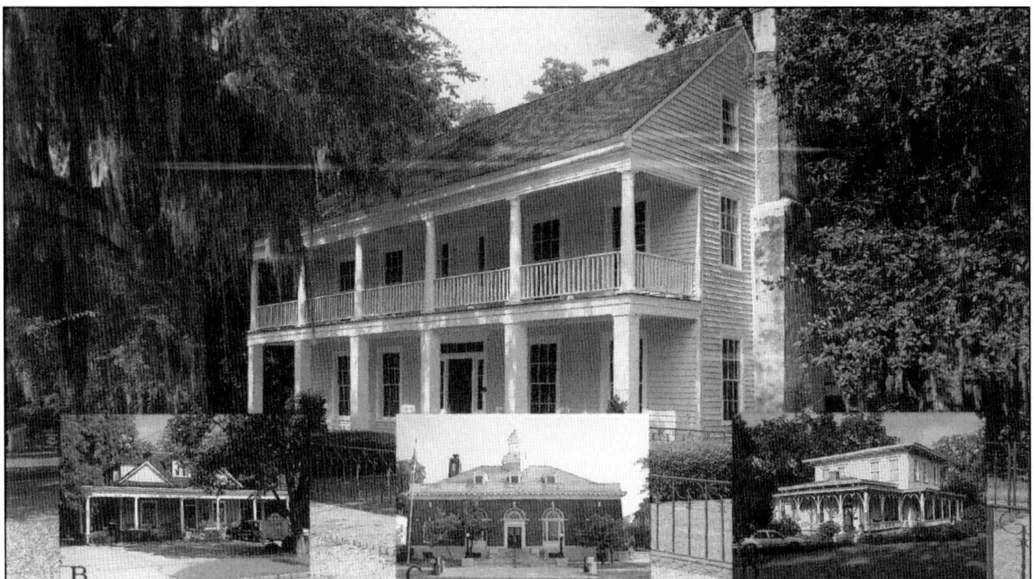

Published in the early 1990s by the Eufaula/Barbour County Tourism Council, this modern postcard displays four of Eufaula's historic buildings. The large center photo is of The Tavern, built in 1836; it is Eufaula's oldest remaining structure. From the bottom, left to right, are Conner-Lawrence Real Estate office (*c.* 1895), Old Post Office Building (*c.* 1912), and St. Mary's Bed and Breakfast (*c.* 1850), which is now a private residence. (Courtesy of Maisie Pugh.)

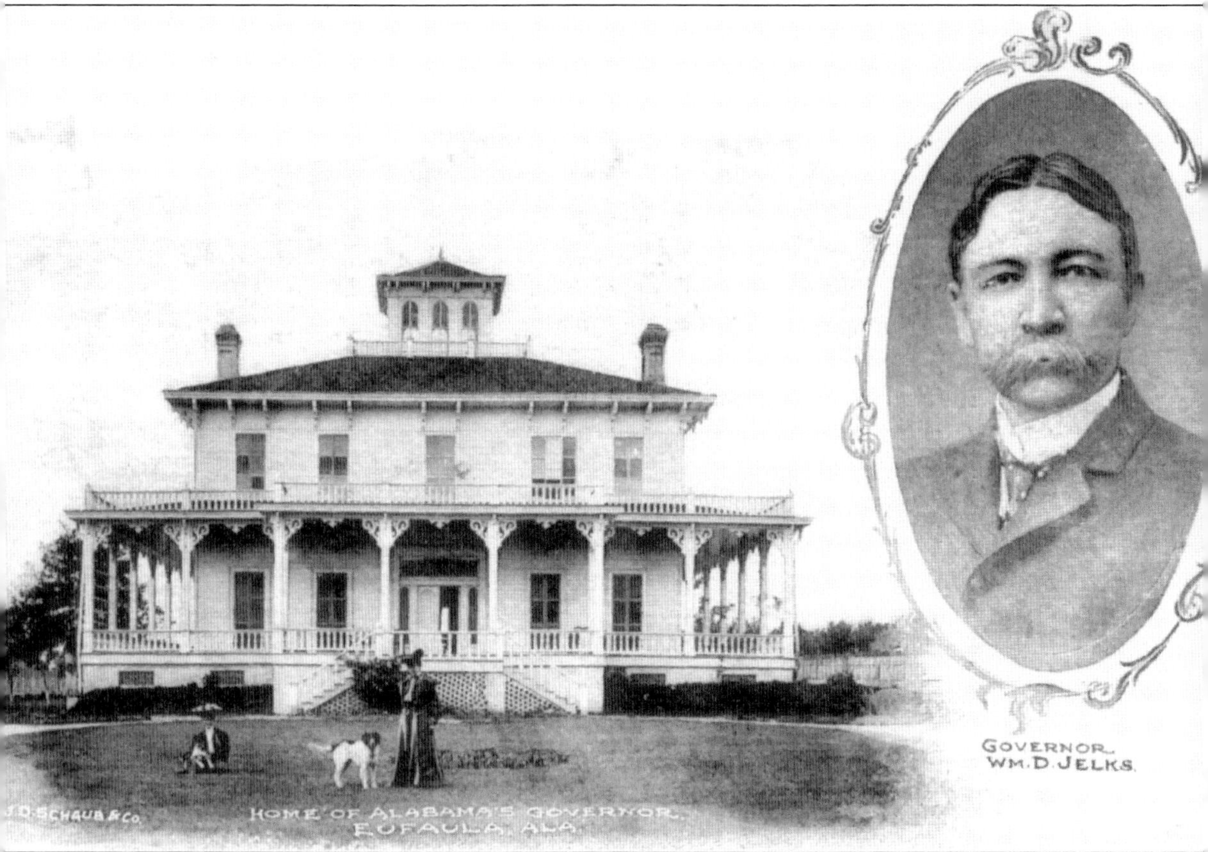

This antebellum ancestral home of Alice Shorter and her husband, Gov. William Dorsey Jelks, was demolished shortly before the Eufaula Heritage Association was organized in 1966. Governor Jelks is among the prominent Alabamians who have been outstanding figures in politics and public affairs. He promoted harmony in the Democratic Party and his administration was noted for its economy and adherence to the business ideal. His talents and contributions are difficult to summarize. Before he was governor, he owned the *Eufaula Times* for nearly 20 years. During his ownership, it had a larger circulation than any other newspaper in the state. While in office he began the child labor legislation. After leaving office in 1907, he organized the Protective Life Insurance Company of Birmingham, Alabama, the first Alabama life insurance company to come into being. The beautiful Protective Life Building now towers over Birmingham as a sentinel. (Courtesy of Rob Schaffeld.)

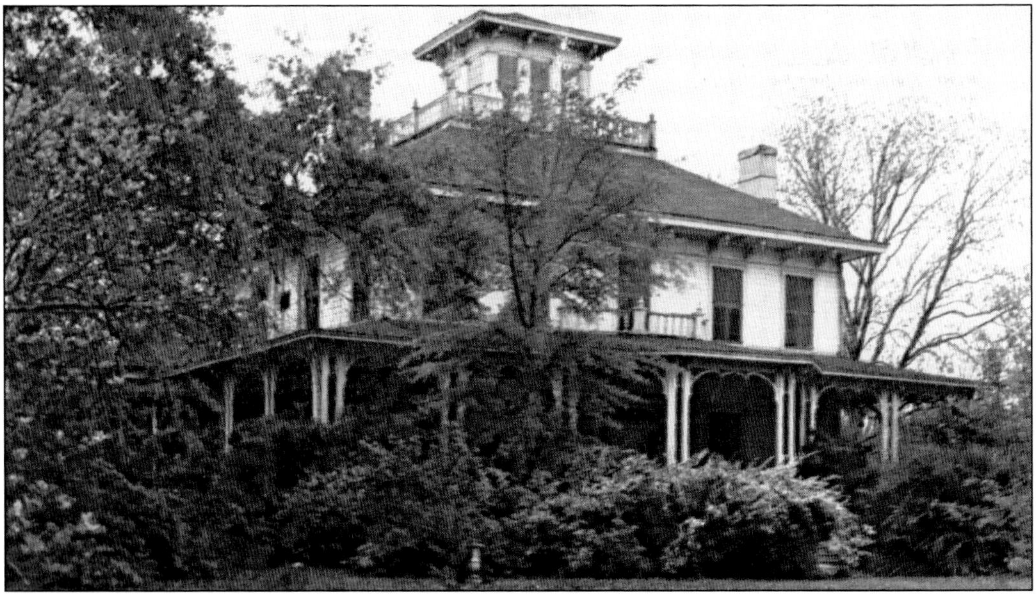

After serving as home for five generations of Youngs and their descendants, Fendall Hall, *c.* 1860, now serves the public as an educational tool. The Alabama Historical Commission purchased the house in 1973 to be preserved as a house museum. The commission has restored and interpreted the house to the style from the 1880 to 1916 occupancy of the home. This postcard predates that restoration. (Courtesy of Eufaula Heritage Association.)

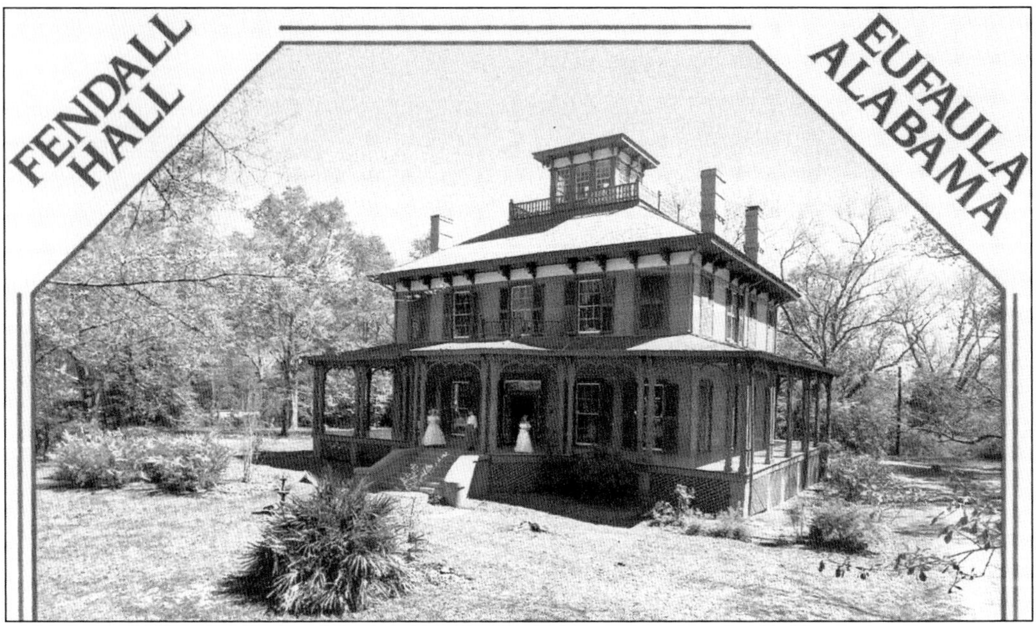

Fendall Hall, owned by the Alabama Historical Commission, has everything you would expect in a Southern suburban mansion—columns, black and white entrance floor, Italian marble fireplaces, period furnishings, heart pine flooring, a blooming landscape, and three rooms of the finest Victorian-era murals found in any home in America. The murals were painted in the 1880s. (Courtesy of the Historic Chattahoochee Commission.)

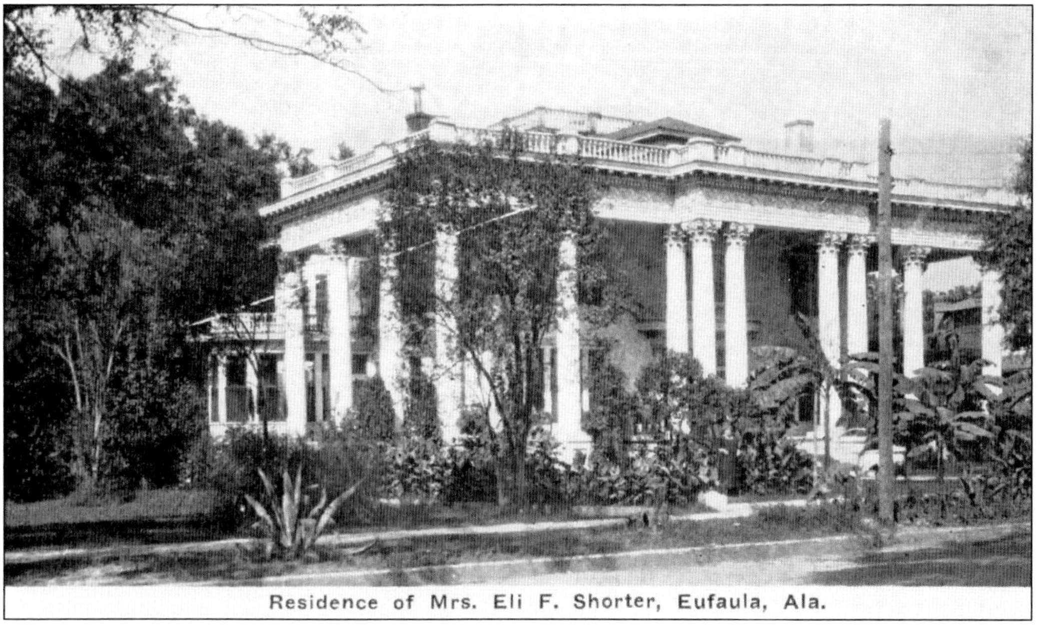

Built in 1894 by Eli Sims Shorter and his wife Wileyna Shorter, this mansion was remodeled to its current Neoclassical Revival style in 1906. Money from Mrs. Shorter's SSS *Tonic* inheritance was used for the remodeling. The home remained in the family until the mid-1960s. (Courtesy of Eufaula Heritage Association.)

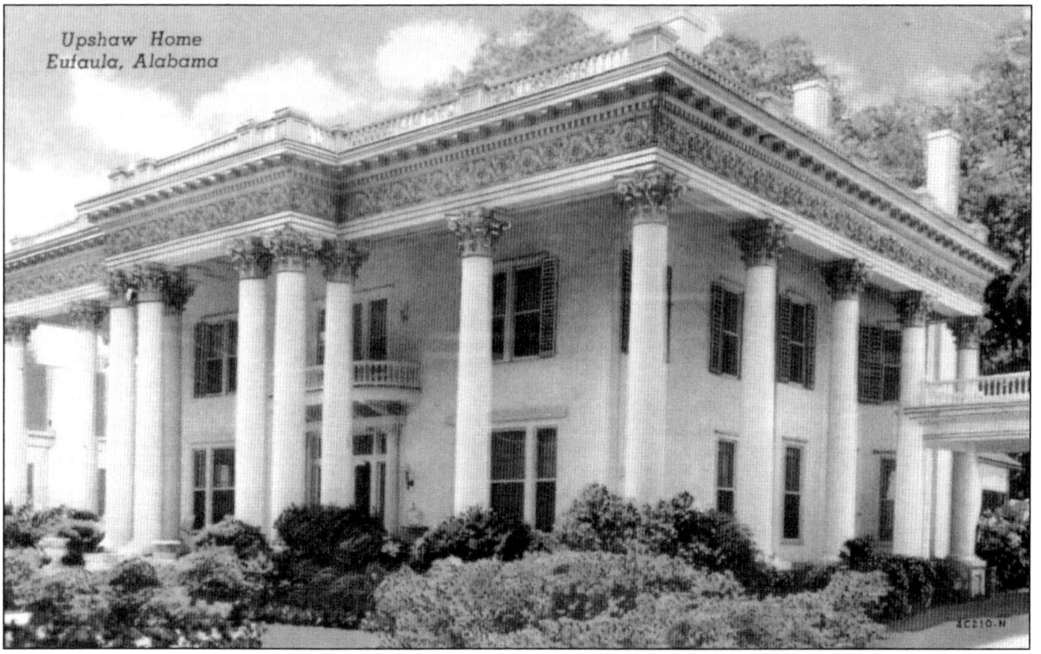

Herman Upshaw came to Eufaula in 1908 and was elected principal of Eufaula High School. In 1912 he married Fanny Shorter, the second daughter of Col. and Mrs. Eli Shorter, builders of this home. Mr. Upshaw became editor of *The Eufaula Tribune* in 1929 and held that position until 1958. (Courtesy of Eufaula Heritage Association.)

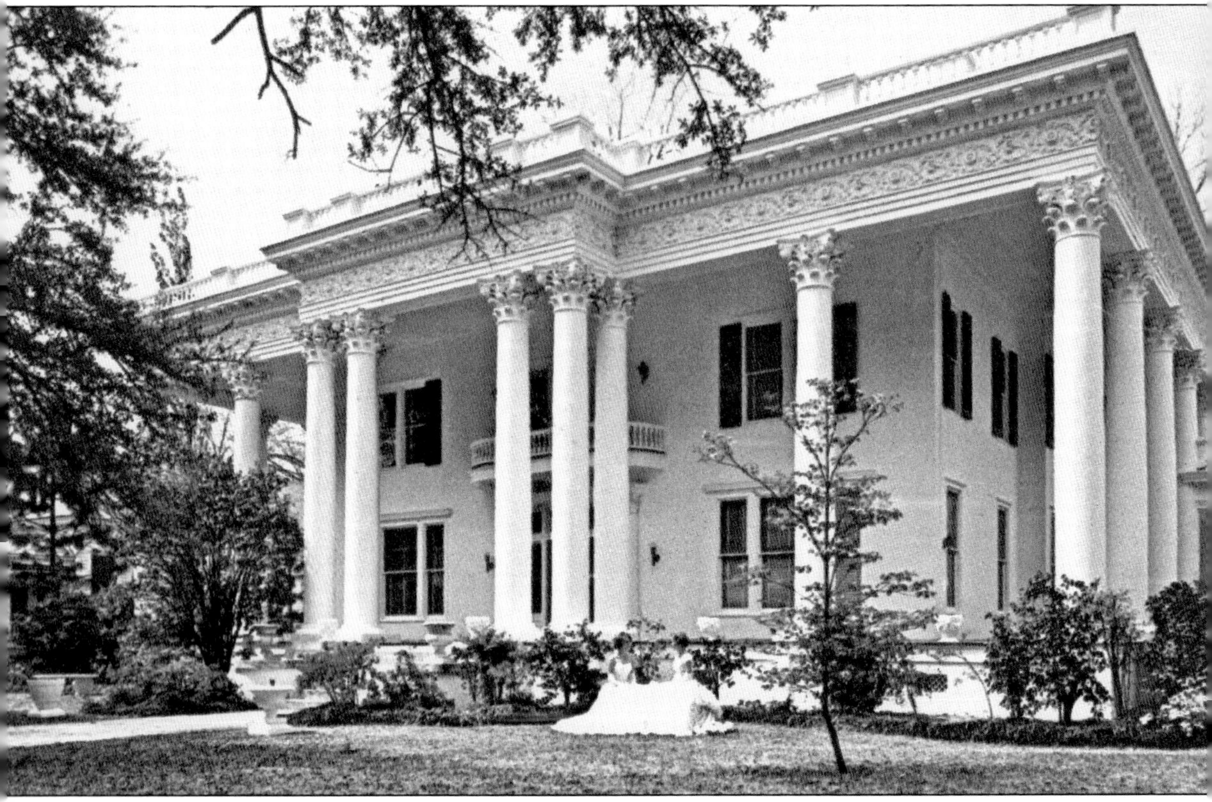

In 1965 the Shorter-Upshaw home was bought at public auction by a group of concerned citizens for $33,000. Two months later, the Eufaula Heritage Association was formed and a Pilgrimage Tour of Homes was planned. Bobbie Helen Herlong and Connie Smith helped promote the tour held April 11–17, 1966. (Courtesy of Rob Schaffeld.)

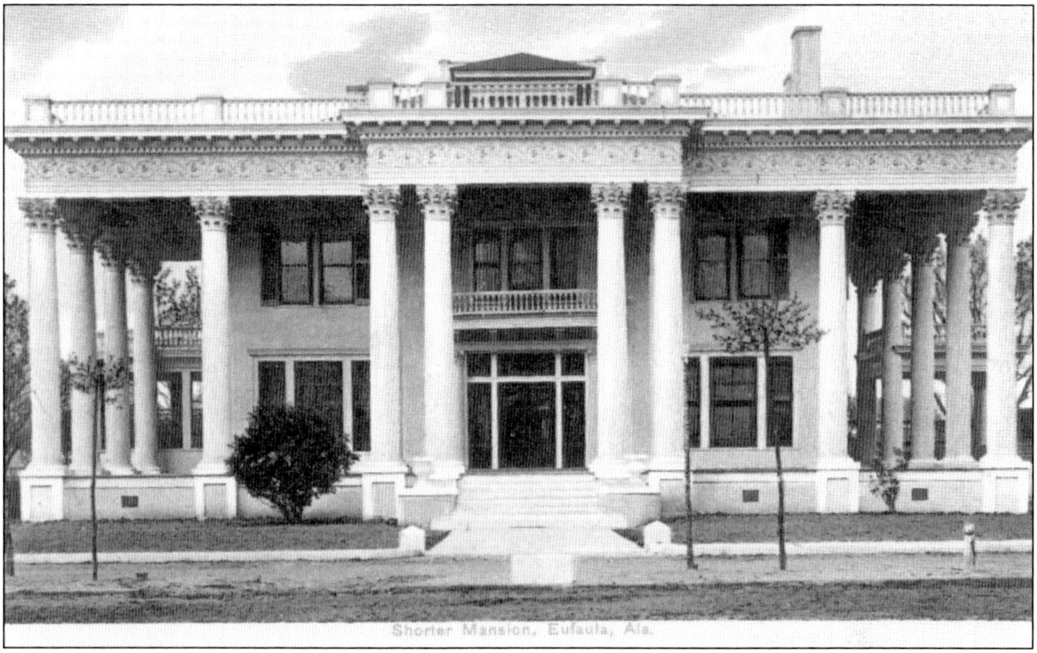

Shorter Mansion was saved in 1965 as a sign of Eufaula's commitment to preservation and civic pride. Today the mansion still serves as headquarters of the Eufaula Heritage Association. The Eufaula Historical Museum is housed on the second floor. The Eufaula Pilgrimage Tour of Homes, started in 1966 as an association fund-raiser, is still held each spring. (Courtesy of Rob Schaffeld.)

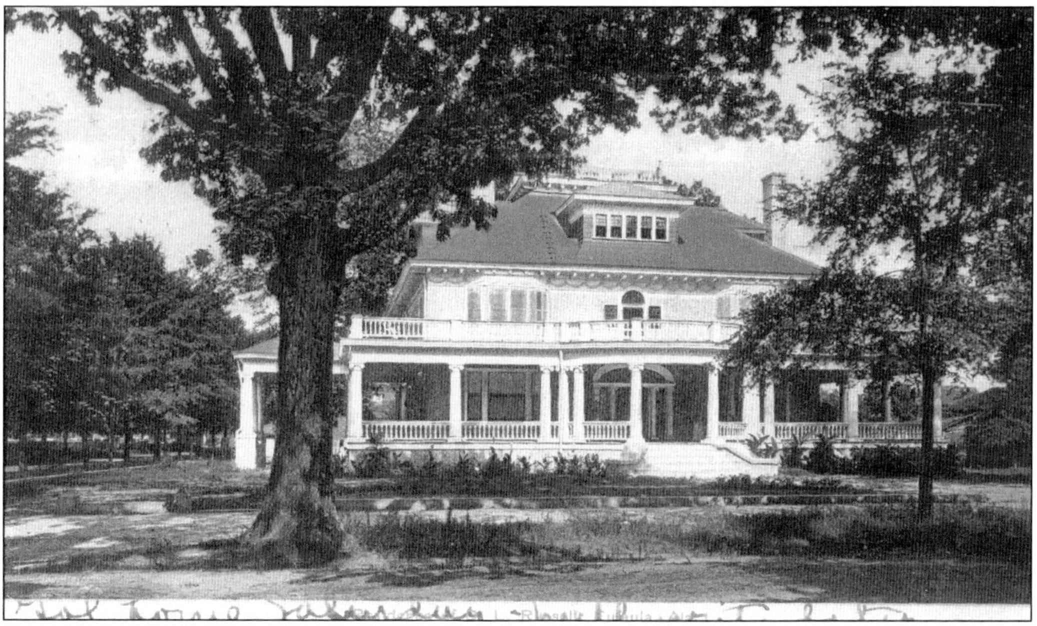

Though the sender is unknown, this postcard of the residence of D.L. Russell is postmarked February 12, 1903, from Eufaula to Savannah, Georgia. The inscription reads, "Got home Saturday—Will write later." (Courtesy of Ken Thomas.)

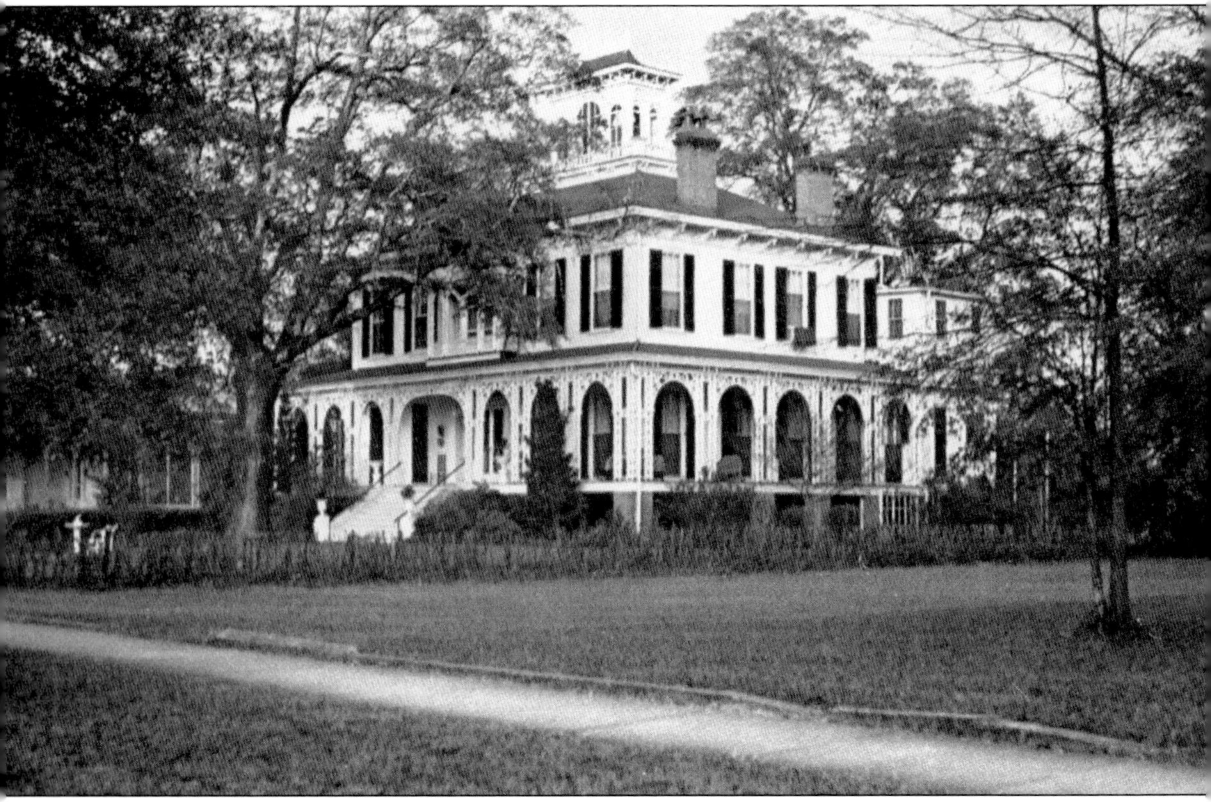

William T. Simpson, a cotton wholesaler, built Dean-Page Hall in 1850. He employed a servant boy to maintain the windows in the belvedere, watching for "weather signs" and steamboats. This Italianate mansion was named by Simpson's daughter Caroline, Mrs. L.Y. Dean. Captain Dean prospered in the mercantile and insurance business. The home features 16 wooden tracery arches hand-carved from heart pine. (Courtesy of Eufaula Heritage Association.)

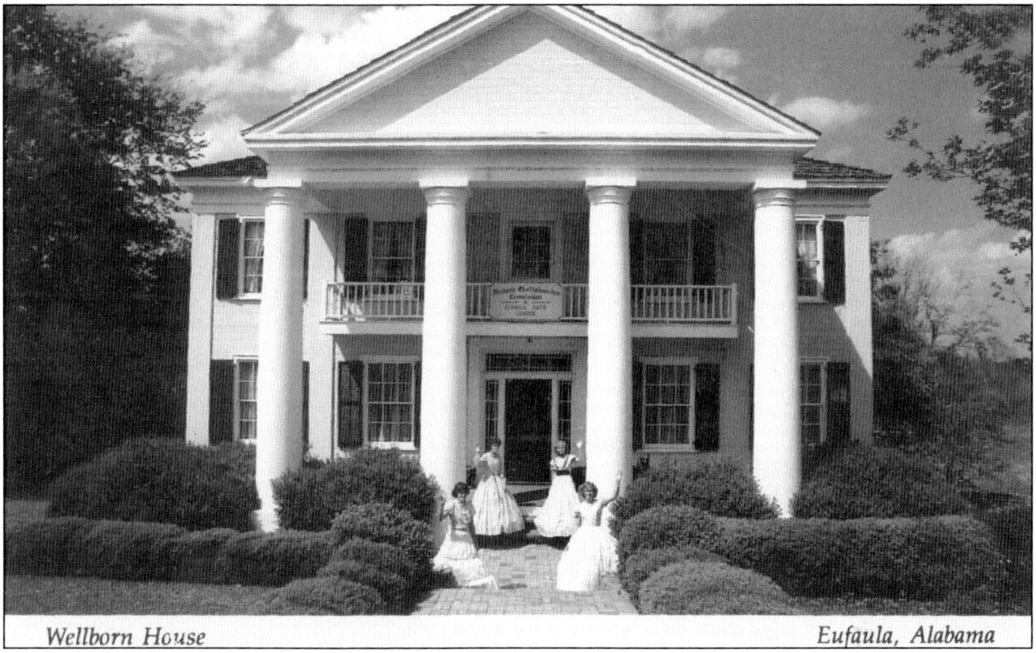

This house, completed in 1837 by Dr. Levi Wellborn, was one of the area's first Greek Revival structures. The house was restored and moved to its present location by the Eufaula Arts Council. It housed a prize-winning art collection and served as the Historic Chattahoochee Commission headquarters. This postcard was printed in 1982. The Wellborn House is now an office complex. (Courtesy of Maisie Pugh.)

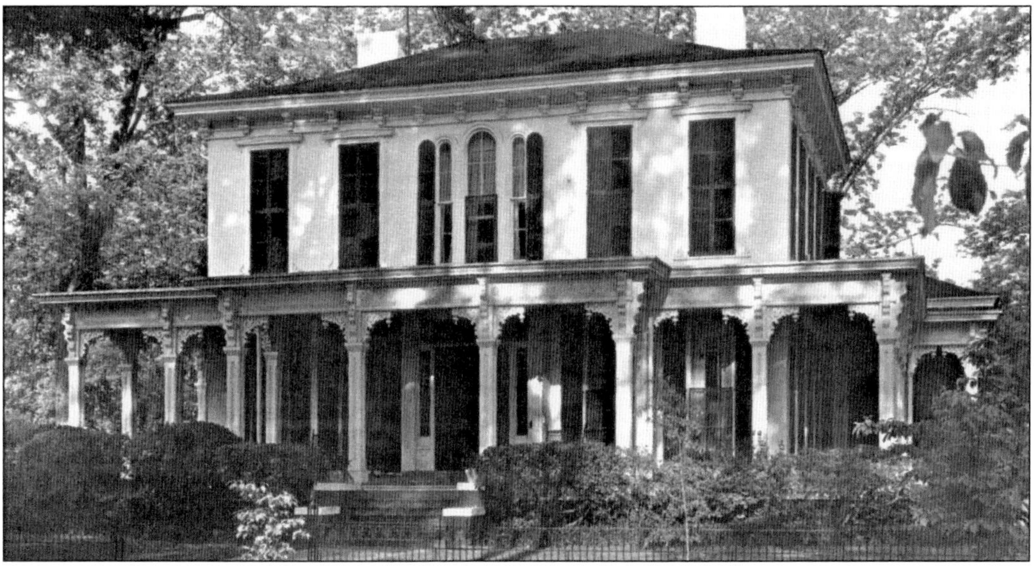

The Drewry-Mitchell-Moorer home was constructed in 1848. Dr. John Drewry was one of the greatest typhoid fever doctors of his time. During epidemics, he used the house as a hospital. The fourth generation of the family now lives here. This lovely Italianate home has a broad veranda on three sides supported by elaborately carved columns. A belvedere on the house burned about 1914 and was not replaced. (Courtesy of Rob Schaffeld.)

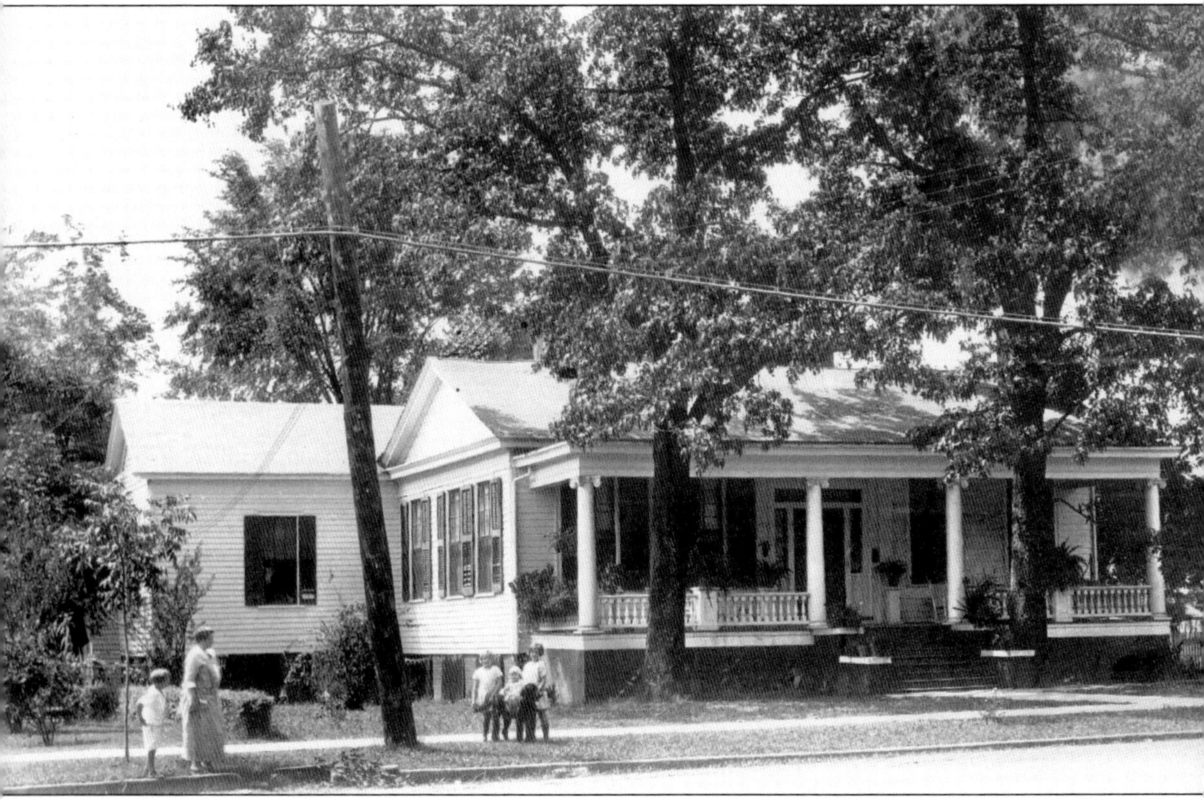

This beautiful cottage-style home in Eufaula's Seth Lore Historic District was the setting of amusement for three small children and their dog in the early 1900s. (Courtesy of Tade Lampley.)

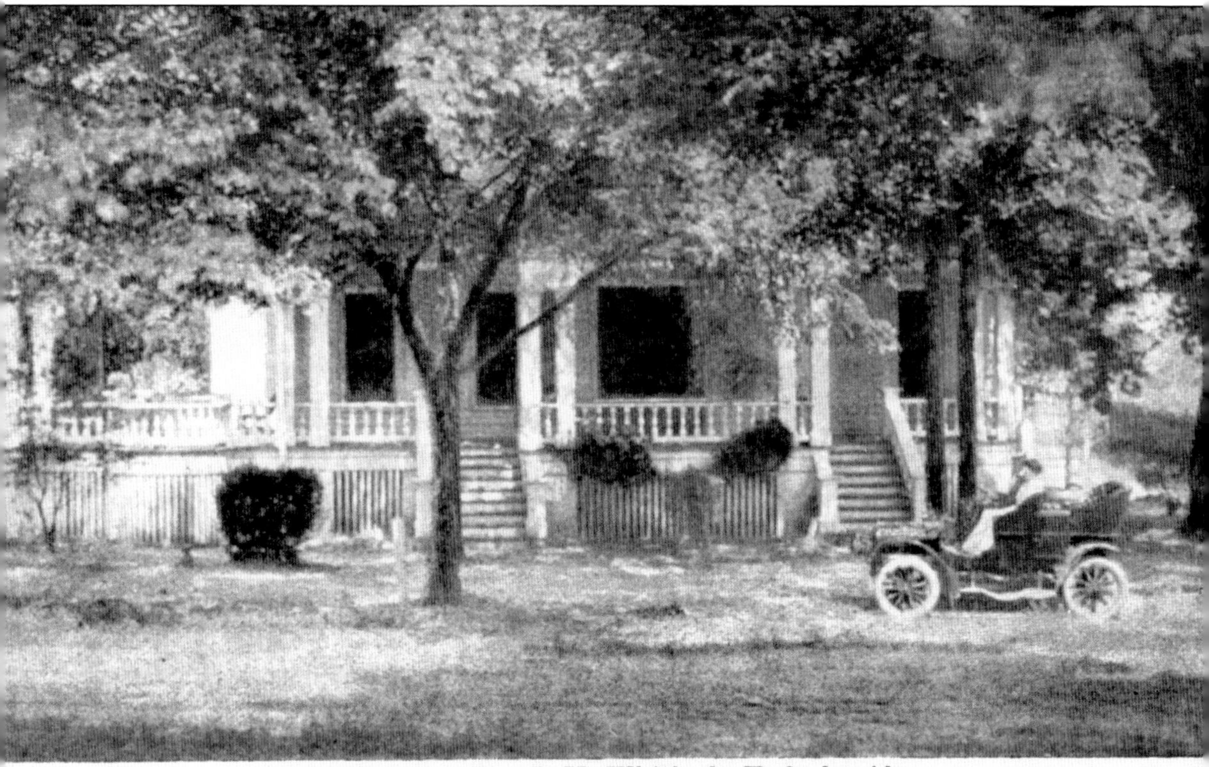

Residence of Mrs. J. H. Whitlock, Eufaula, Ala.

Clara Griffeth, of Columbia, Alabama, married John H. Whitlock in February 1886. She came to Eufaula with her new bridegroom who, in the previous year, had opened the J.H. Whitlock Jewelry Store. She was a beloved woman who devoted much of her time to church work at St. James Episcopal Church. She was also a leader of the United Daughters of the Confederacy. Mr. Whitlock died in 1900 and Mrs. Whitlock in 1925. Their home stood on Orange Avenue. (Courtesy of Rob Schaffeld.)

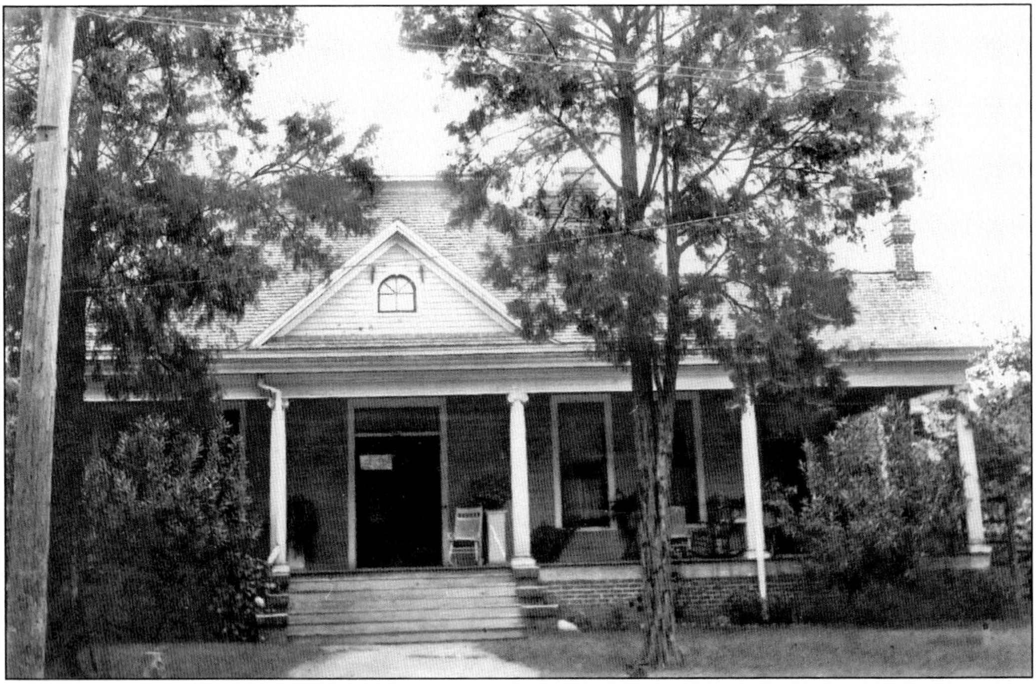

Depicting a historic home in Eufaula, this postcard was addressed to Mrs. W.M. Flewellen, Greensburough, Alabama. It was postmarked September 19, 1912. (Courtesy of Doug Purcell.)

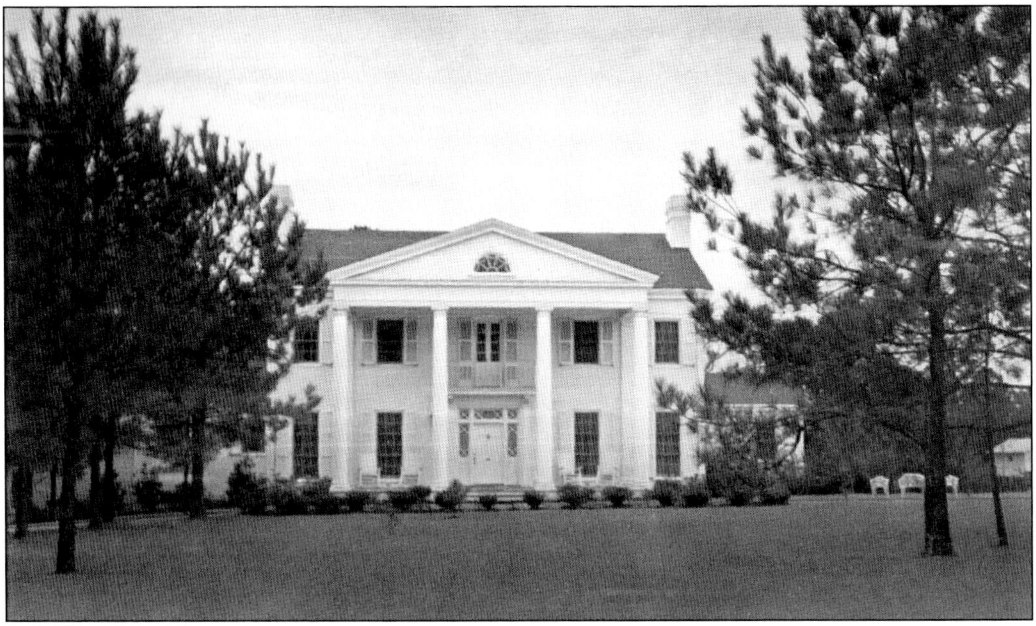

The M.C. Dixon home was constructed in the early 1950s on Country Club Road in Eufaula. The second generation of the family now lives in the home. Its builder, Mr. M.C. Dixon, started M.C. Dixon Lumber Company in 1928 in Clayton. In 1935 he and his brother purchased an existing lumber plant in Eufaula. The third Dixon generation now runs Dixon Lumber Company. (Courtesy of Doug Purcell.)

Four

Disasters

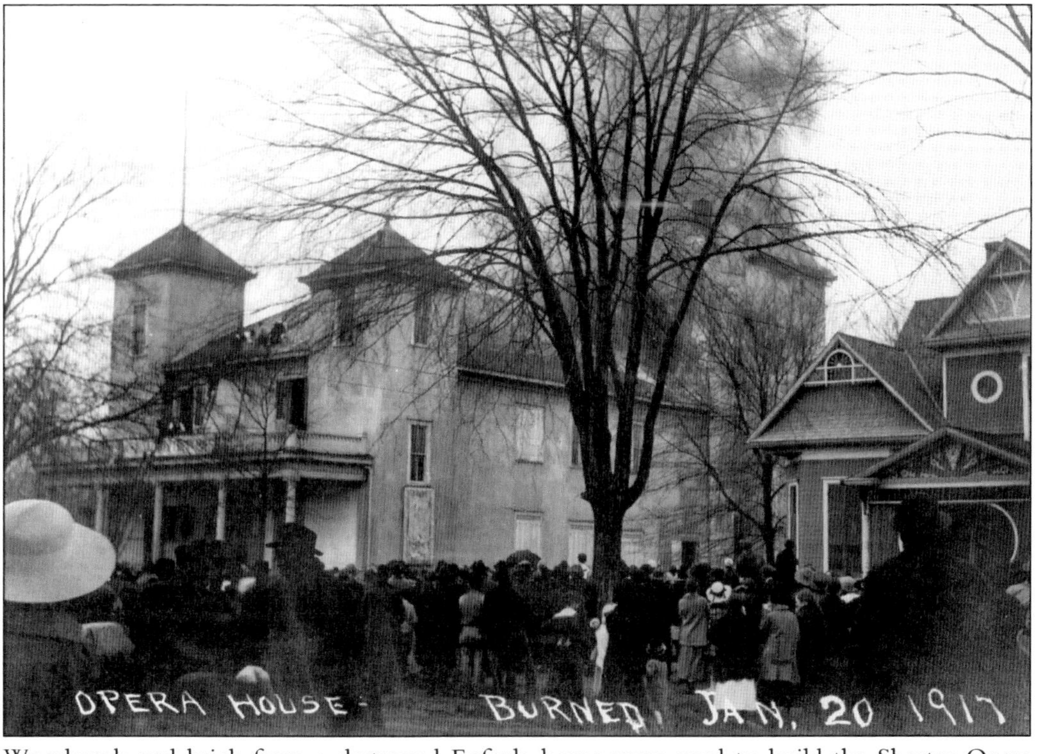

Woodwork and brick from a destroyed Eufaula home were used to build the Shorter Opera House in 1867, later known as the Eufaula Opera House. The facility was large enough to present plays and drama to a capacity of approximately 700 people. On January 20, 1917, the Opera House burned while citizens looked on. (Courtesy of Eufaula Heritage Association.)

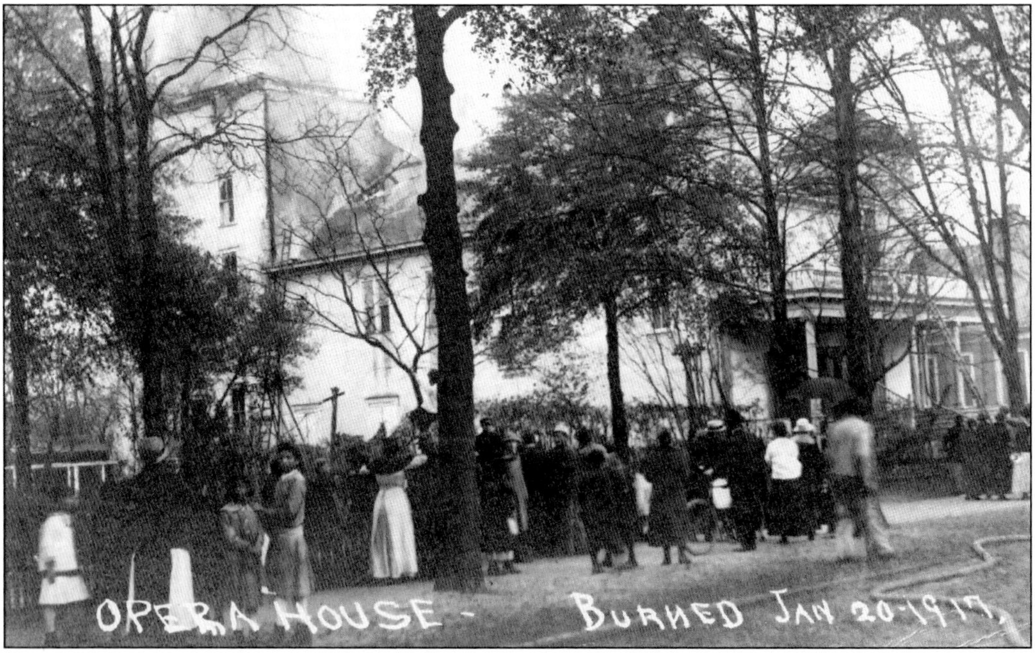

In 1886 the planning committee for Jefferson Davis's visit met at the Opera House on West Broad Street. In 1917 Eufaulians gathered in the street to watch the Opera House burn. (Courtesy of Eufaula Heritage Association.)

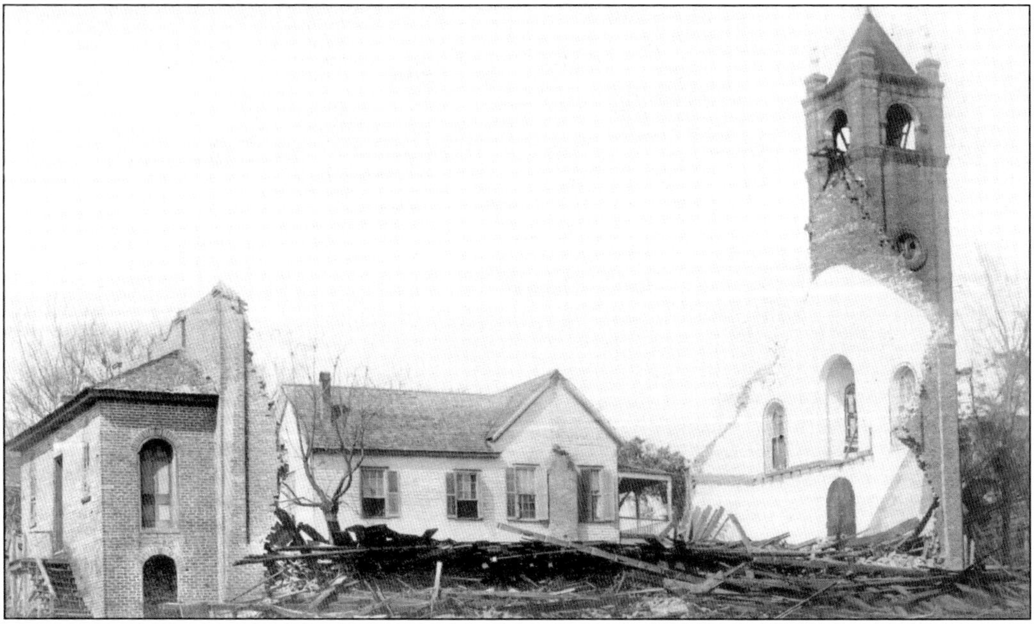

The Holy Redeemer Catholic Church was the first building struck on March 5, 1919, at three in the afternoon by the tornado that came through that day. The cupola and a portion of the back wall was all that was left standing in the place where the church once stood. The church was rebuilt on the original site and still stands on the corner of McRae Street and West Broad. (Courtesy of Rob Schaffeld.)

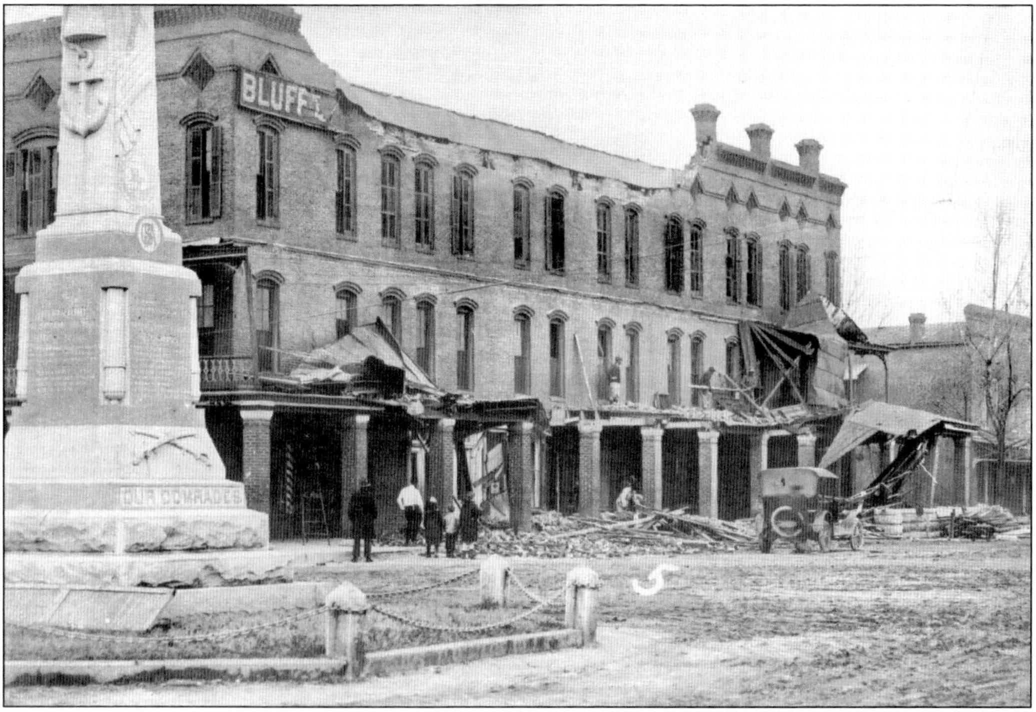

The Bluff City Inn, built in 1885 by W.N. and J.H. Reeves, suffered much damage from the tornado of March 5, 1919. (Courtesy of Rob Schaffeld.)

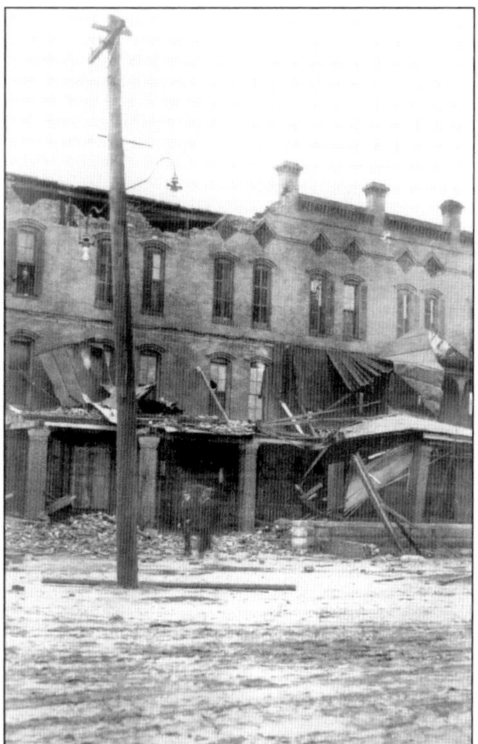

After leaving the Catholic church, the tornado moved toward the Bluff City Inn before it moved on towards Ross Hardware. The drive-through on the front of the inn was destroyed and not replaced. (Courtesy of Rob Schafeld.)

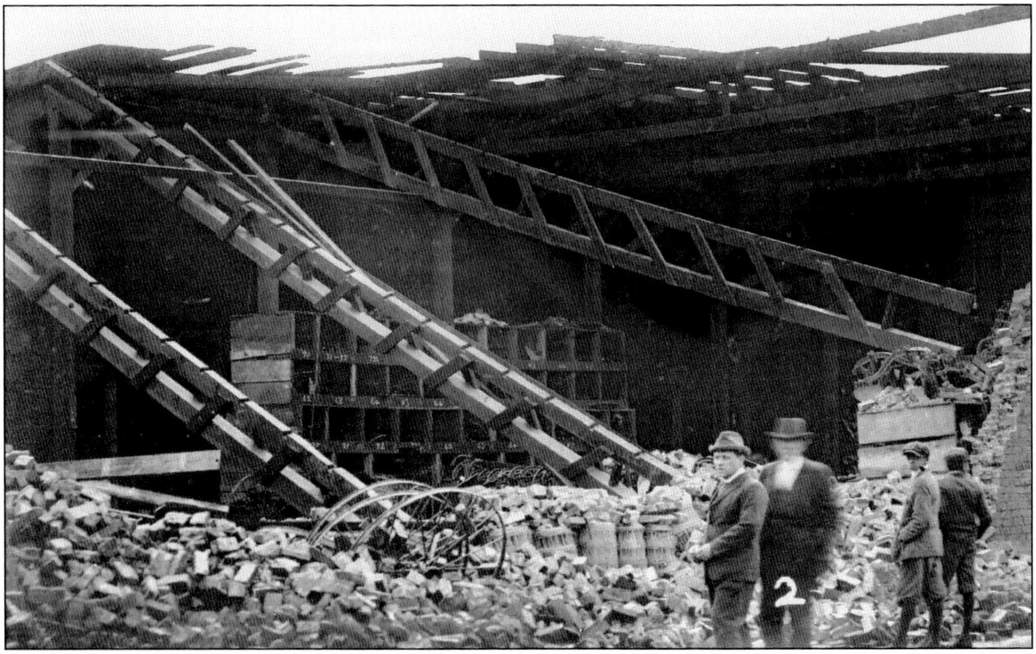

Citizens assess the damage to Ross Hardware Company caused by the tornado that hit Eufaula mid-afternoon March 5, 1919. (Courtesy of Mary Gray.)

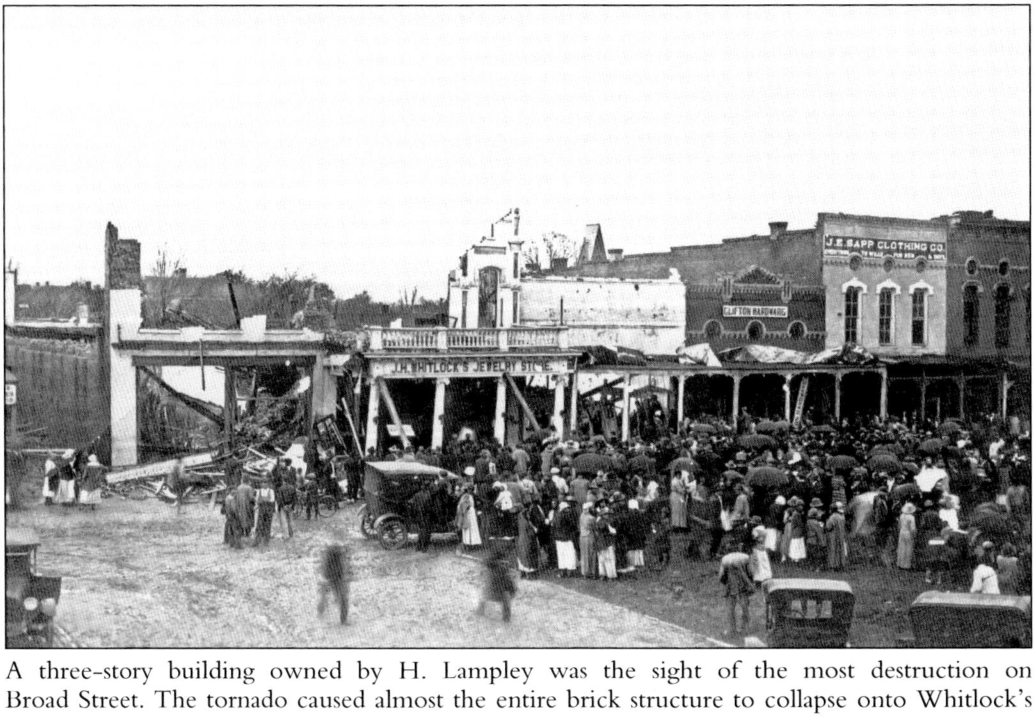

A three-story building owned by H. Lampley was the sight of the most destruction on Broad Street. The tornado caused almost the entire brick structure to collapse onto Whitlock's Jewelry next door. It also partially destroyed Hamilton's Café and J.C. McRae's. (Courtesy of Rob Schaffeld.)

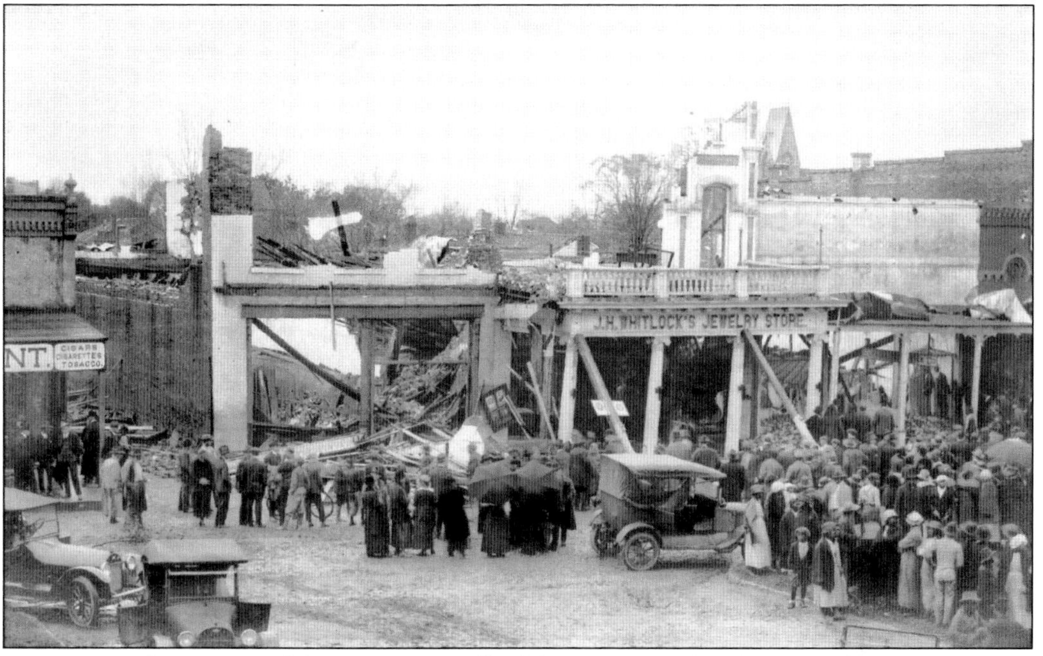

Notice in a closer view of the same scene all of the townspeople who are gathered around the debris. They gathered to work through the night in order to find survivors and dead. Four bodies were removed from the rubble. (Courtesy of Rob Schaffeld.)

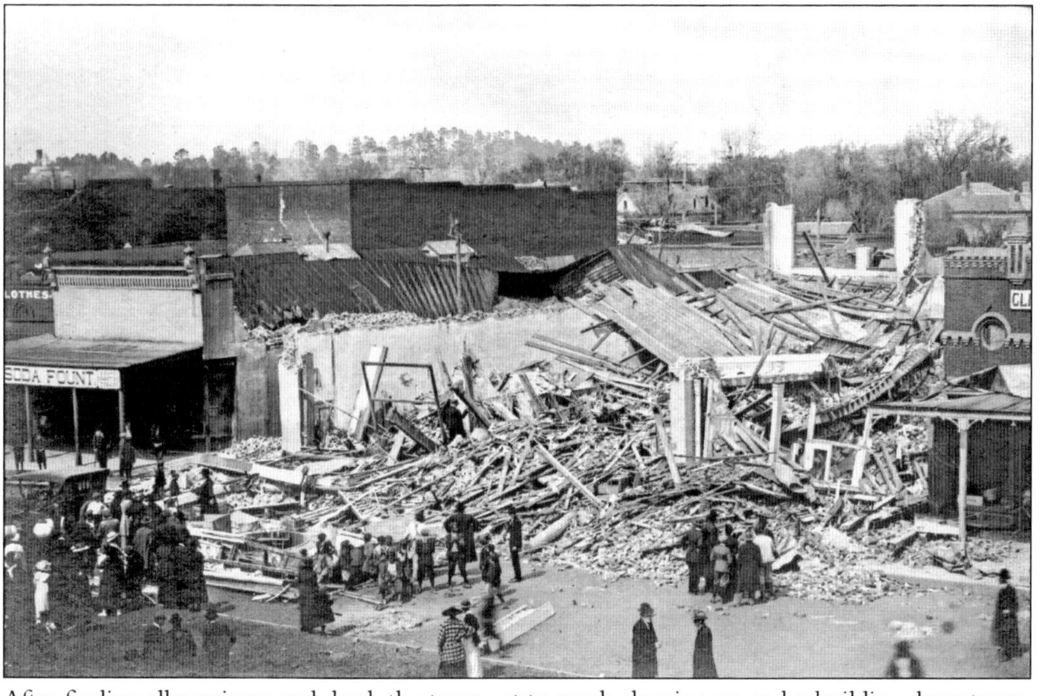

After finding all survivors and dead, the town set to work cleaning up and rebuilding downtown. This postcard depicts the beginning of the demolition of what was left on Broad Street. (Courtesy of Rob Schaffeld.)

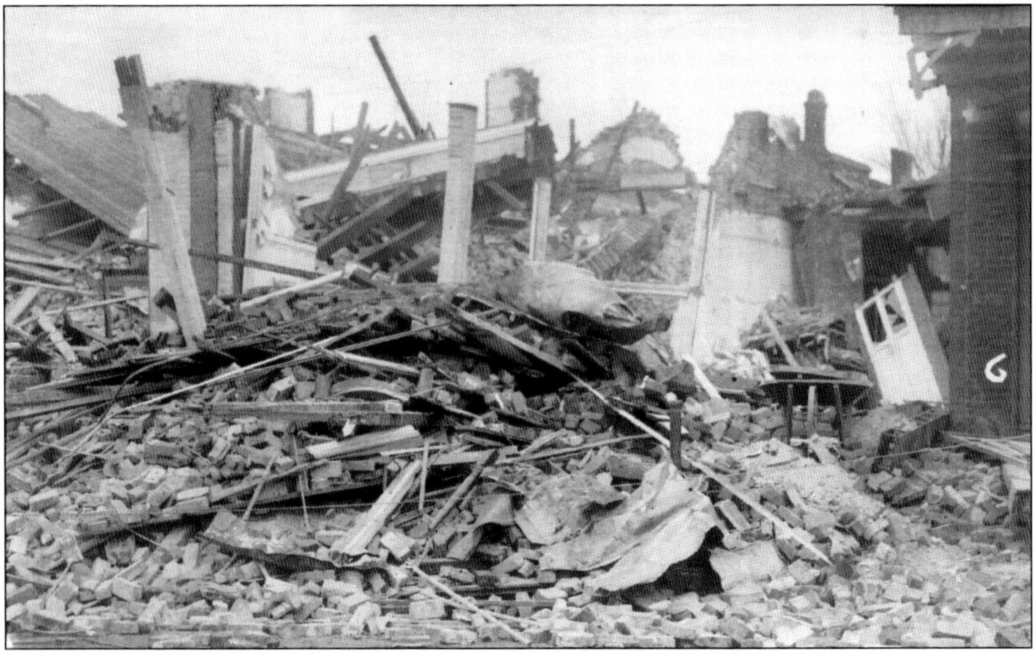

Though this site is unidentifiable, we again see the destruction of the tornado. After all the community losses were totaled, they were estimated at about $500,000. (Courtesy of Rob Schaffeld.)

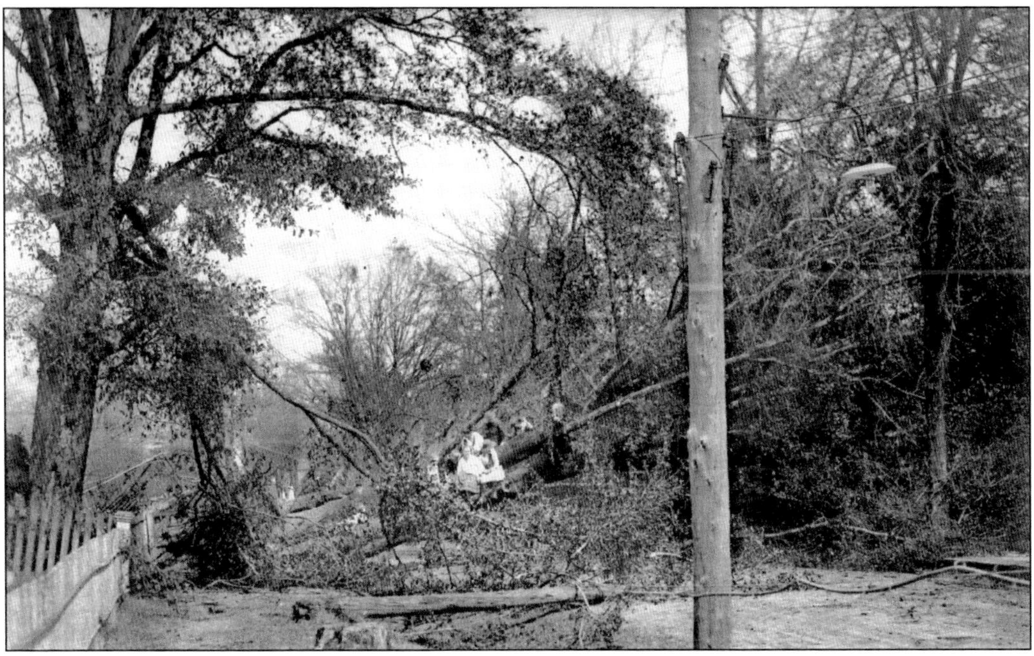

Chimneys were blown down from every house in the destructive path of the tornado. The huge uprooted trees blocked many of the streets, but they provided a playground for neighborhood children. (Courtesy of Rob Schaffeld.)

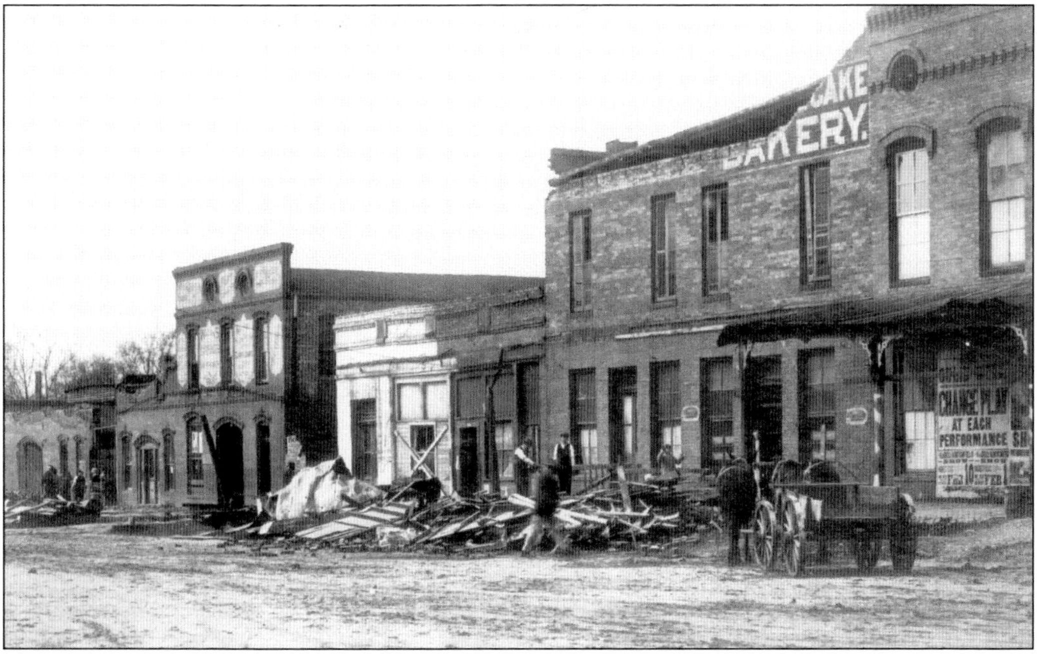

The downtown streets were the sight of much damage, much destruction, and much clean up. It was not long, though, before Eufaulians banded together to rebuild their lovely downtown. (Courtesy of Mary Gray.)

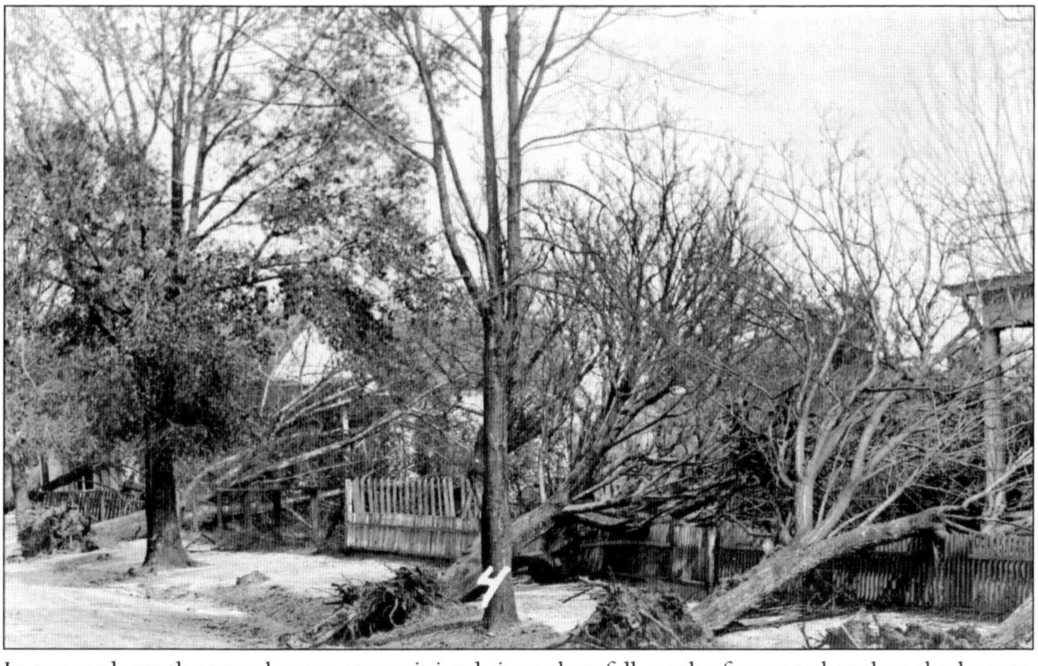

In some places the tree damage was minimal since they fell on the fences rather than the houses. (Courtesy of Mary Gray.)

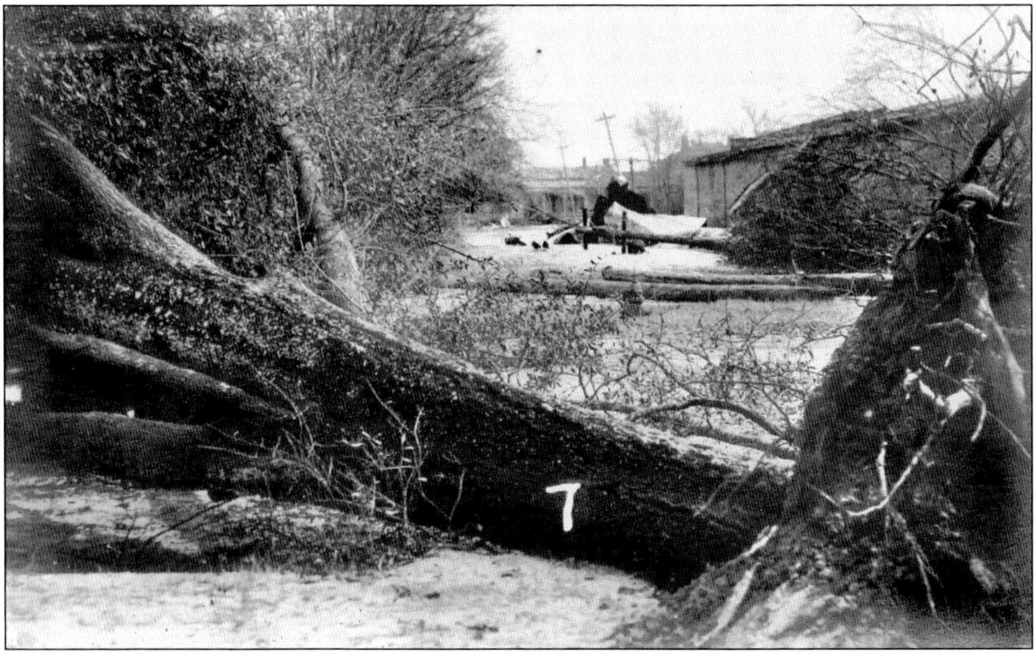

The outer edge of the storm blew over trees, barns, and quite a few outbuildings. (Courtesy of Rob Schaffeld.)

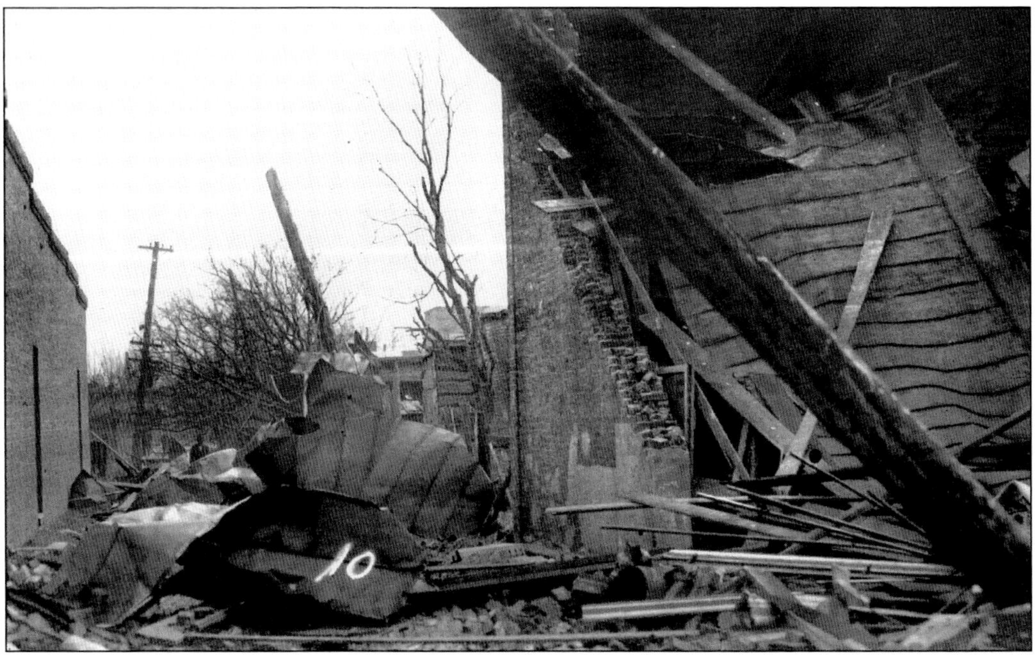

The damage of the tornado of 1919 was like nothing Eufaula had ever seen before or has seen since. (Courtesy of Rob Schaffeld.)

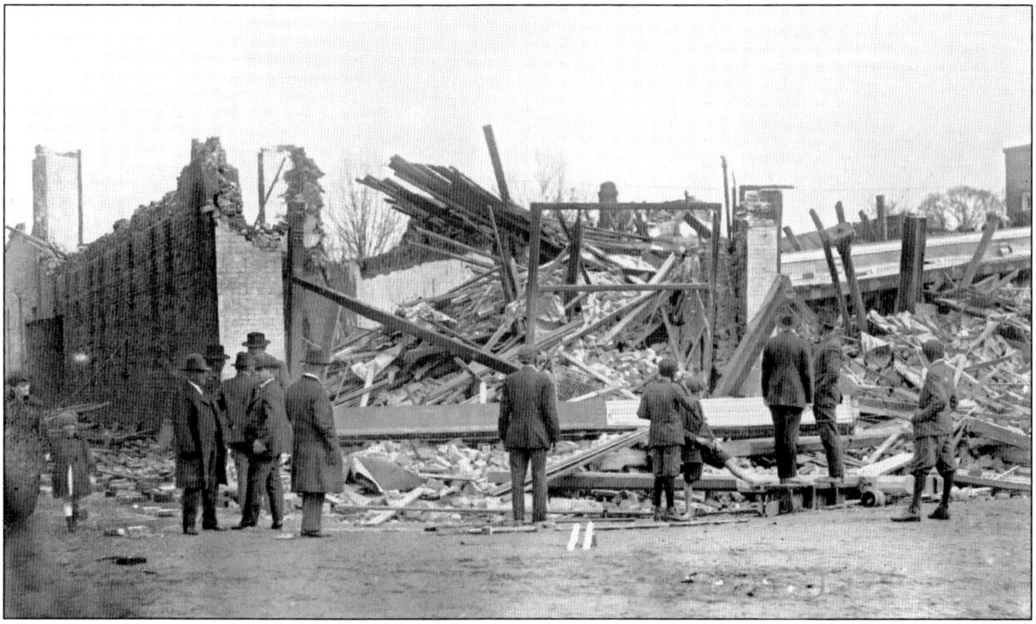

Townspeople survey the amazing amount of rubble from the 1919 tornado with a sobering realization of the damage. (Courtesy of Mary Gray.)

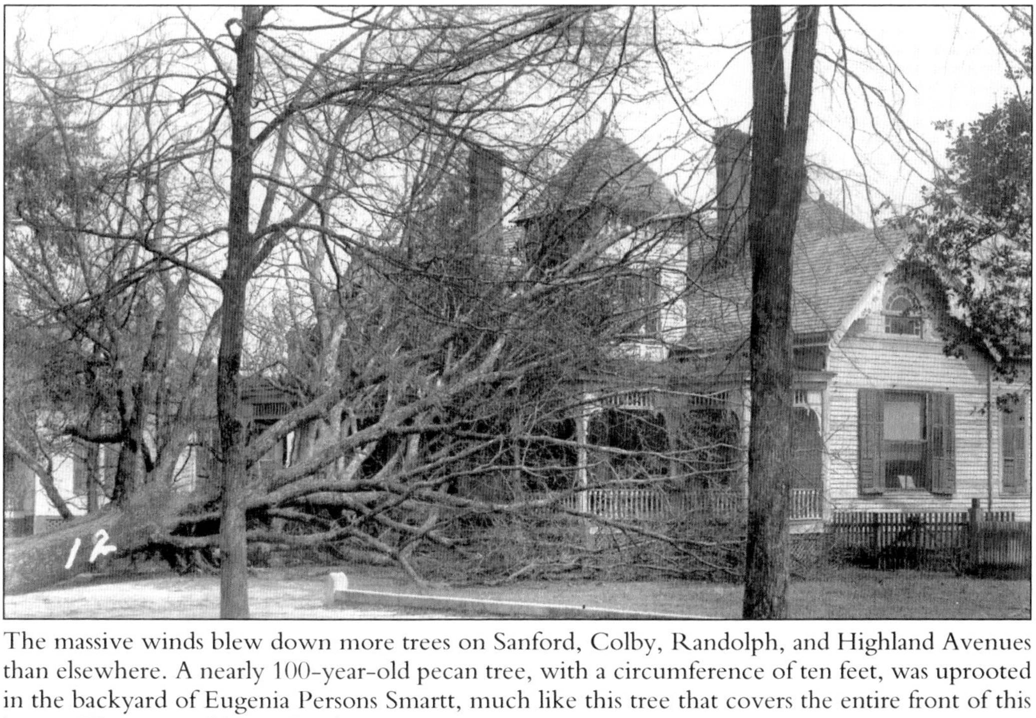

The massive winds blew down more trees on Sanford, Colby, Randolph, and Highland Avenues than elsewhere. A nearly 100-year-old pecan tree, with a circumference of ten feet, was uprooted in the backyard of Eugenia Persons Smartt, much like this tree that covers the entire front of this home. (Courtesy of Mary Gray)

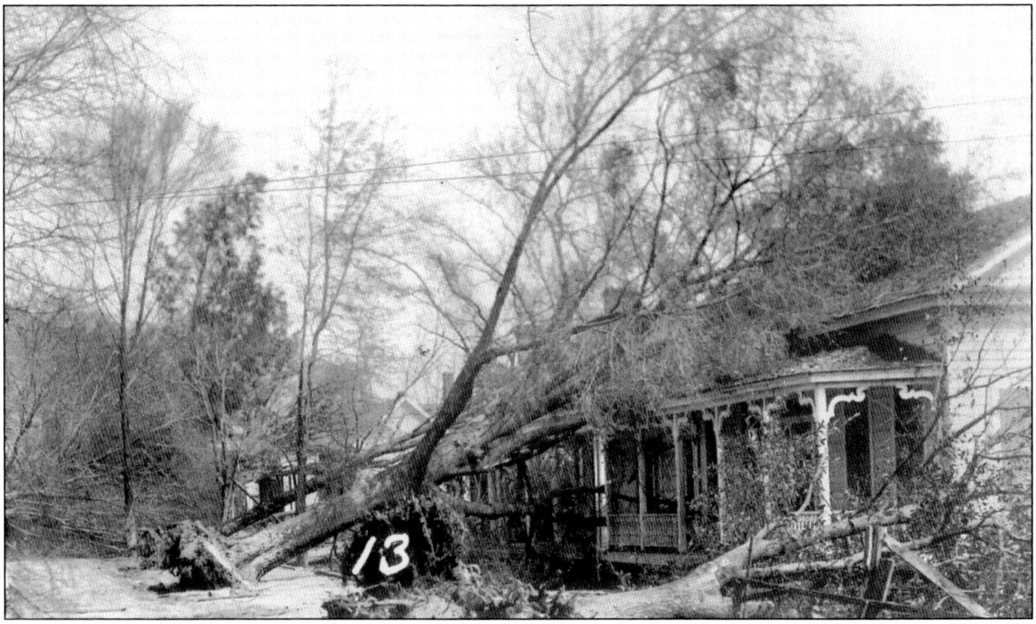

In the destruction of the tornado of 1919, many trees were uprooted and entire trees were lying on houses. (Courtesy of Rob Schaffeld.)

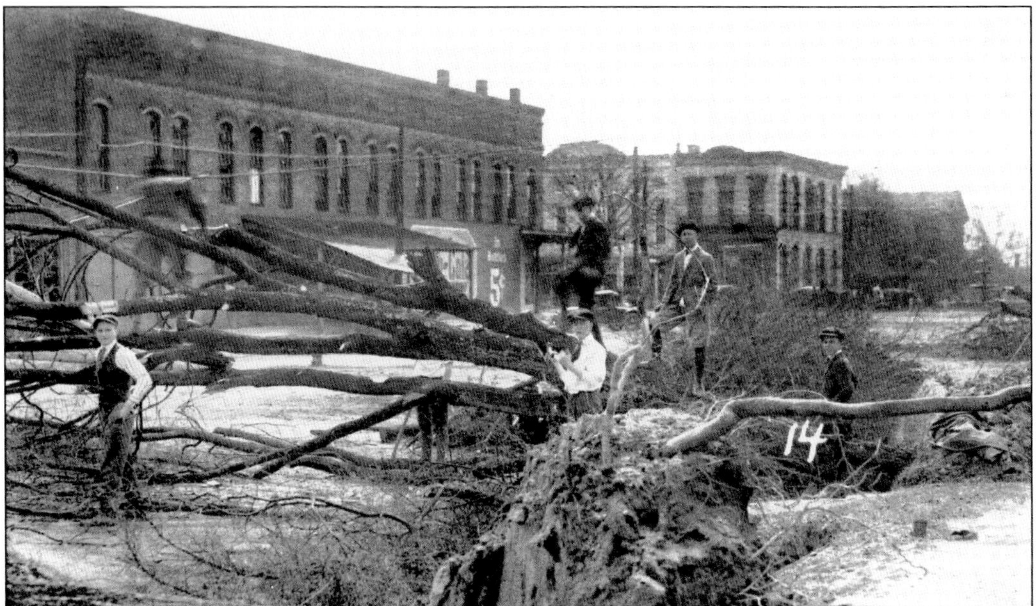

This is a photo showing damage from Randolph Avenue looking south to Broad Street. (Courtesy of Rob Schaffeld.)

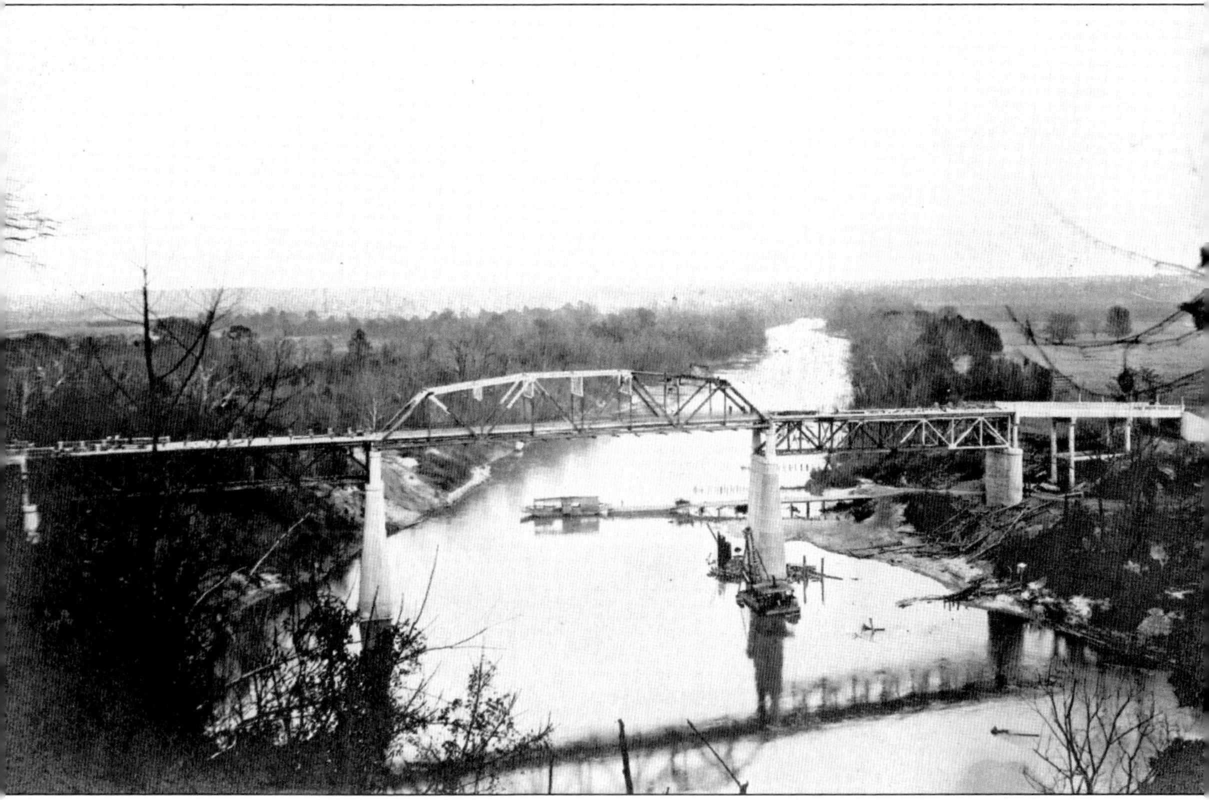

The damaging tornado hit Eufaula one last time when it took a stab at the River Bridge before it moved into Georgia. The bridge was not completely destroyed and the old columns were used in the construction of a new iron bridge built in the same place.(Courtesy of Rob Schaffeld.)

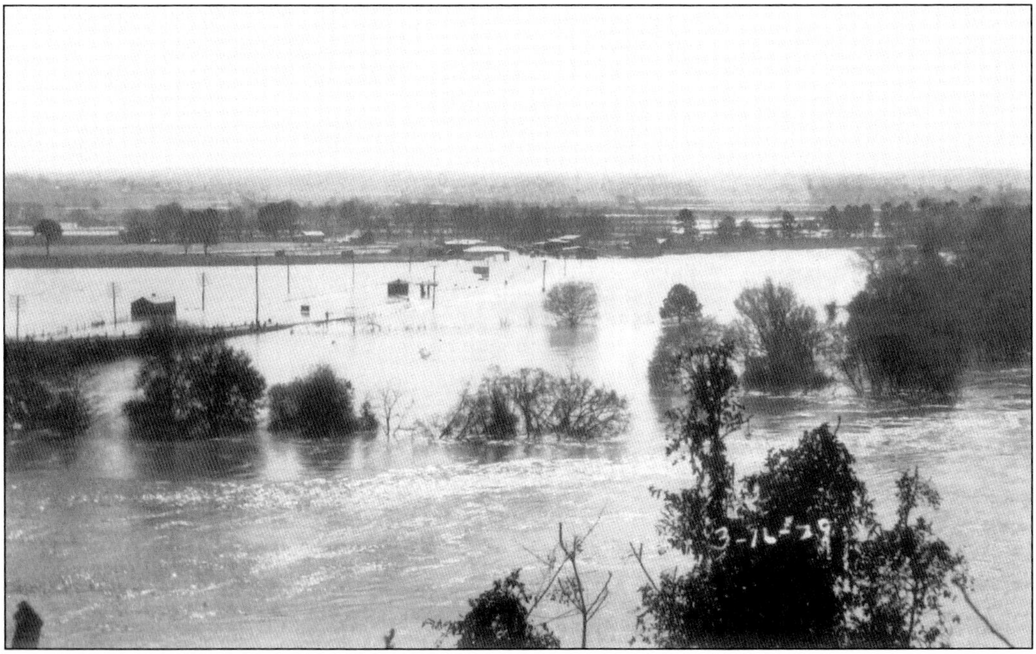

This scene is of the 1929 flood of the Chattahoochee River looking from Georgia westward towards Eufaula. (Courtesy of Rob Schaffeld.)

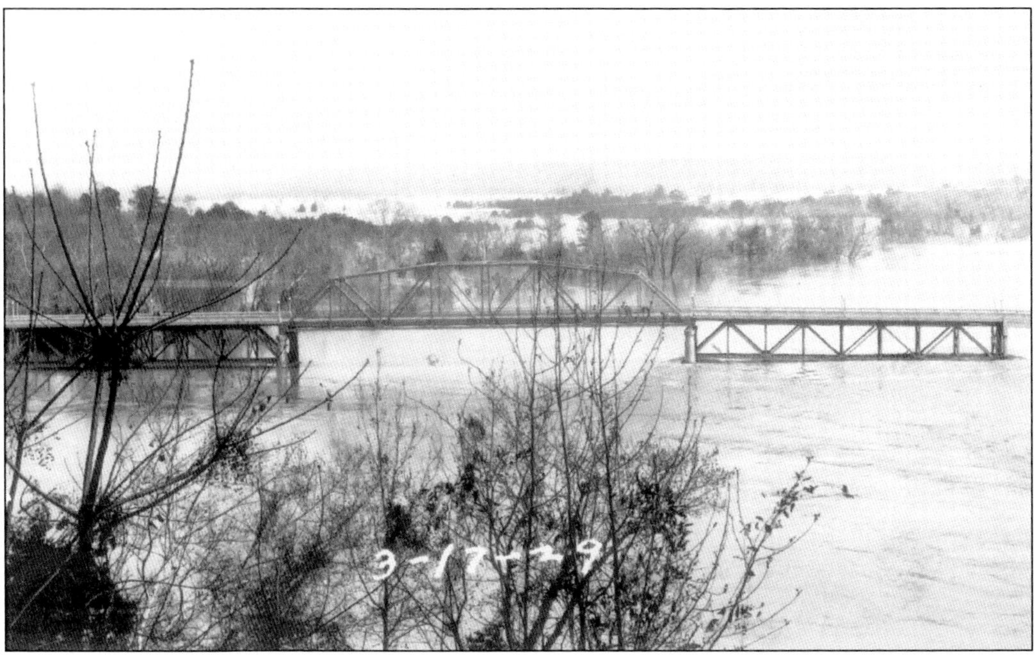

The flood of 1929 covered the Georgia Flats. Memories of this flood may have been a factor in convincing residents along the Chattahoochee that a dam was needed for flood control. (Courtesy of Mary Thomas.)

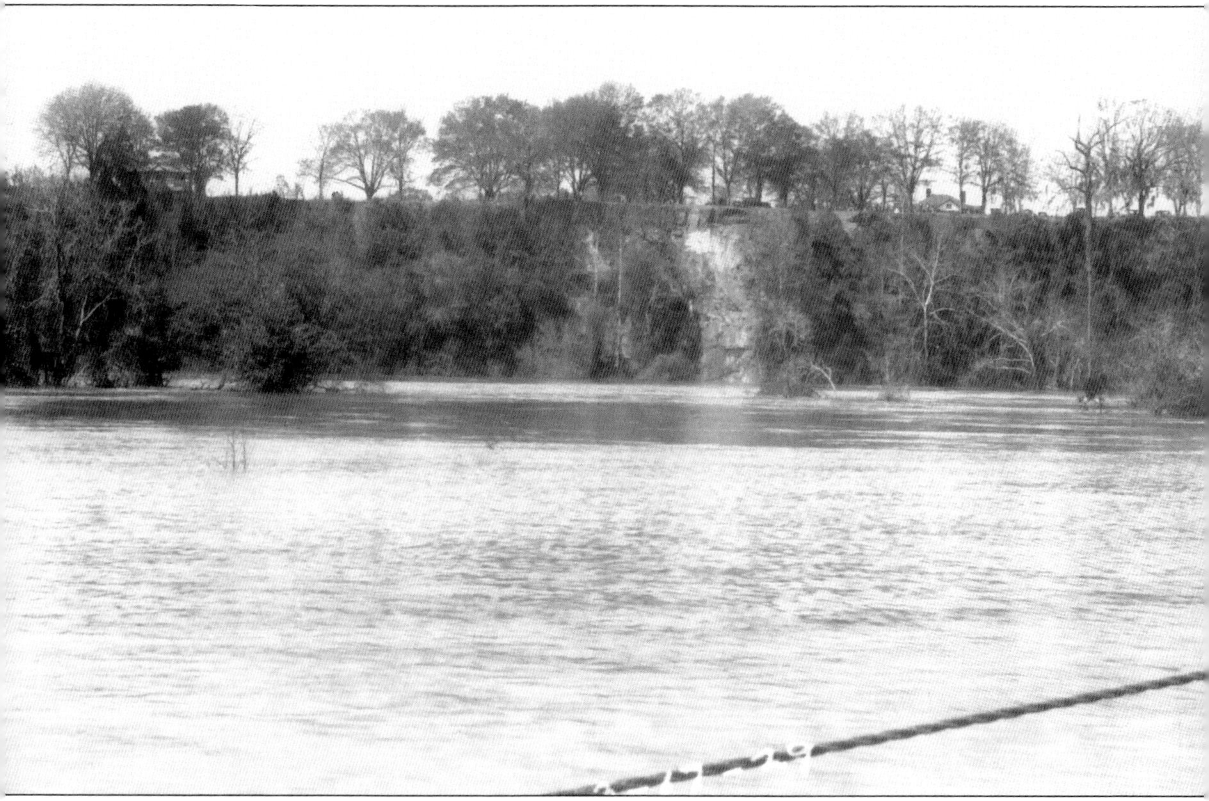

Eufaula's high bluffs served it well during the flood of 1929 as it avoided much of the destruction that plagued surrounding cities. This is a scene from the west bank of the Chattahoochee River. (Courtesy of Rob Schaffeld.)

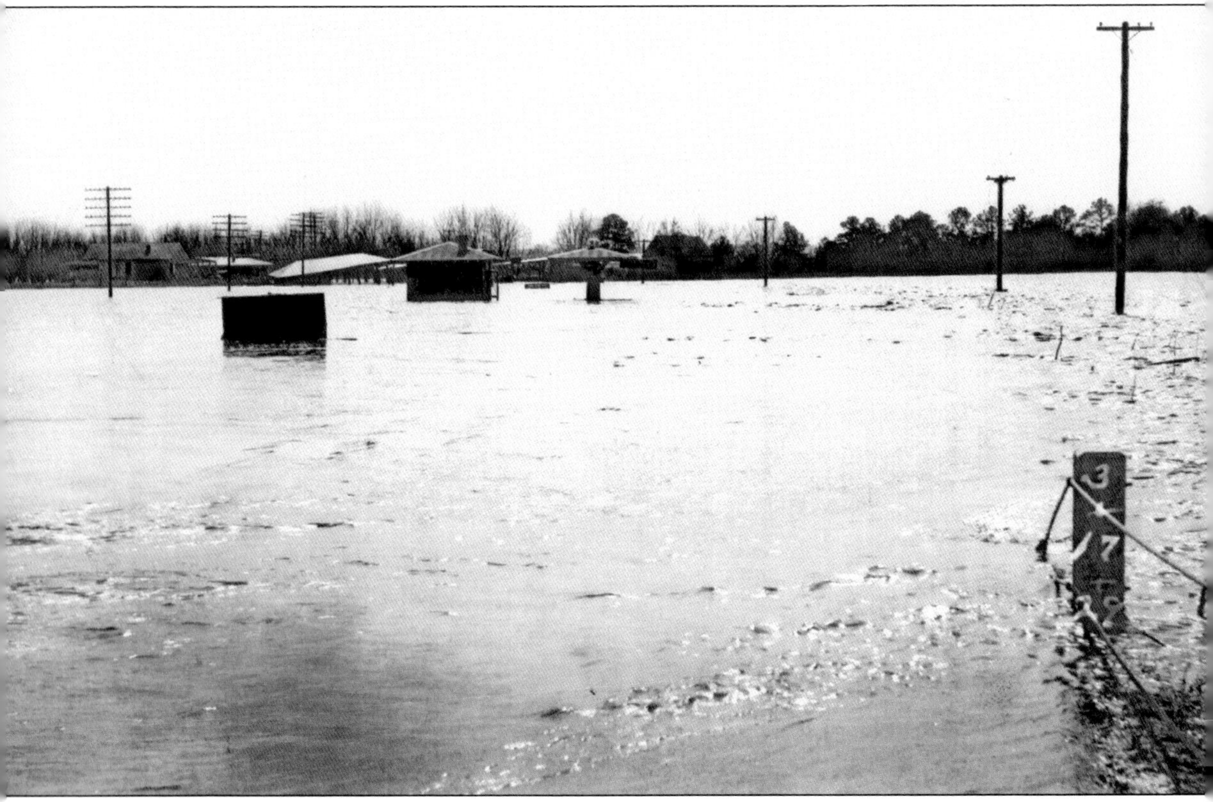

March 1929 floodwaters caused the Chattahoochee River to rise to 63.9 feet, its highest point in history. The spreading waters covered the fields on the Alabama side of the bridge from St. Francis bend nearly to the roadway leading to the city. (Courtesy of Rob Schaffeld.)

Five

Churches

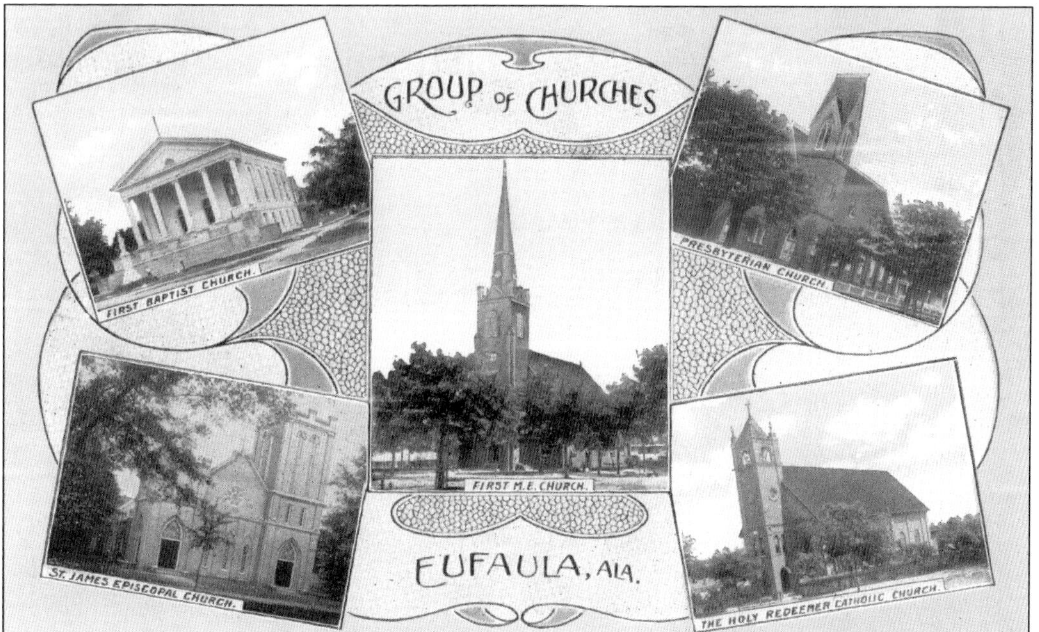

Barbour County is steeped in religion, evidenced by the many beautiful churches throughout the county. Five churches of Eufaula are shown in this grouping: First Baptist Church, First Presbyterian Church, St. James Episcopal Church, First M.E. Church, and the Holy Redeemer Catholic Church. Because of structural changes that occurred in the churches, this card can be dated between 1912 and 1919. (Courtesy of Eufaula Heritage Association.)

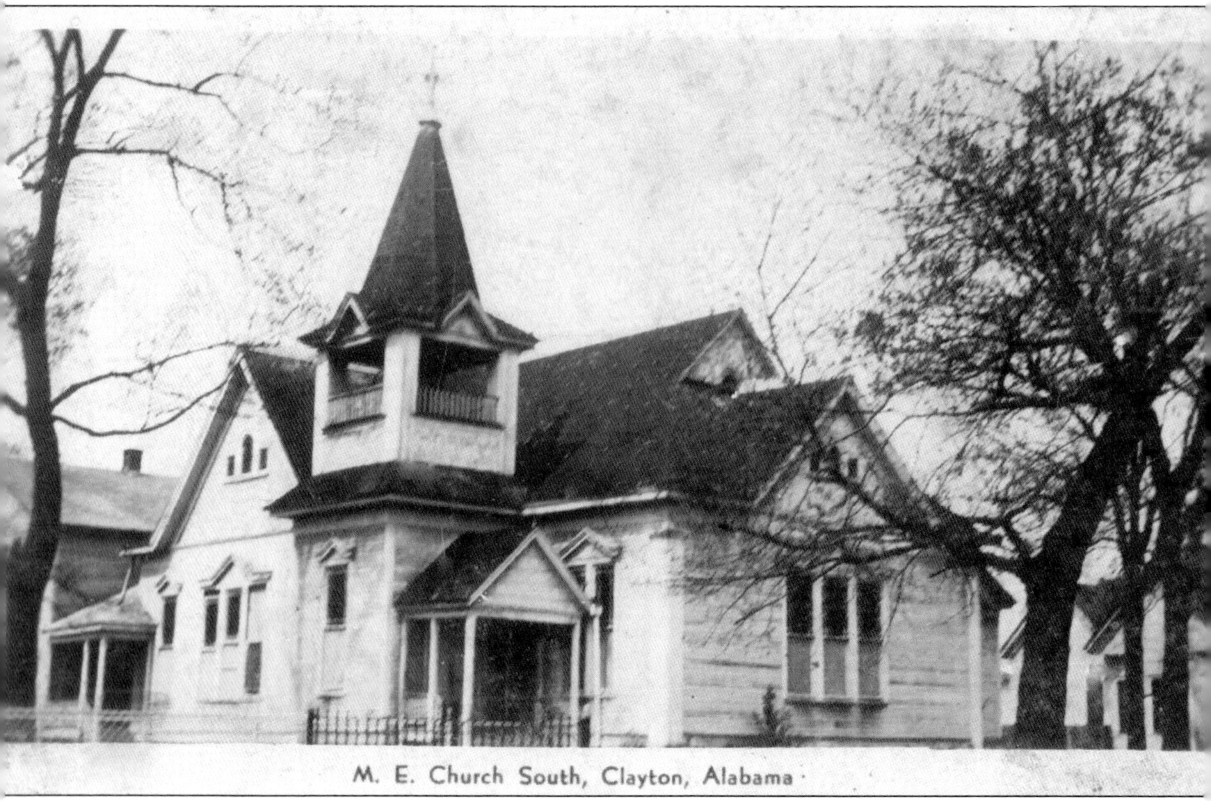

Clayton United Methodist Church has served the area for 180 years. James Clark donated land on Midway Street in 1846 for the construction of a Baptist and a Methodist church and a shared cemetery. Several variations of the frame structure were constructed. The Methodist church was remodeled in 1934. (Courtesy of Jean Fenn.)

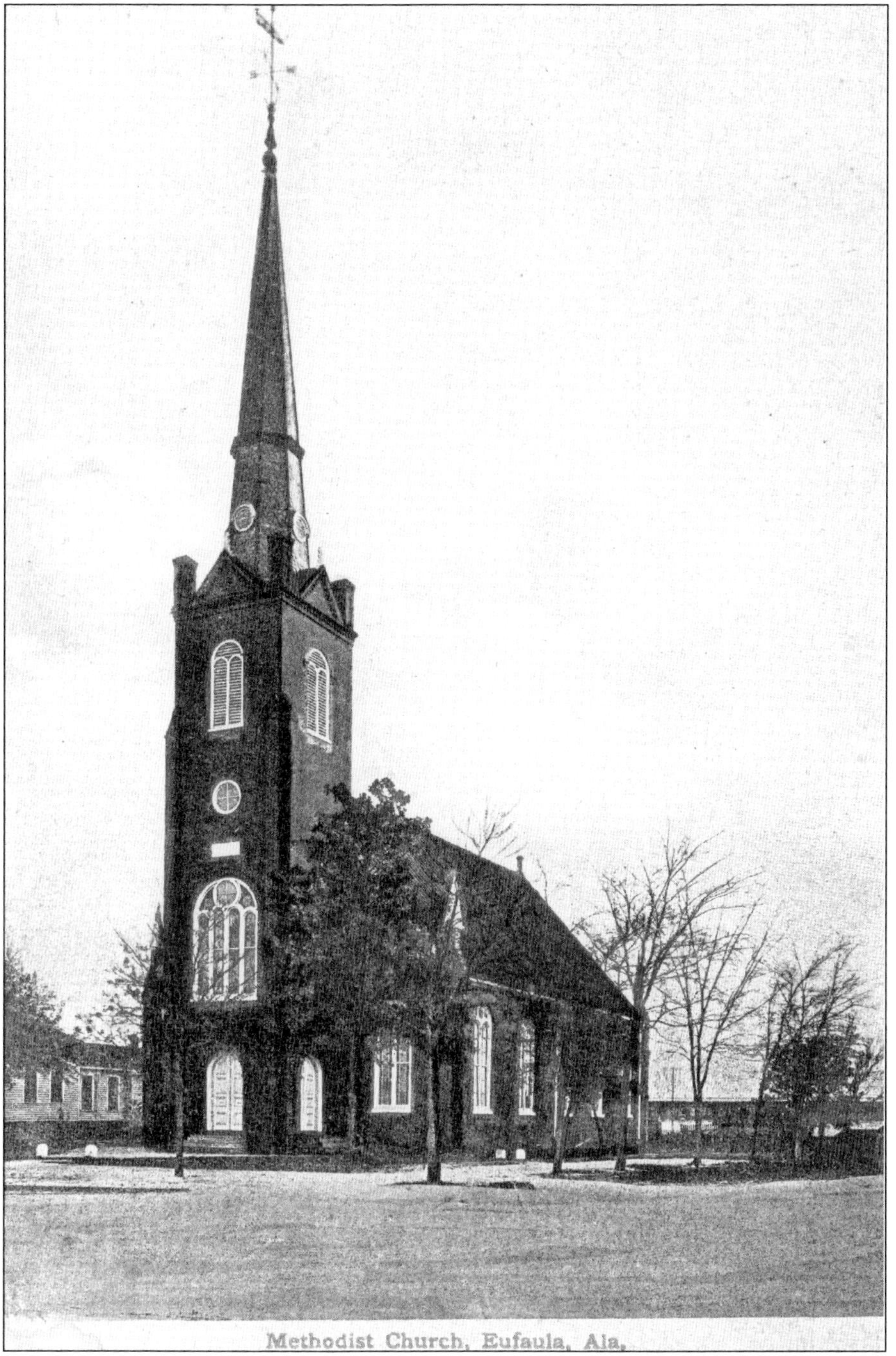

E.B. Young was the head of the building committee appointed to oversee the construction of the Methodist church, complete in 1879. Ann Young, wife of E.B. Young, had her last public appearance at the dedication ceremony of the church. The first funeral in the church was for Ann Beall Fendall Young. The church building is located behind the current First United Methodist Church minus the steeple, which was destroyed by lightning in 1910. (Courtesy of Doug Purcell.)

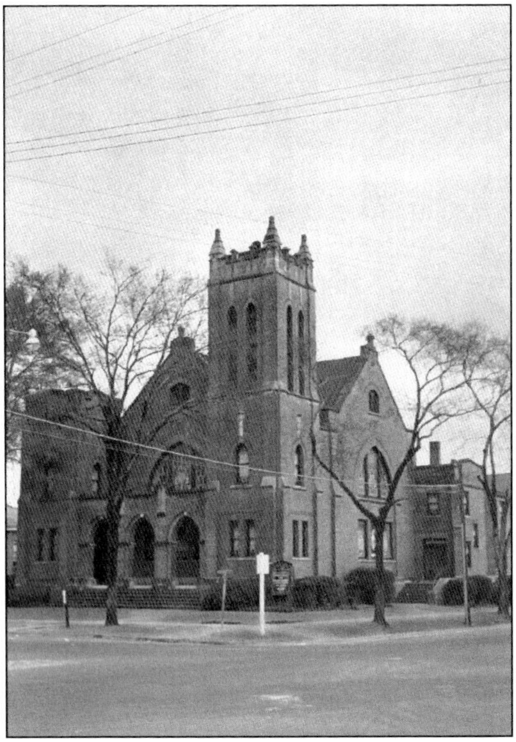

This First United Methodist Church building was constructed to replace the one damaged by lightning in 1910 at the same location. It was dedicated in 1917 and still stands at the corner of East Barbour Street and South Eufaula Avenue. Mr. John P. Fry was the chairman of the building committee appointed to oversee the construction. (Courtesy of Doug Purcell.)

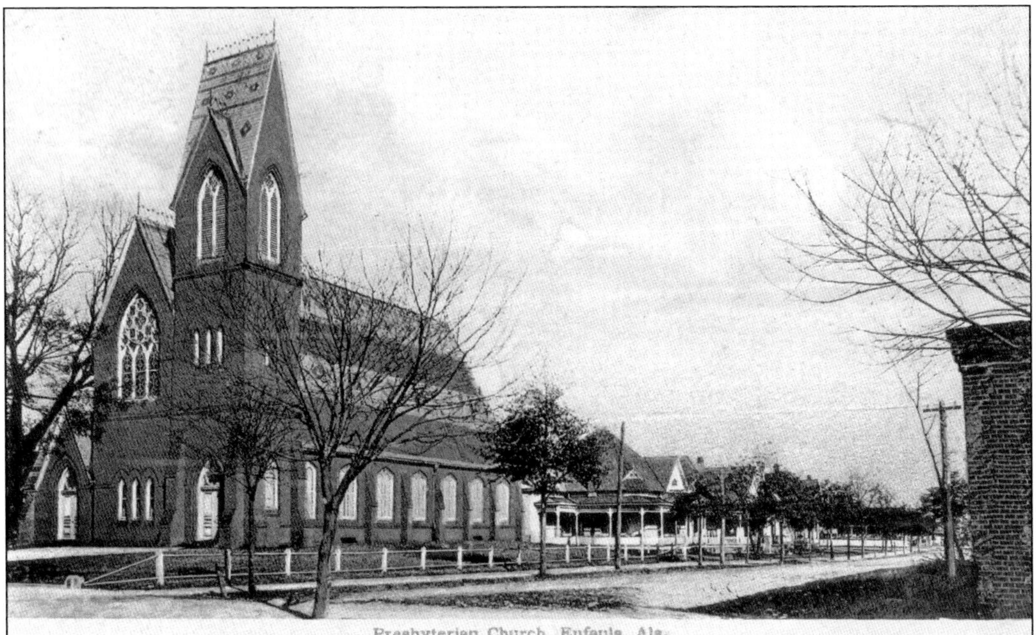

The First Presbyterian Church has served the Eufaula community at this location since 1869. This card pre-dates 1919 when the Gothic-style church was damaged by the tornado of 1919. The Tiffany stained glass window in front was purchased in New York City by Elder John McNab. (Courtesy of Frank Mixon.)

The First Baptist Church was organized on January 24, 1837, as Irwinton Baptist Church. The original church stood on the northwest corner of Union and Livingston Street. This building was constructed later at the corner of Barbour and Randolph Streets. The steeple was destroyed by lightning in 1907. (Courtesy of Rob Schaffeld.)

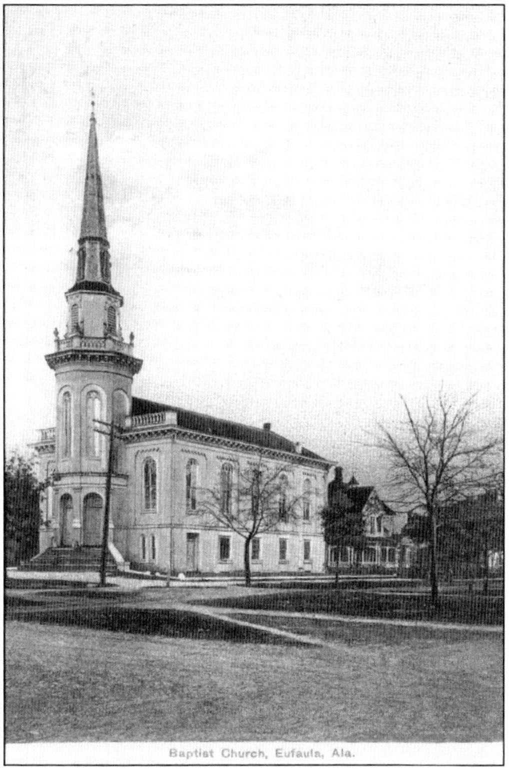

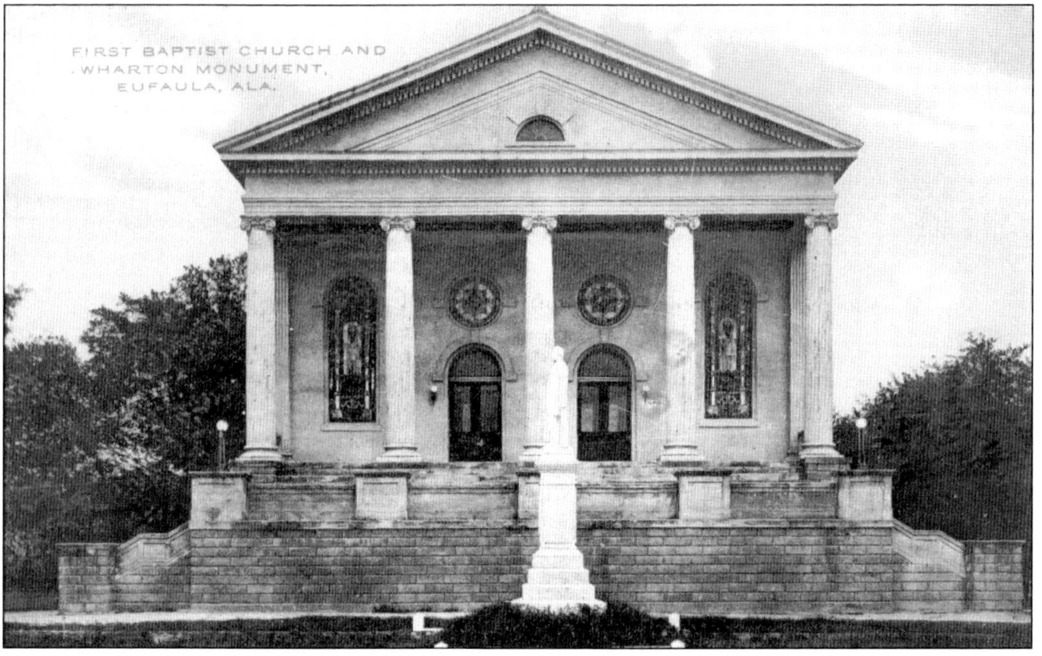

The town erected a monument to the Rev. Morton Bryan Wharton, First Baptist Church minister, after his death in 1908. Wharton served as ambassador to Saxe-Coburg in Germany. He was born in Orange County, Virginia. (Courtesy of Rob Schaffeld.)

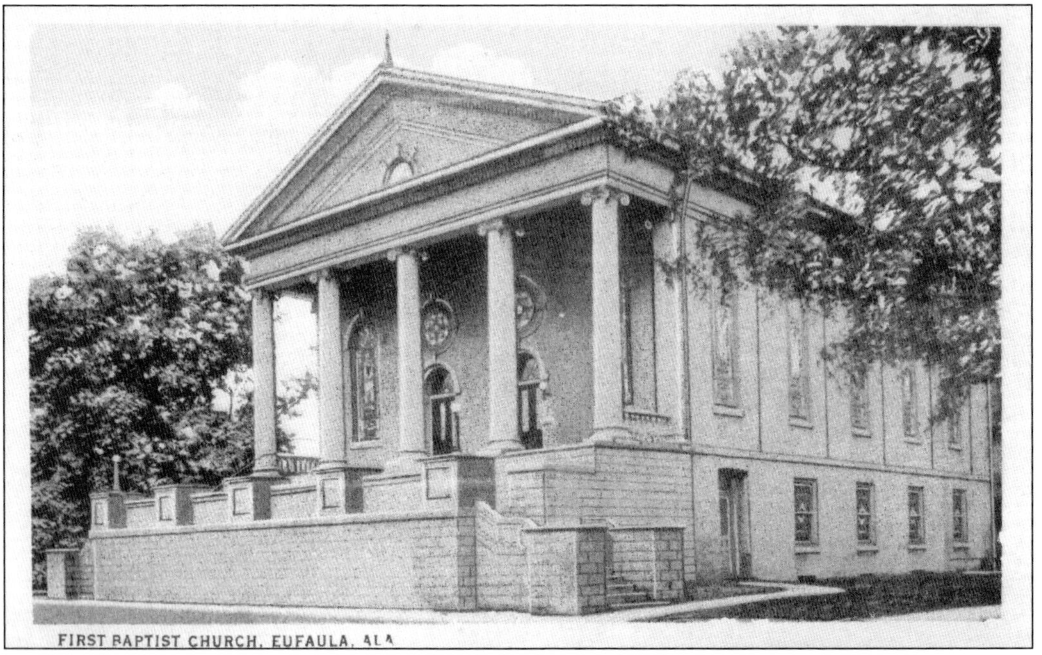

This postcard is a side view of the First Baptist Church located on the corner of Randolph and Barbour Streets. The present front columns, steps, and other changes were added after lightning in 1907 destroyed the original front and steeple. The cost of the remodeling was $30,000. (Courtesy of Eufaula Heritage Association.)

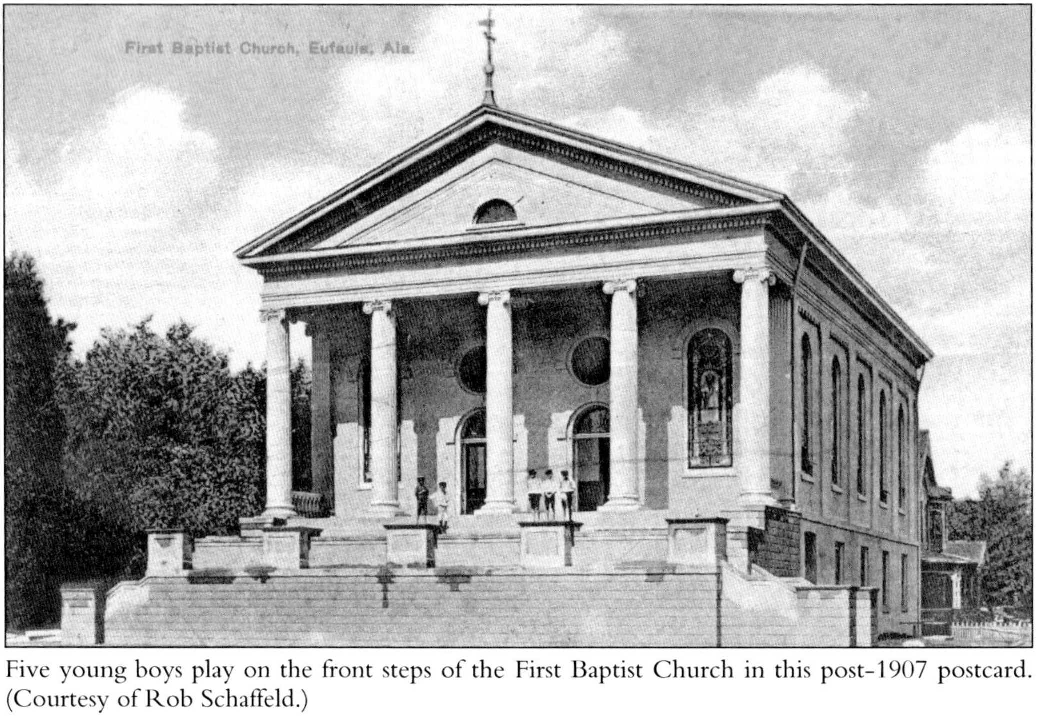

Five young boys play on the front steps of the First Baptist Church in this post-1907 postcard. (Courtesy of Rob Schaffeld.)

Six

Novelties

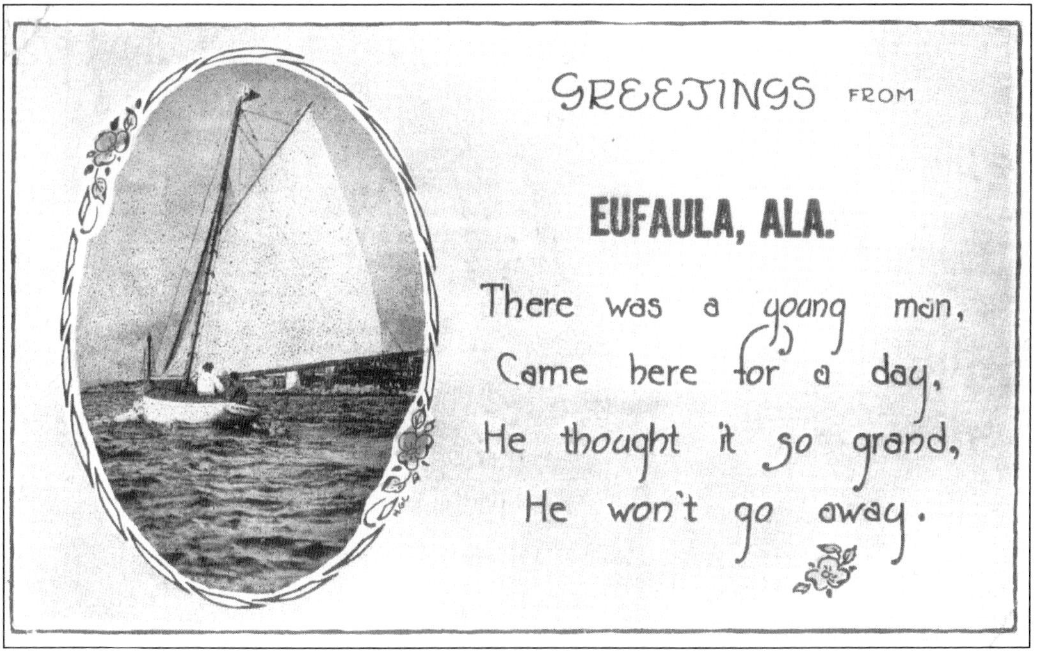

Capitalizing on Eufaula's recreational opportunities along the Chattahoochee River, this novelty card shows two people sailing. Though the front says "Greetings from Eufaula, Ala." along with a cute little rhyme, this is not a scene from Eufaula but a generalized "greeting" card. (Courtesy of Rob Schaffeld.)

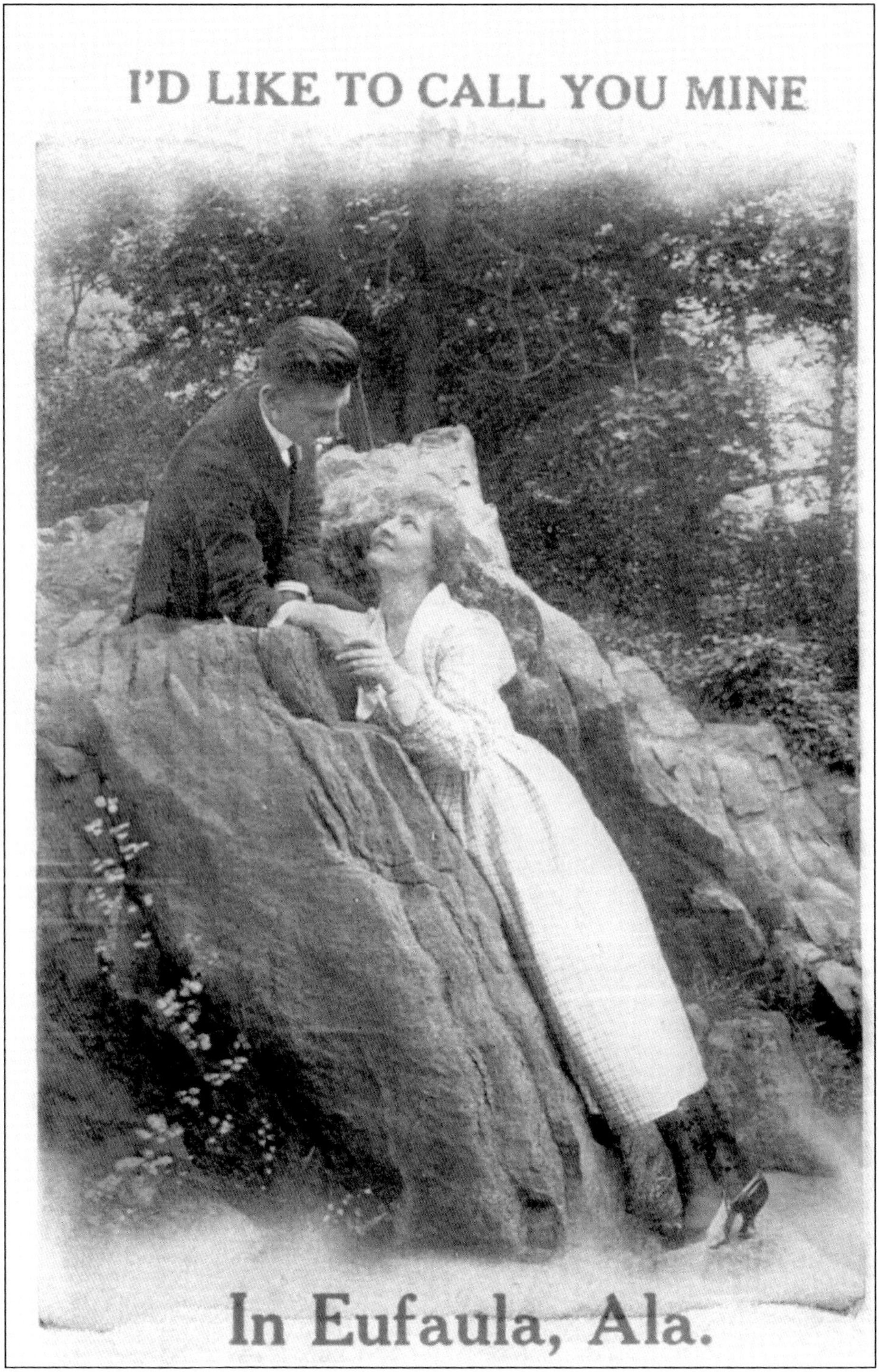

Dated October 1, 1920, Miss Lela Mae Anderson of Eufaula received this postcard saying, "Hello! How you be these cool days? From—Guess Who?" Such novelty cards were quite popular in the Roaring 1920s. (Courtesy of Doug Purcell.)

This is another novelty card from "Ruby," in Troy, to Lela Mae Anderson, of Eufaula. This enchanting and romantic card was postmarked August 1922. (Courtesy of Doug Purcell.)

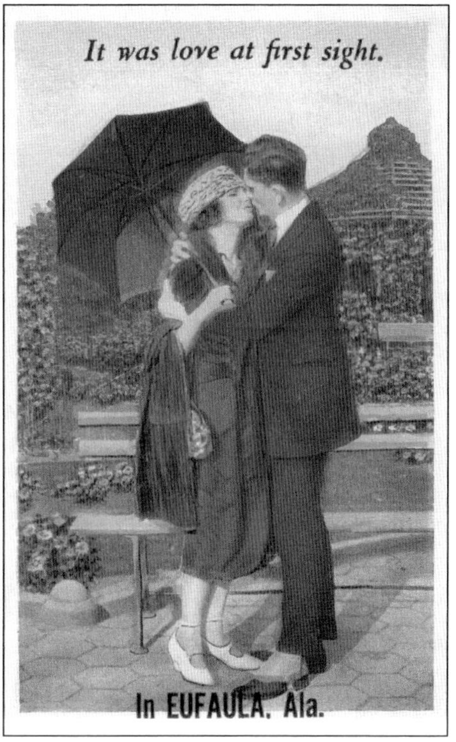

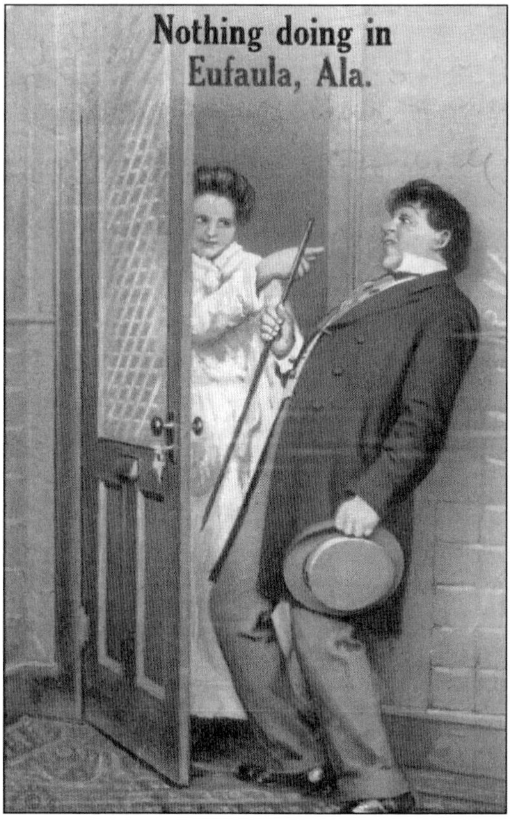

This "no nonsense" postcard had no postmark, but was addressed to Miss Vera Bush of Belcher, AL (Alabama). (Courtesy of Doug Purcell.)

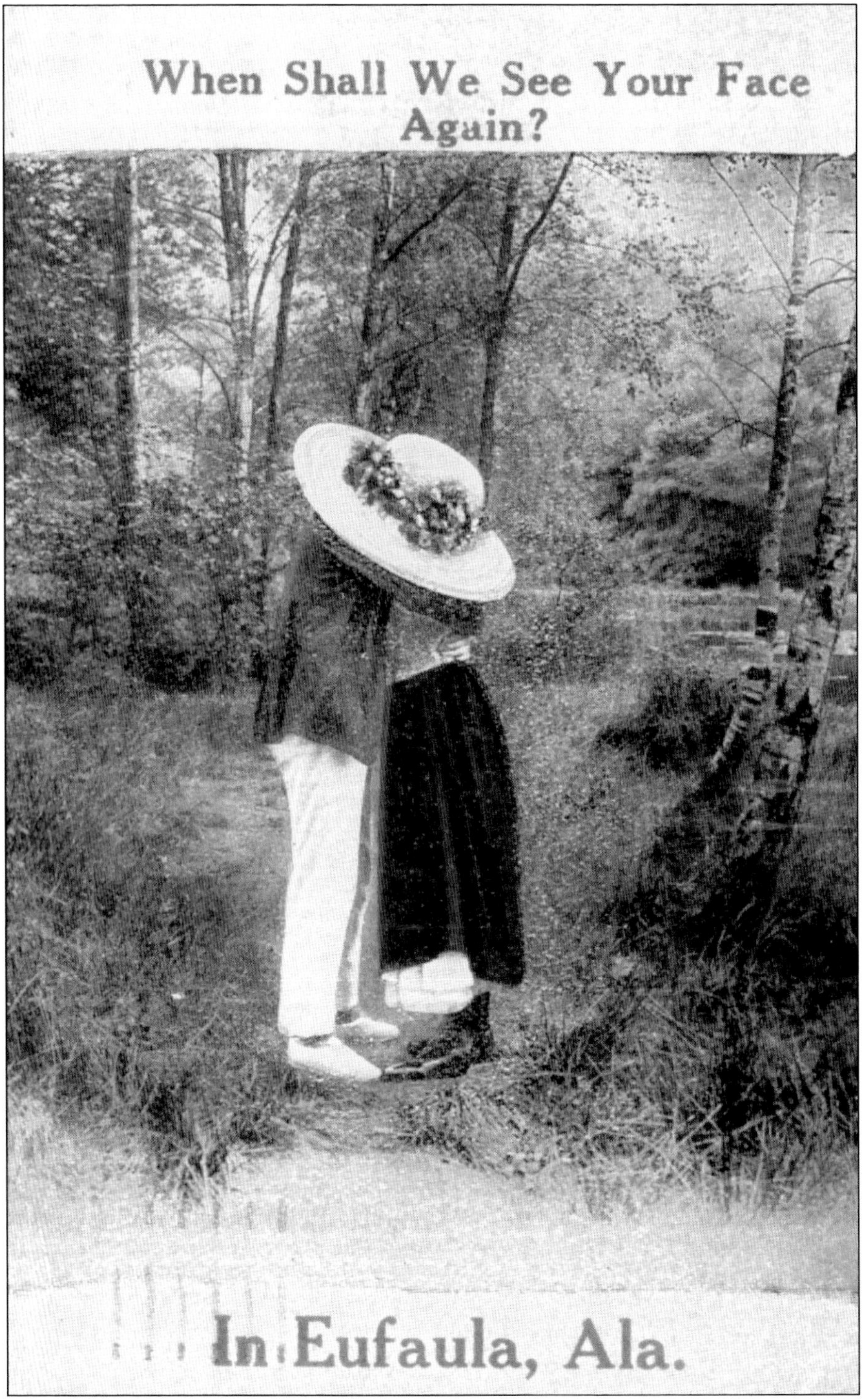

This generic postcard was postmarked August 31, 1920, from Troy, Alabama, to Miss Lelia Mae Anderson of Eufaula, Alabama. It is a romantic invitation to come back to Eufaula. (Courtesy of Doug Purcell.)

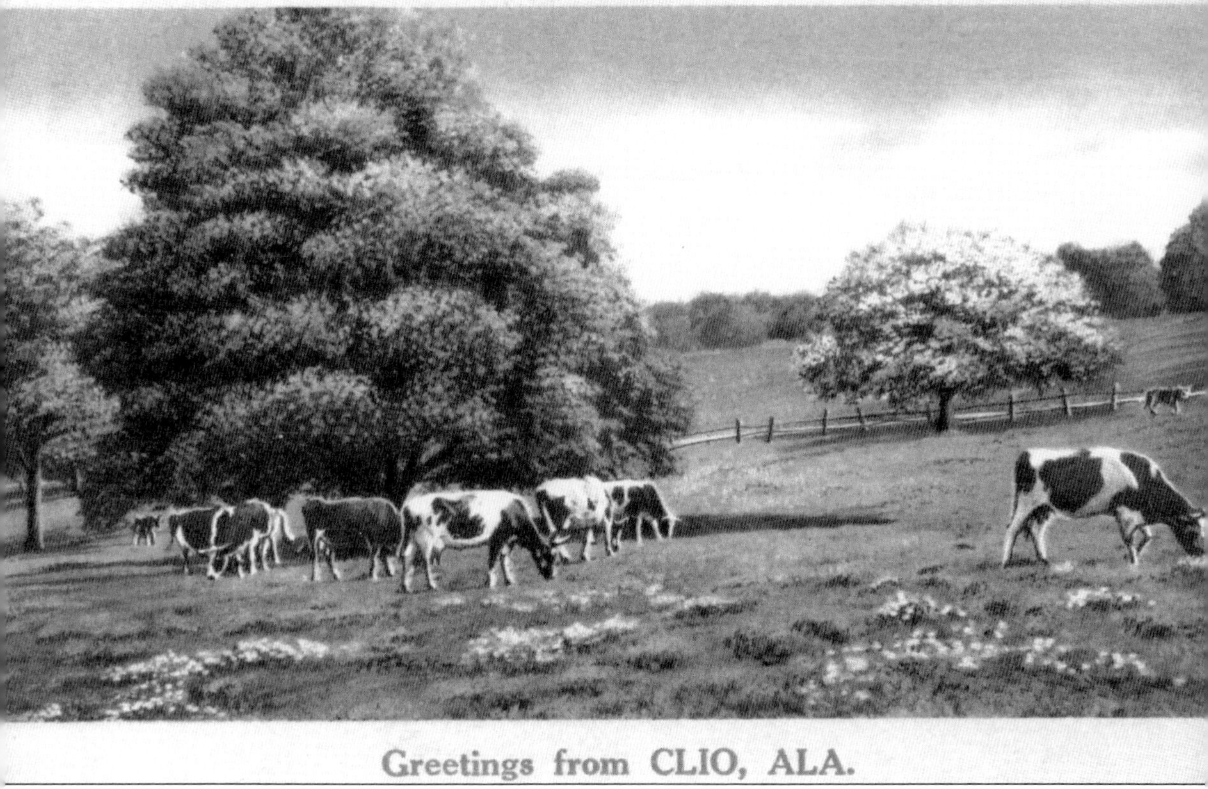

This postcard, with its painted pastoral scene, takes you back in time to Clio, Alabama, in western Barbour County. (Courtesy of Ben Spurlock.)

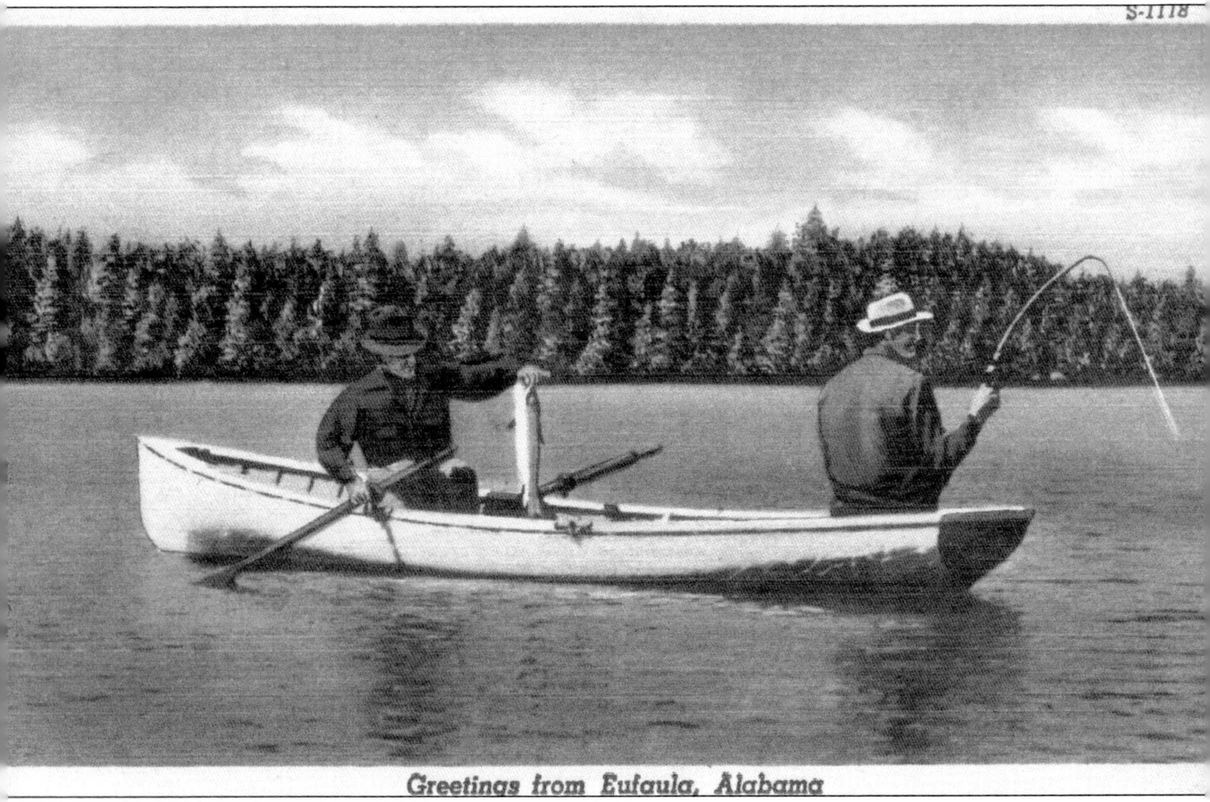

Fishing along the Chattahoochee River is a favorite past time for citizens and visitors of the area. This "Anytown U.S.A." card shows two men fishing, though the scene is not from the Chattahoochee River. (Courtesy of Rob Schaffeld.)

Seven

MONUMENTS

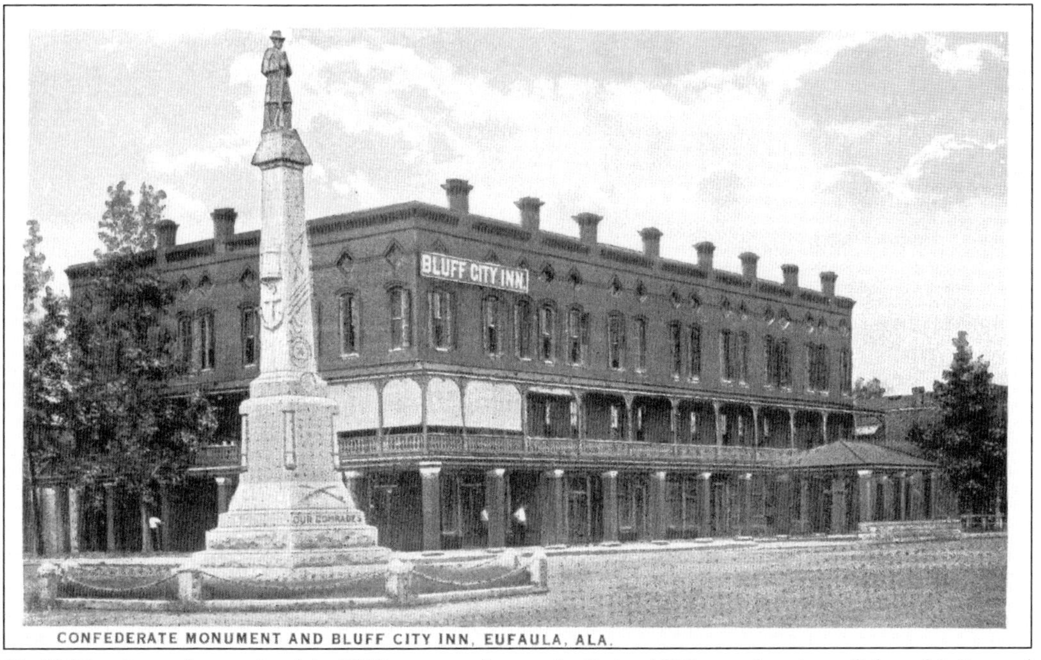

Bluff City Inn, shown in this 1928 postcard, was built in 1885 on the site of the old Central Hotel. It was during this time that a large addition was built on the north end, increasing its size to 70 rental rooms and several apartments. The Confederate Monument that was placed by the United Daughters of the Confederacy in 1904 is shown in the foreground. (Courtesy of Rob Schaffeld.)

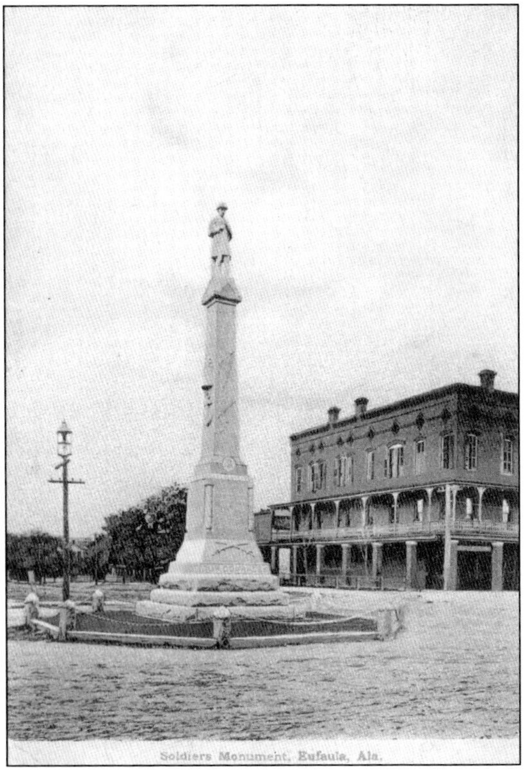

This Soldier's Monument, also known as the Confederate Monument, was dedicated on Thanksgiving Day 1904. The monument is 35 feet tall and made of Georgian granite and Italian marble. (Courtesy of Ben Spurlock.)

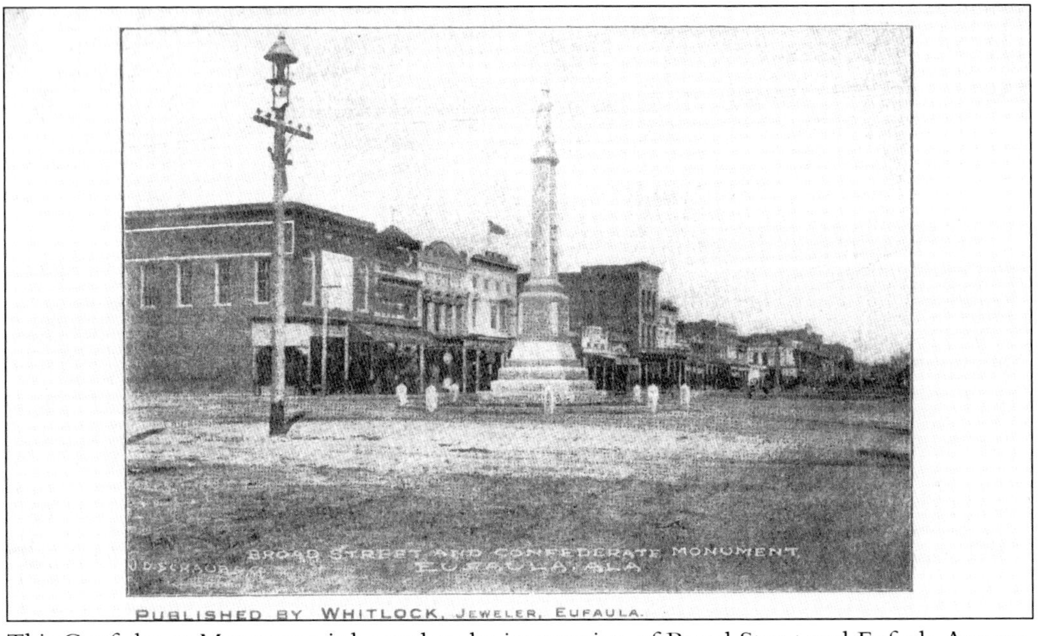

This Confederate Monument is located at the intersection of Broad Street and Eufaula Avenue. The dedication included a parade with a band playing *Bonnie Blue Flag*, and carriages carrying Mayor Dent and members of the City Council. The "Line of March" was west along Broad Street from the courthouse to the monument. (Courtesy of Rob Schaffeld.)

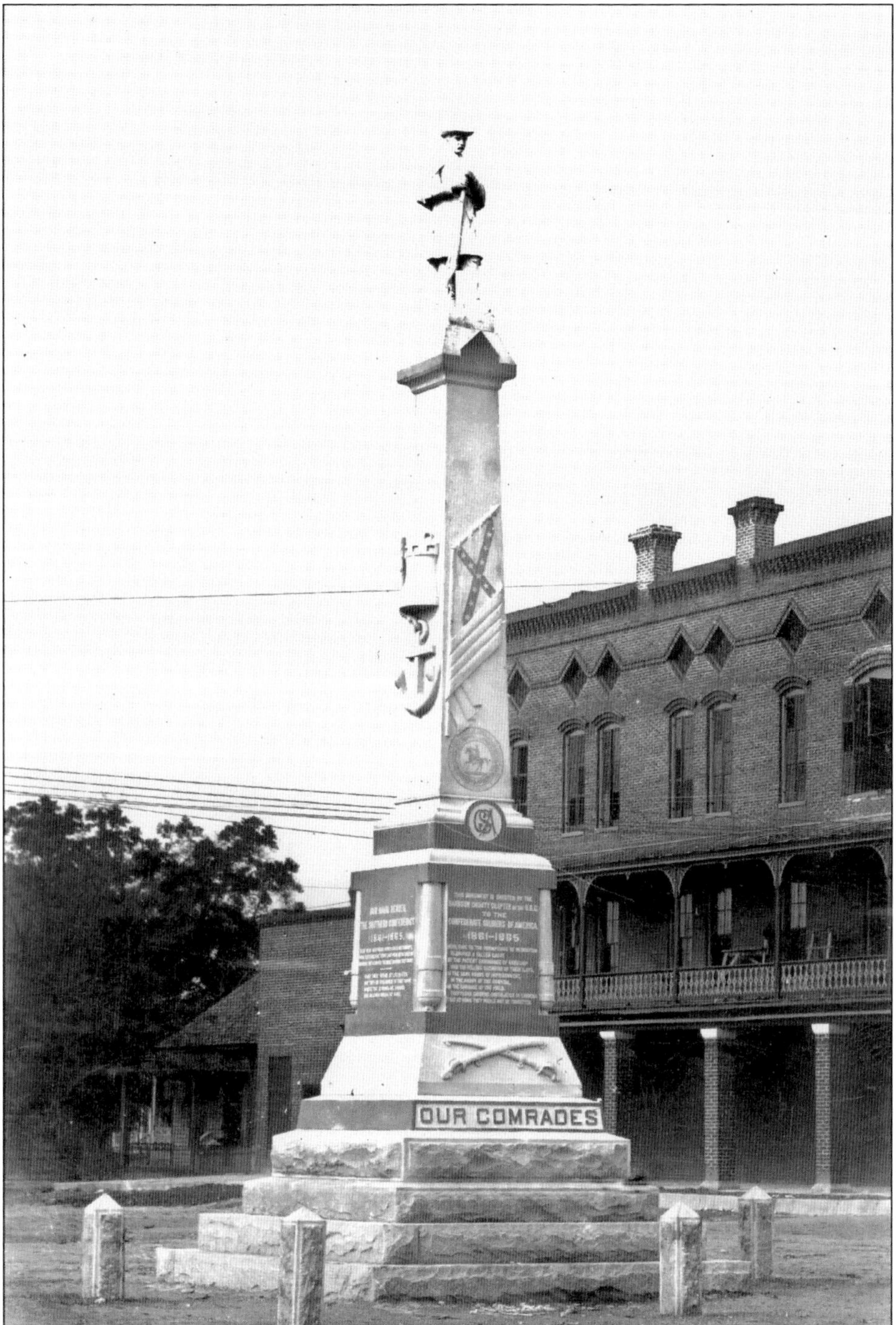

The Confederate Monument in Eufaula is a memorial to the soldiers who fought in the Confederate Army. The memorial was made possible by the fund-raising efforts of the United Daughters of the Confederacy. The soldier in the monument does not face north but east towards new horizons. (Courtesy of Tade Lampley.)

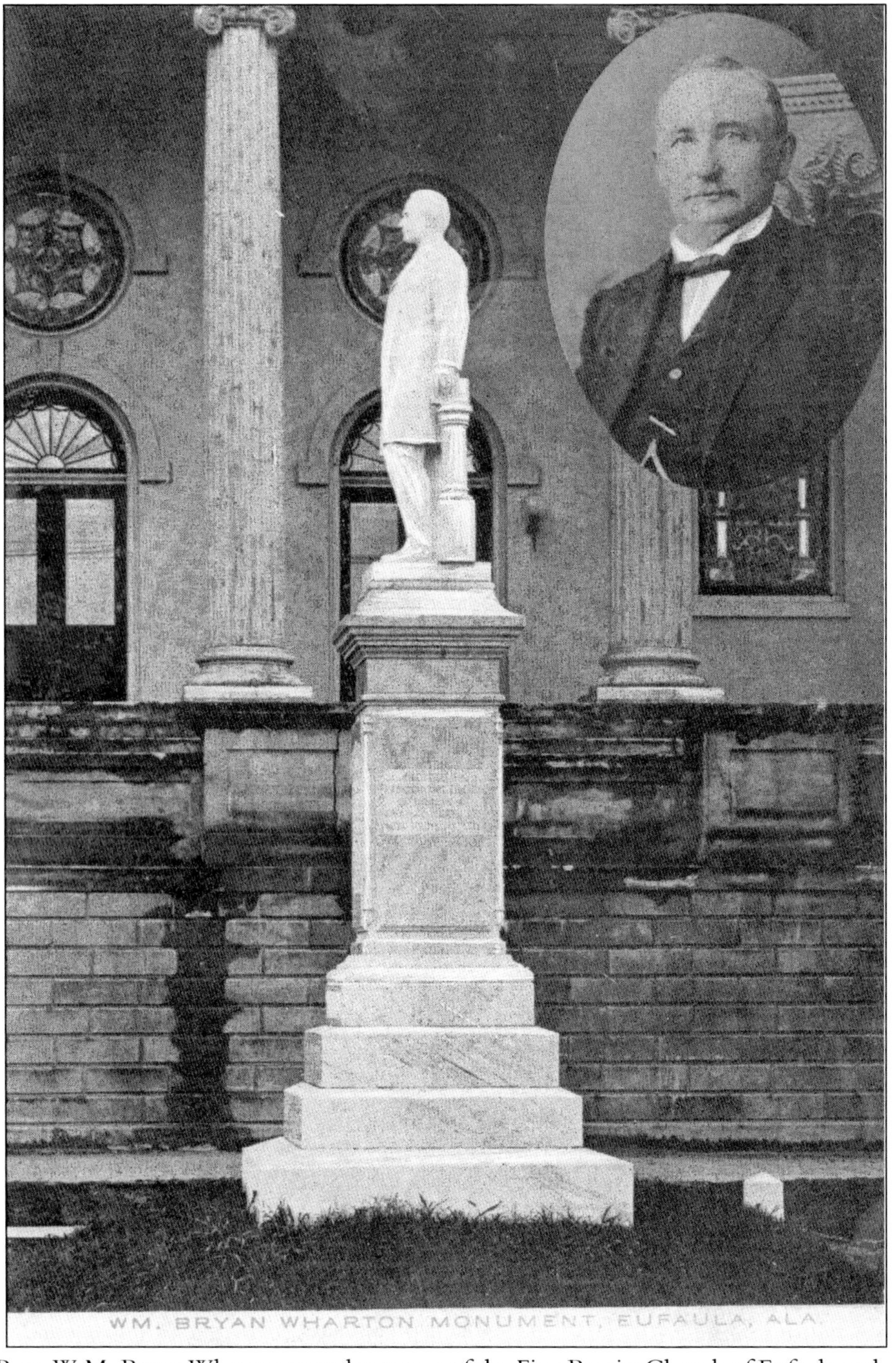

The Rev. W.M. Bryan Wharton served as pastor of the First Baptist Church of Eufaula at the turn of the century. For his tremendous contributions, the pictured marble statue was dedicated in his honor in 1912. In 1964, the statue was moved from the front of the church to its present location at the intersection of Barbour Street and Randolph Avenue. Wharton's photograph is an inset on this postcard. (Courtesy of Tade Lampley.)

Eight

Travel and Transportation

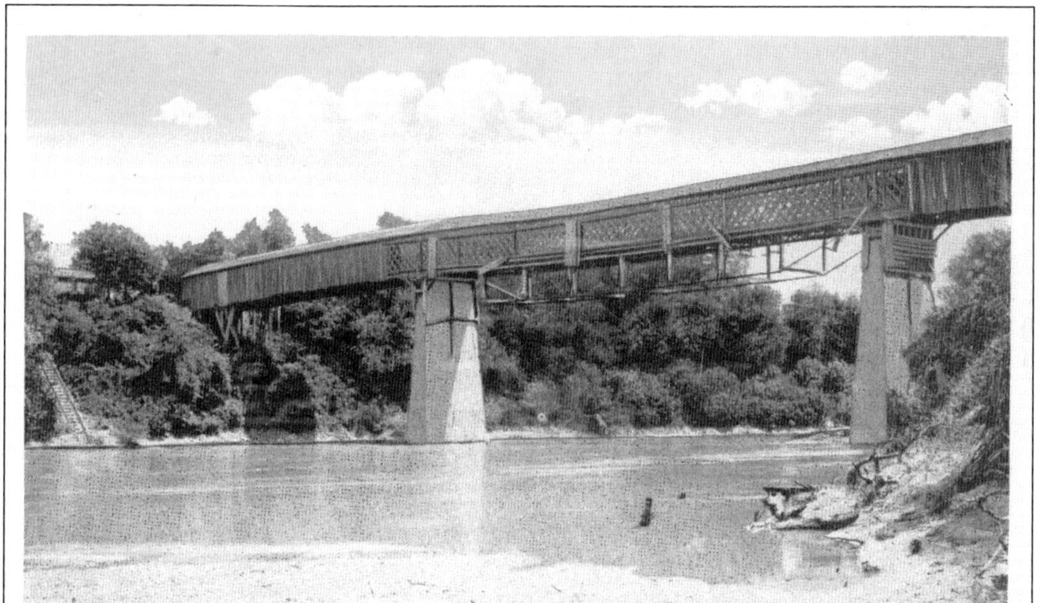

Built in 1837 by a group of businessmen led by E.B. Young, the lattice-covered bridge linked Eufaula with Georgia. The bridge's designer was former slave Horace King, who had become a master bridge builder. It survived many floods only to be eventually swept away by floodwaters. King salvaged the fallen bridge, and with the townspeople's help, it was rebuilt on the remaining piers. (Courtesy of Rob Schaffeld.)

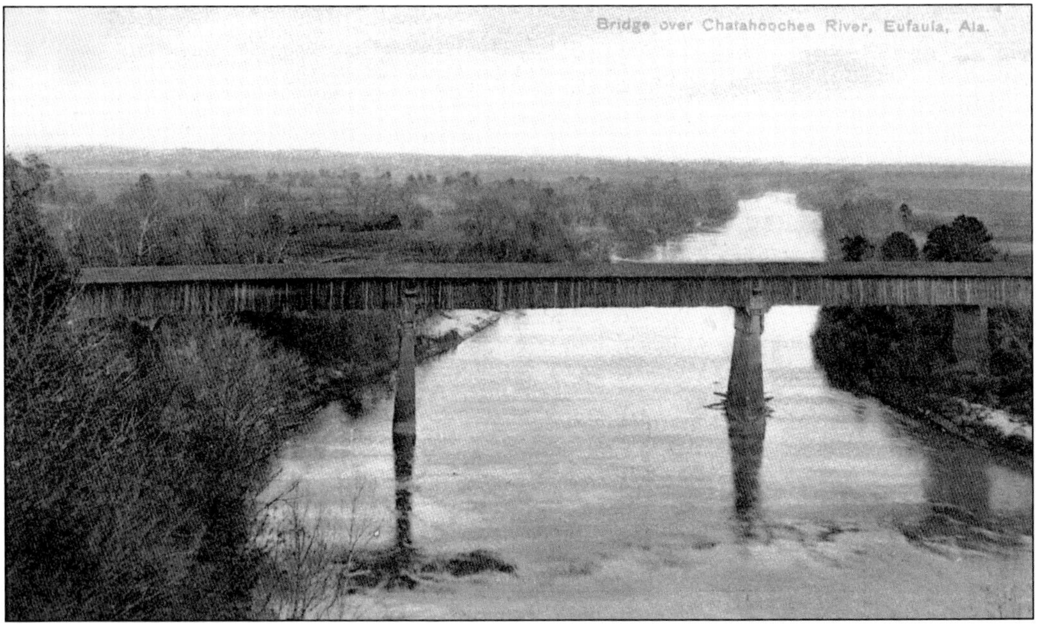

After the original bridge was destroyed by floodwaters, Edward Young and the citizens gathered the salvaged material to rebuild the bridge. The second covered bridge was built using those materials and the original piers and approaches. (Courtesy of Rob Schaffeld.)

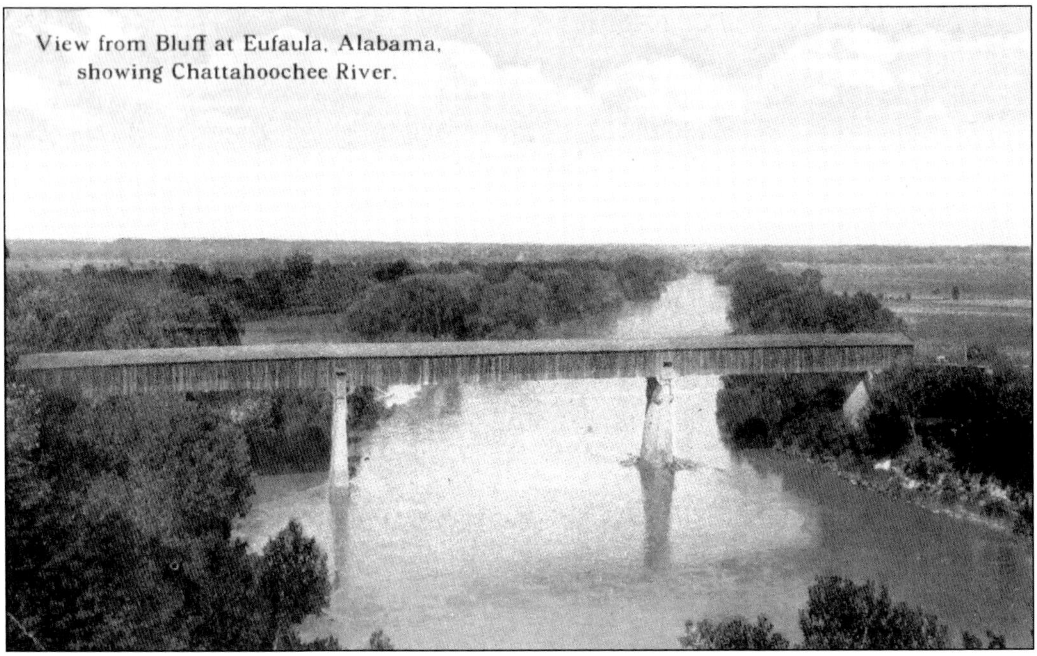

One of the most scenic sites in the area overlooks the covered bridge crossing the Chattahoochee River from Eufaula to Georgetown, Georgia. Steamboats traveling up or down river would often have to lower their stacks to go under the bridge. (Courtesy of Rob Schaffeld.)

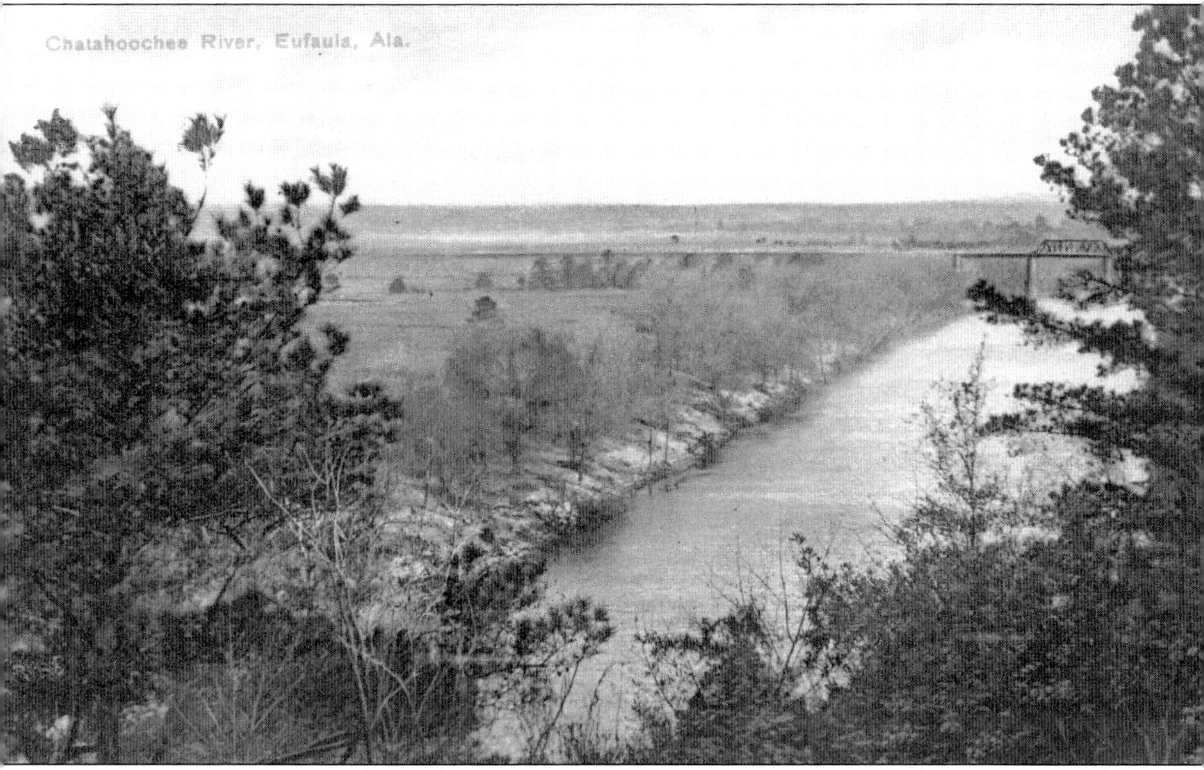

The natural wild beauty of the Chattahoochee River is showcased on this card. The Barbour County area and the entire Chattahoochee Valley owe much to the river. A system of locks and dams was placed along the river in the mid 1900s, breathing a new life of recreation into the area. (Courtesy of Hank Johnson.)

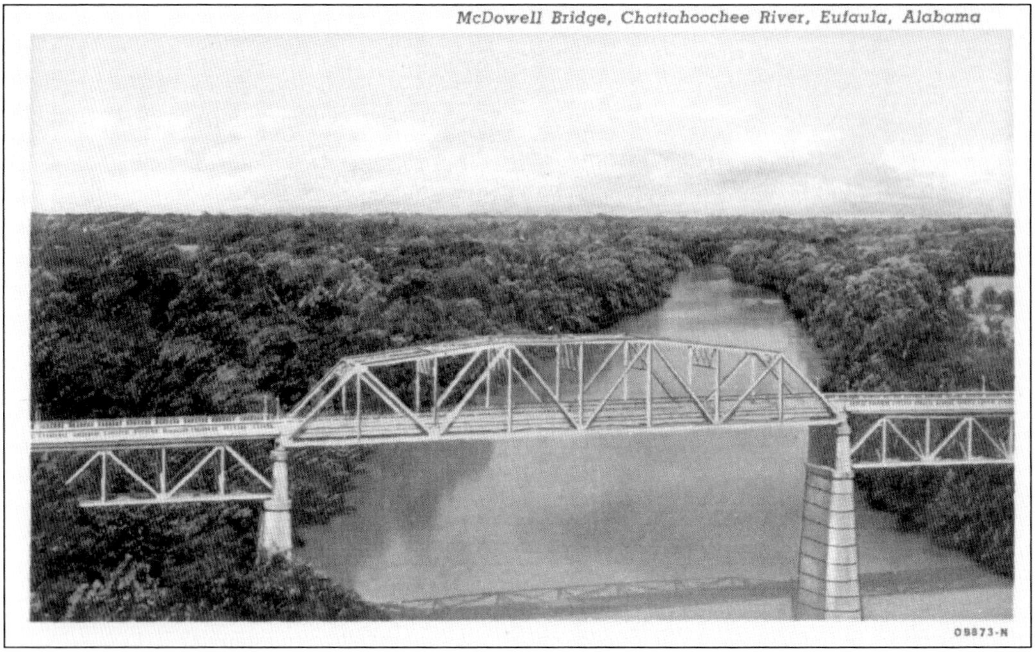

The cantilever bridge was completed in December 1925 at a cost of $125,000. The old wooden bridge had become unsafe. Charles S. McDowell, mayor of Eufaula, had the idea of a new steel and concrete bridge. After being elected to the Alabama Senate, he lobbied for its construction. (Courtesy of Rob Schaffeld.)

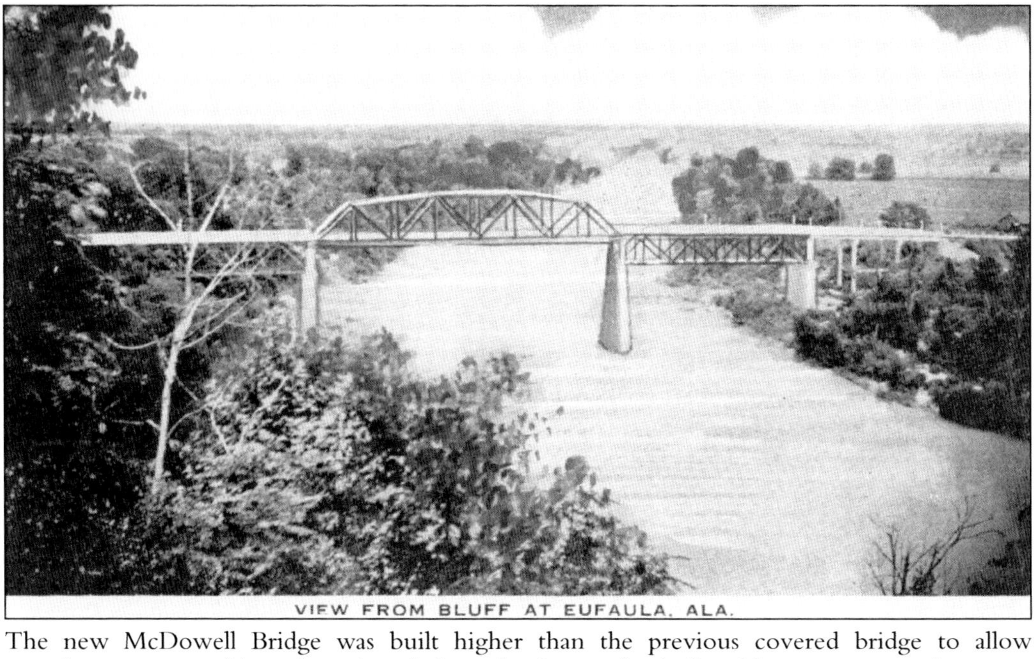

The new McDowell Bridge was built higher than the previous covered bridge to allow steamboats to pass without lowering their stacks. It was also built wider to accommodate two-way automobile traffic instead of horse and buggy traffic; a sign of the changing times. (Courtesy of Ben Spurlock.)

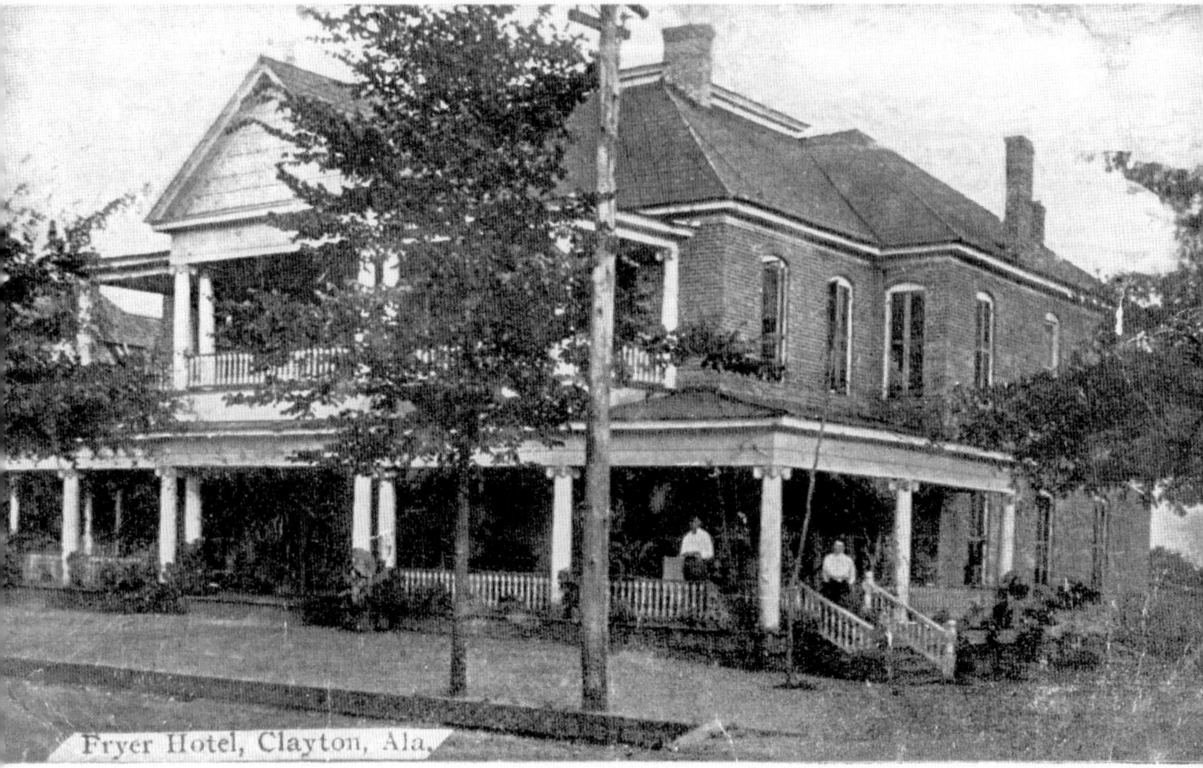

Completed in 1905 by Mr. Tom Fryer, the Fryer Hotel stood on Eufaula Avenue in downtown Clayton. Fryer family members ran the hotel, well-known as a nice hotel and restaurant, until it was sold to Bennie Frank Ventress in the late 1950s. Shortly thereafter, it was sold to Clayton Banking Company who razed the building. Southland Bank now operates on the site. (Courtesy of Rob Schaffeld.)

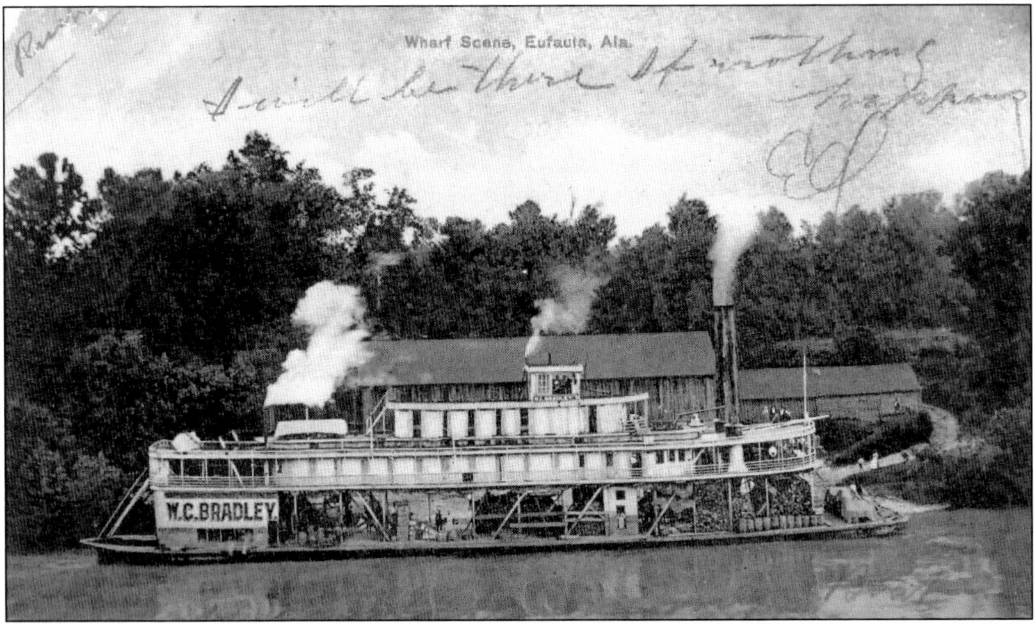

Eufaula's prosperity was due in large part to its location on the Chattahoochee River. Steamboats brought goods from all over and took the wares of area farmers to the world. The *W.C. Bradley* was one of those steamboats. In 1924, the Eufaula Grocery Company (owned by W.C. Bradley) gave their wharf at Eufaula to the city of Eufaula. This postcard is postmarked January 13, 1910, to Miss Vera Bush, Belcher, Alabama. (Courtesy of Doug Purcell.)

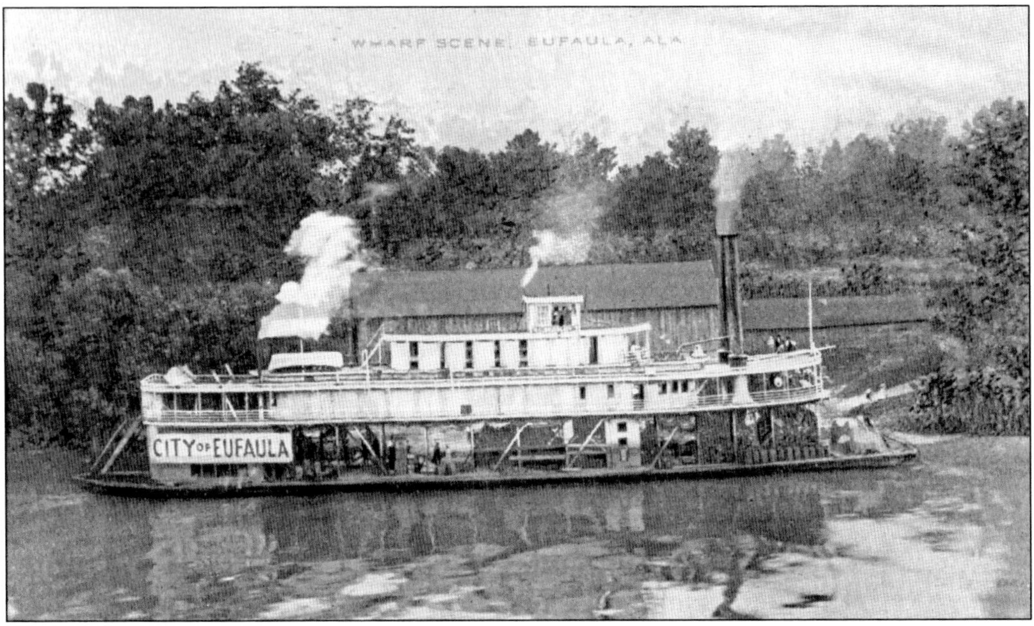

The *City of Eufaula* steamboat traversed the treacherous Chattahoochee River delivering goods to the area and shipping cotton to Apalachicola, Florida, then to ports such as New Orleans, New York, and the world. A closer look shows W.C. Bradley as the owner of the *City of Eufaula*. (Courtesy of Eufaula Heritage Association.)

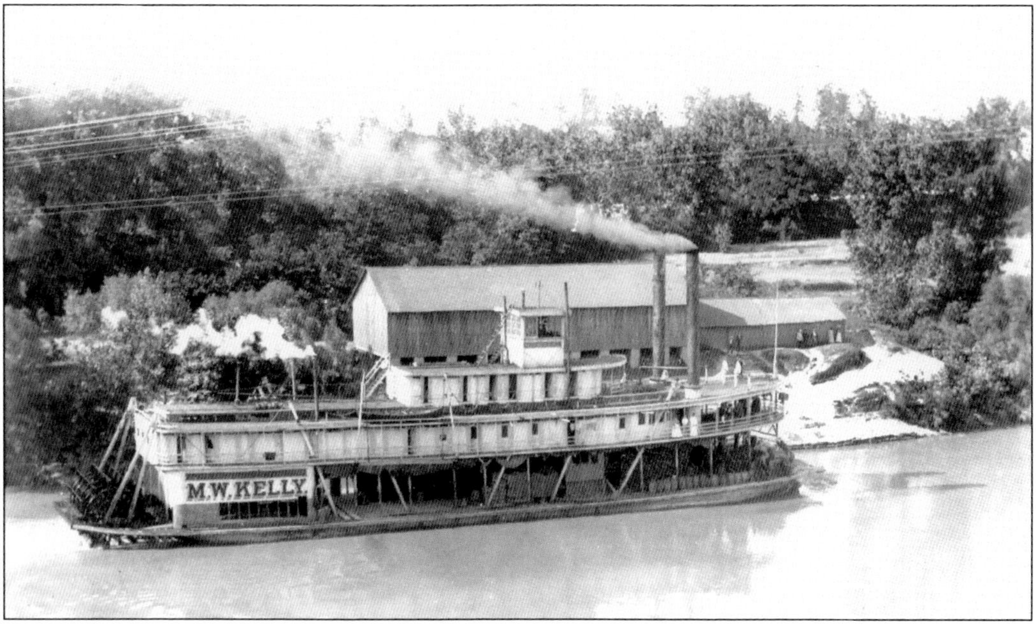

The *M.W. Kelly* was a common site at the Eufaula Wharf. It would be loaded with cotton to be shipped downriver. In 1849, at the insistence of local citizens, the City of Eufaula passed an ordinance opposing the loading or unloading of boats on the Sabbath. This ordinance was tested and a boat captain was made to pay a fine of $50, plus costs, for violating the Sabbath ordinance. (Courtesy of Mary Gray.)

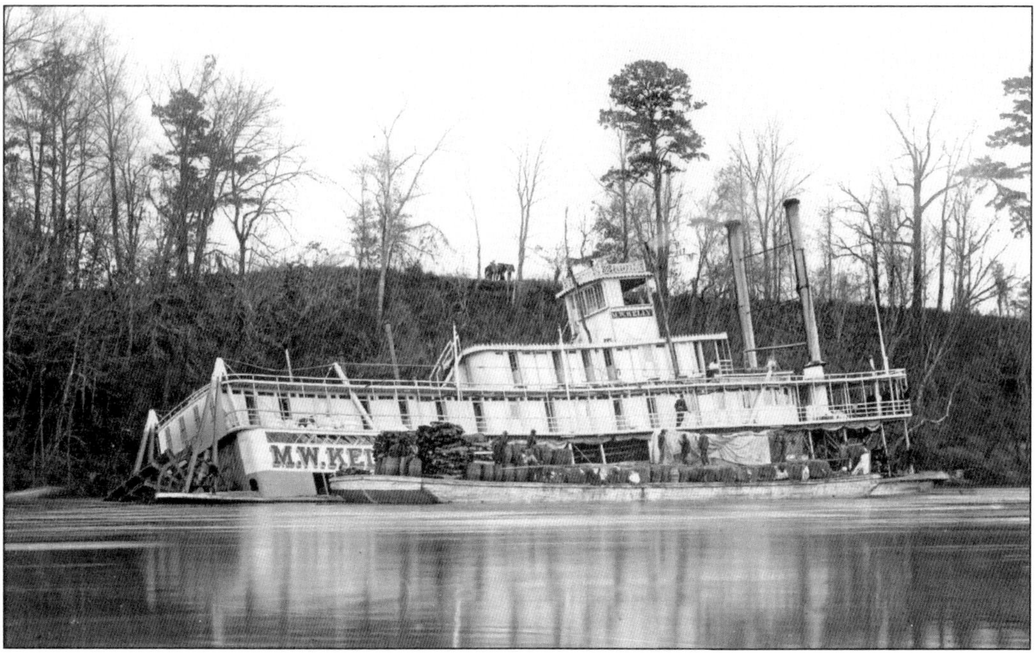

The waters of the Chattahoochee could be quite treacherous at times. They were swiftly moving and shallow in places. Like many others, the *M.W. Kelly* met its demise on these waters. Here, goods are shown being transferred off the wrecked steamboat. (Courtesy of Mary Gray.)

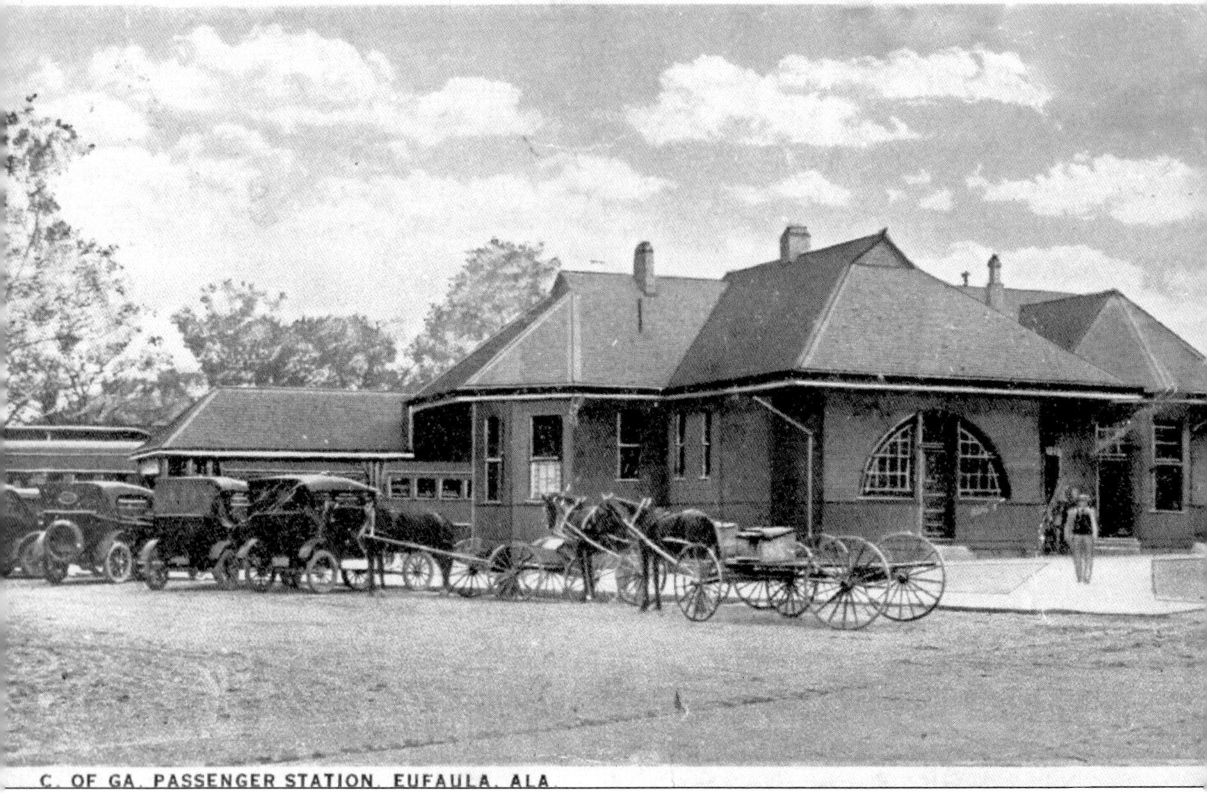

Rail service was extended to Eufaula and by 1870 two rail lines served the area. In 1952, passenger service was halted and the Central of Georgia passenger station razed. (Courtesy of Rob Schaffeld.)

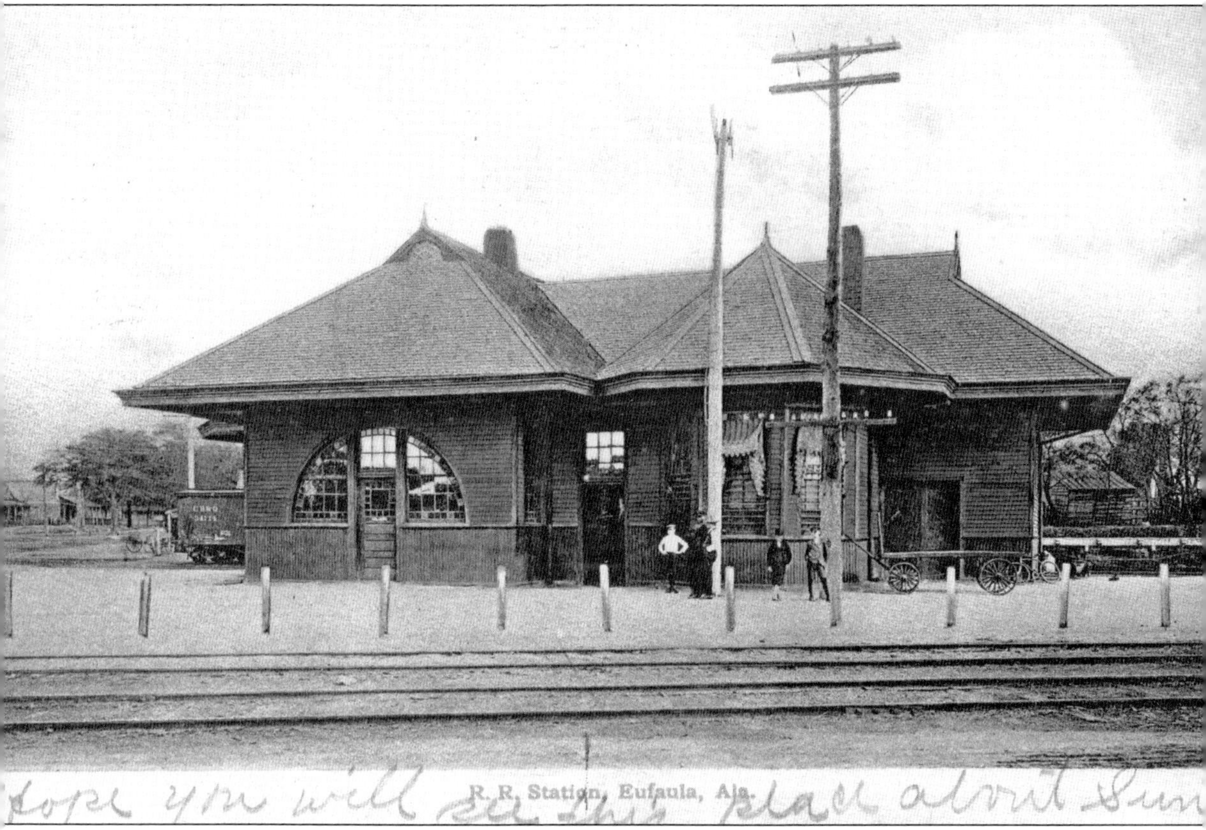

A woman known only as Connie sent this postcard to Mr. Robert Porter Hatfield Sr., of Batesville, Alabama. It is believed he was planning a trip via train from Batesville to Eufaula. Hatfield may have been working at the Batesville depot at the time. The card is postmarked October 1, 1909. (Courtesy of Janet Scroggins.)

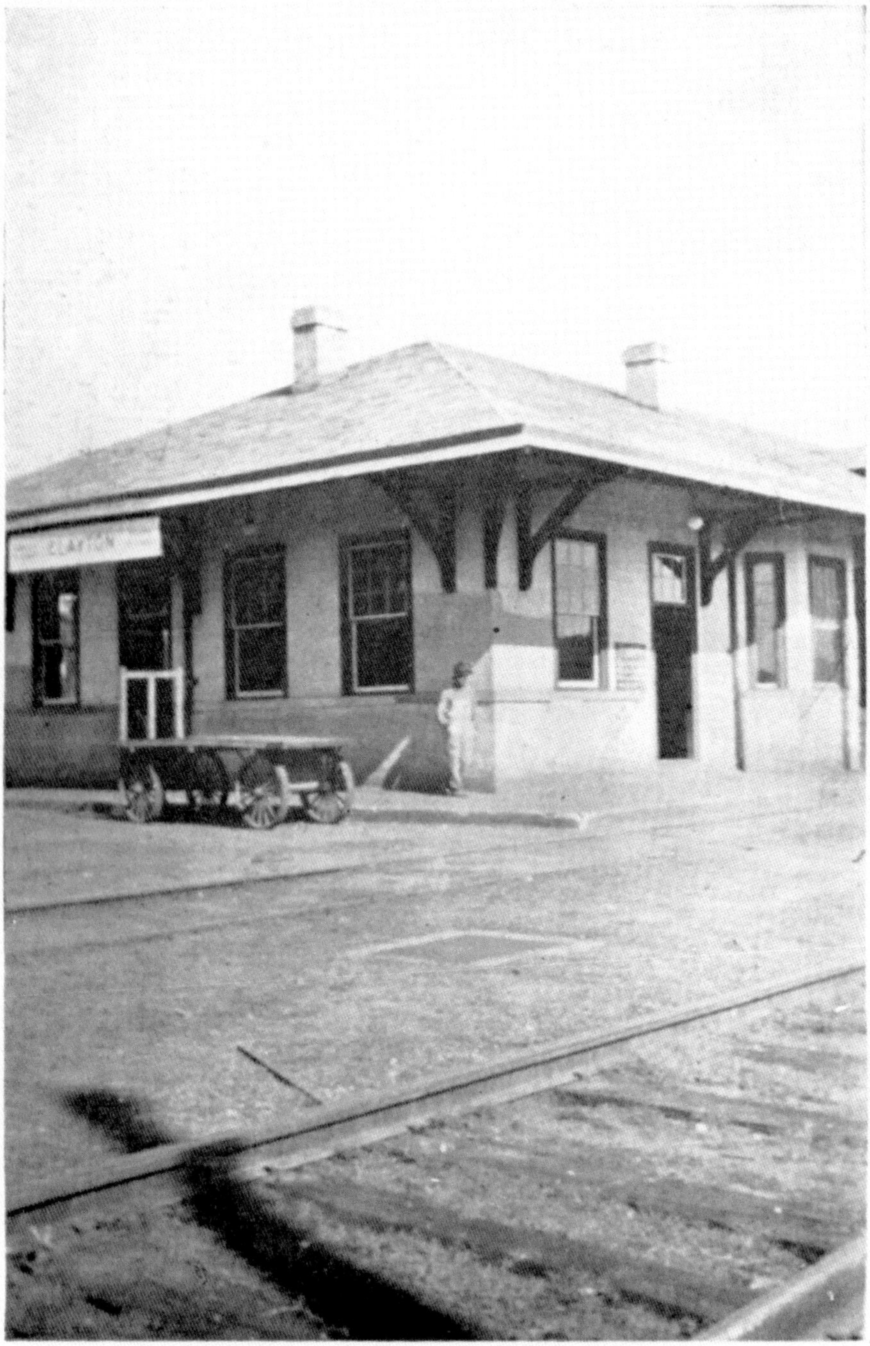

Depot, Clayton, Ala.

The Vicksburg and Brunswick Railroad line began its run from Eufaula to Clayton in the 1870s. In 1889, the Central of Georgia established the Clayton Depot. The roof of the depot has twice burned and been replaced. The depot served mostly as a freight service until 1980, when the station was closed and the track removed. (Courtesy of Betty Greene.)

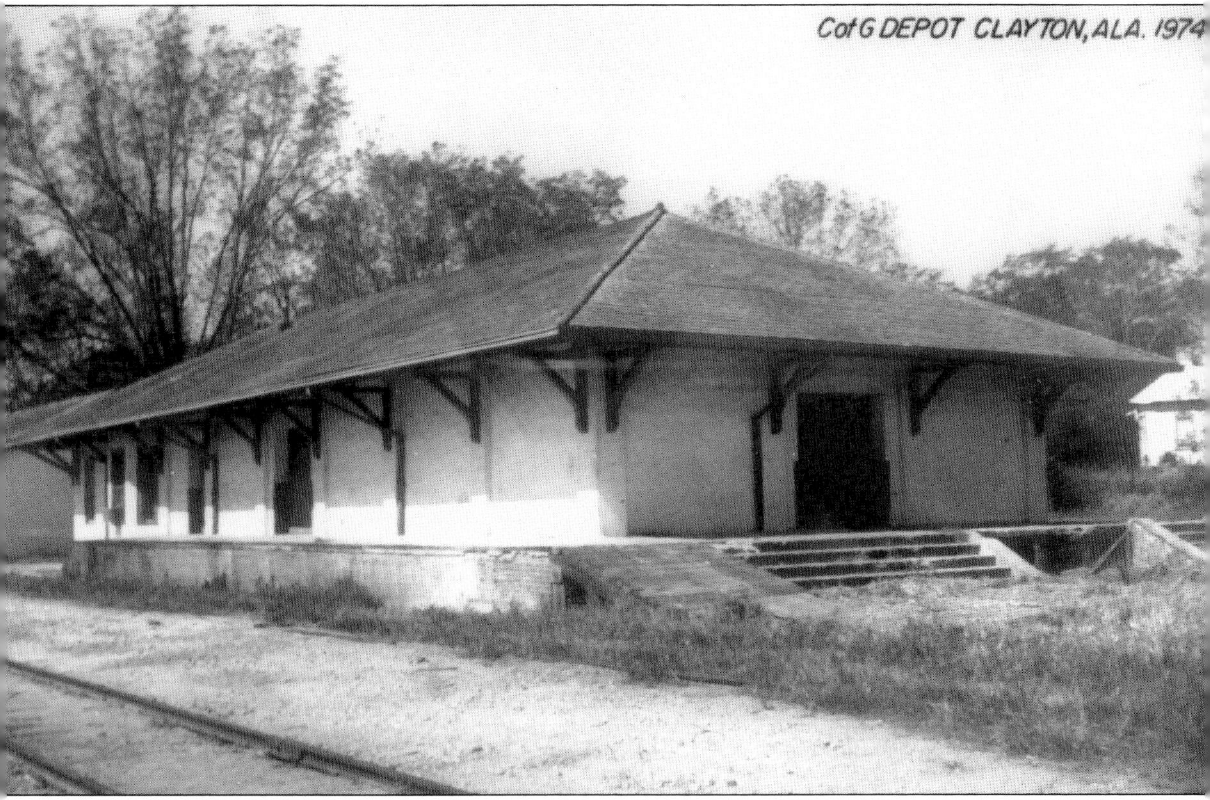

After its closing in 1980, the Clayton Depot remained unoccupied until its renovation. In December 1999 the depot reopened its doors, functioning as the Municipal Complex for the Town of Clayton. Today it houses Clayton Town Hall, the Clayton Water Works and Sewer Board, and Clayton Rescue Squad. (Courtesy of Steve Riley.)

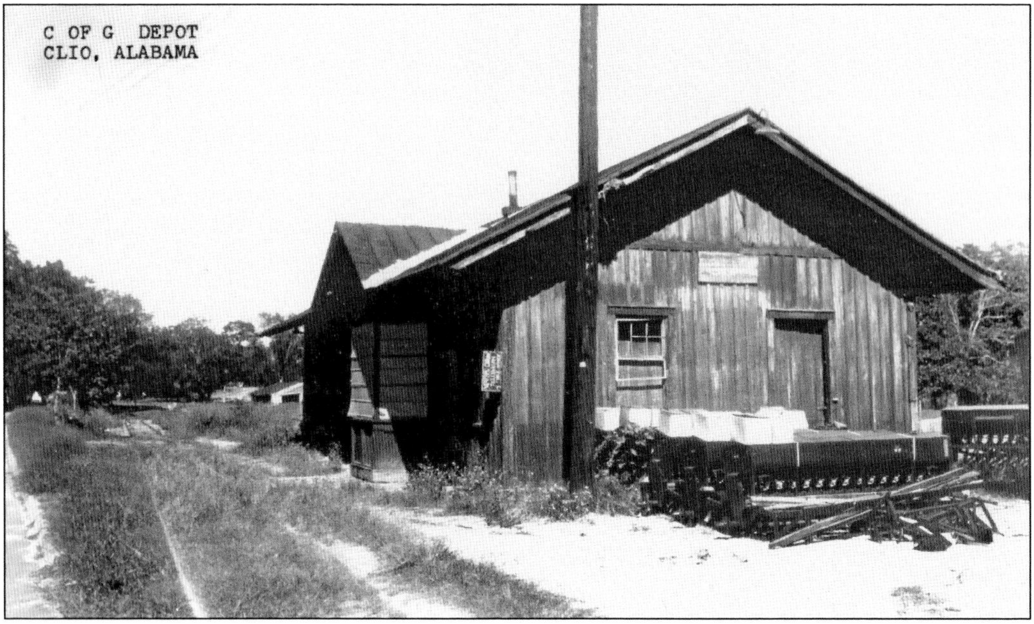

Built *c.* 1890, the Central of Georgia depot in Clio was active until the early 1980s. Today this depot serves as "The Grill," a local eatery. (Courtesy of Steve Riley.)

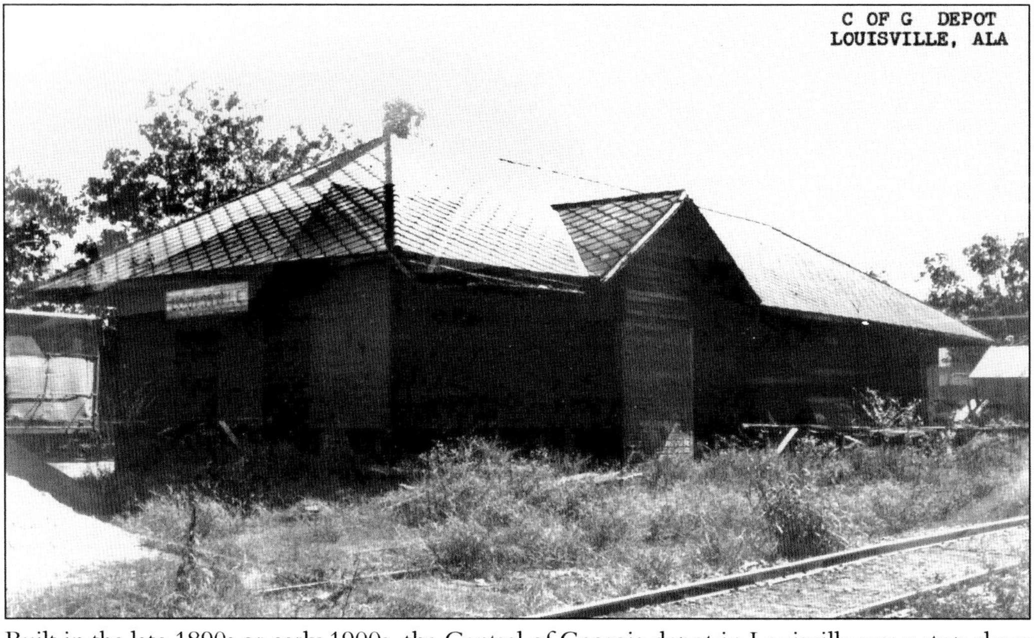

Built in the late 1890s or early 1900s, the Central of Georgia depot in Louisville was a stop along the Eufaula to Ozark route. Though this photo postcard was taken after its close, a boxcar still sitting as if waiting for cargo. This building still stands one block off Main Street in Louisville. (Courtesy of Steve Riley.)

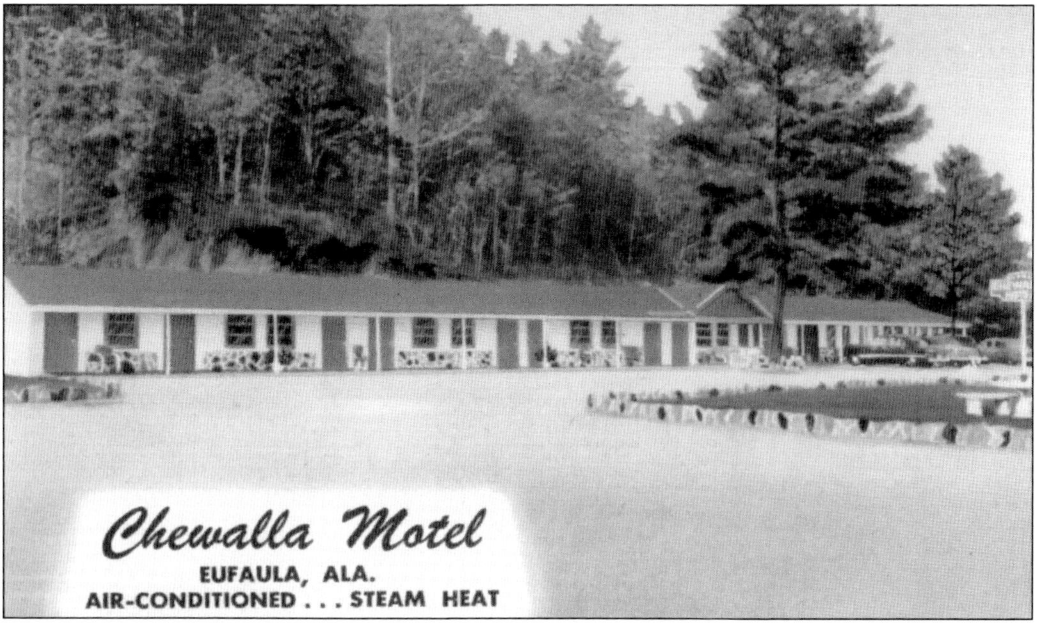

Built in 1952 by Robert Hornsby, the Chewalla Motel was Eufaula's first motel. This card advertised, "air conditioned . . . steam heat." There were 14 units. (Courtesy of Rob Schaffeld.)

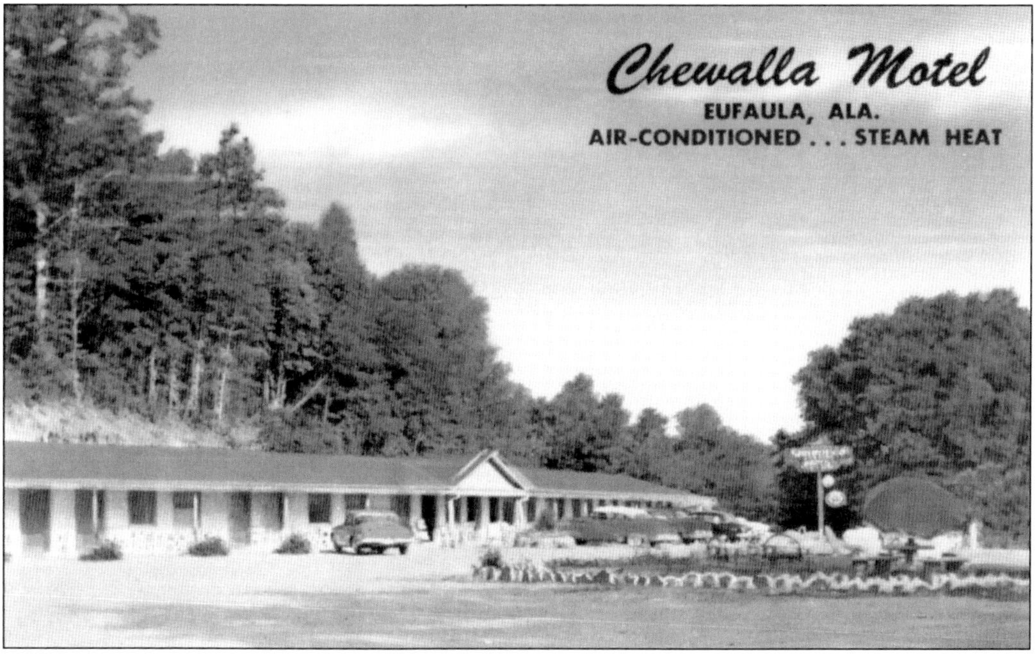

As travel became increasingly a part of the American landscape, "tourist courts" such as the Chewalla Motel were popping up around the country. (Courtesy of Rob Schaffeld.)

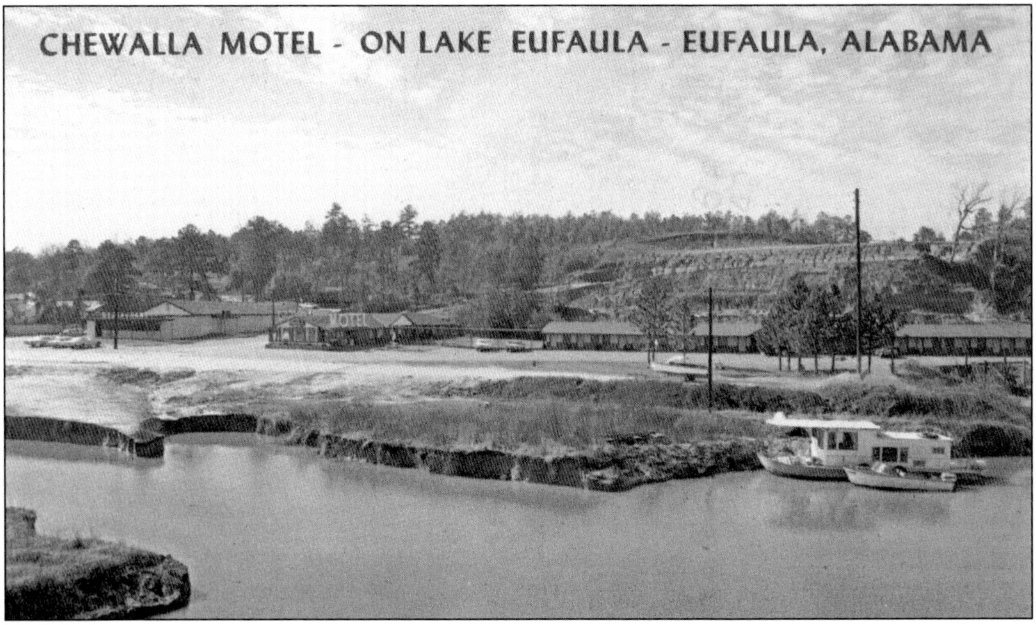

The Chewalla Motel is located directly on Chewalla Creek on Lake Eufaula. Boat travel and recreation breathed new life into Eufaula after the Chattahoochee River was impounded in the early 1960s. (Courtesy of Rob Schaffeld.)

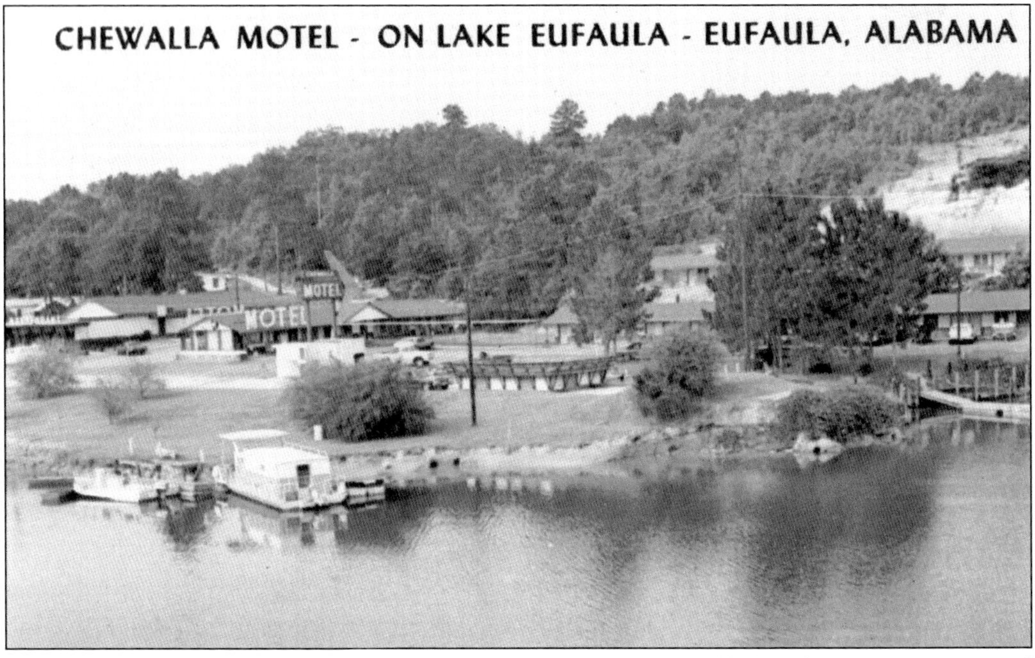

As Eufaula grew so did the Chewalla Motel. More units were added and a restaurant opened next door. Known today as the Lakeside Motor Lodge, the motel still welcomes guests to Lake Eufaula. (Courtesy of Rob Schaffeld.)

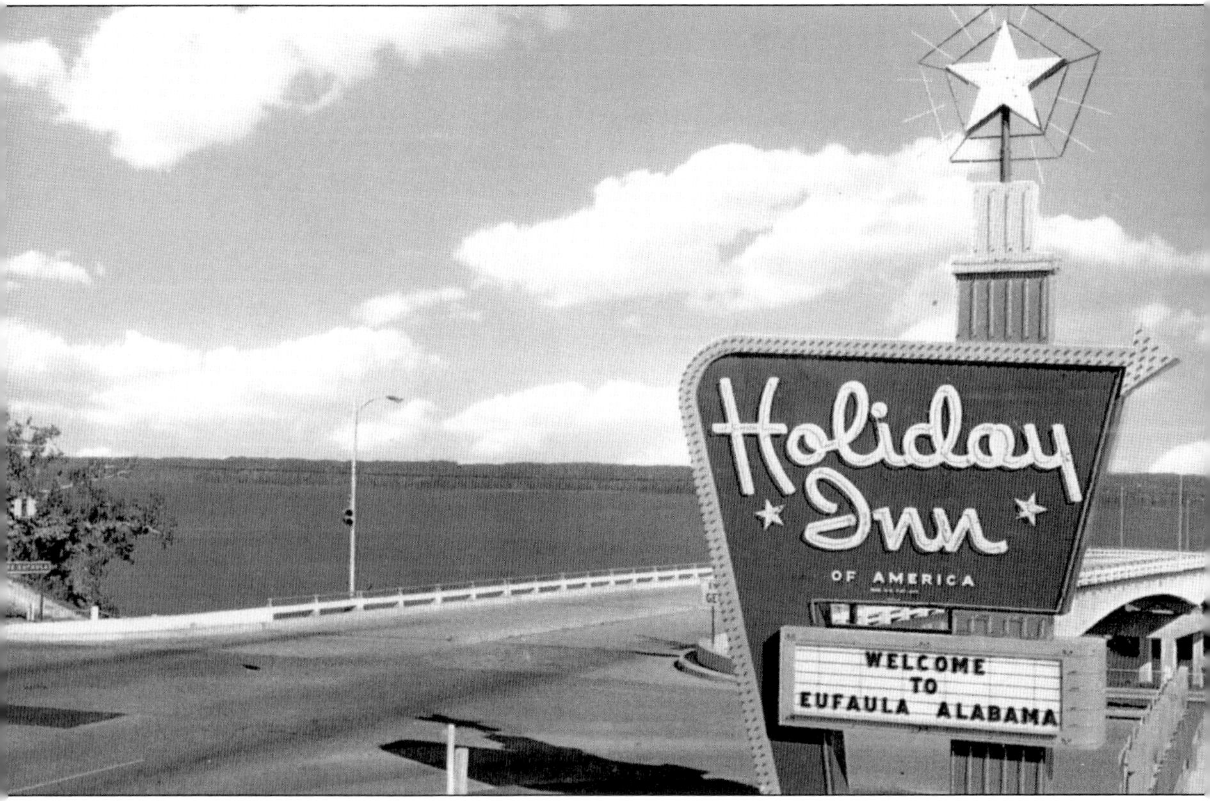

The Holiday Inn gave visitors to Eufaula a comfortable room with a view when it opened in 1962. Sitting high atop the bluff, the Holiday Inn overlooked the newly forming Lake Eufaula/ Walter F. George. The hotel is now a Ramada Inn and still offers a wonderful view of the lake. (Courtesy of Rob Schaffeld.)

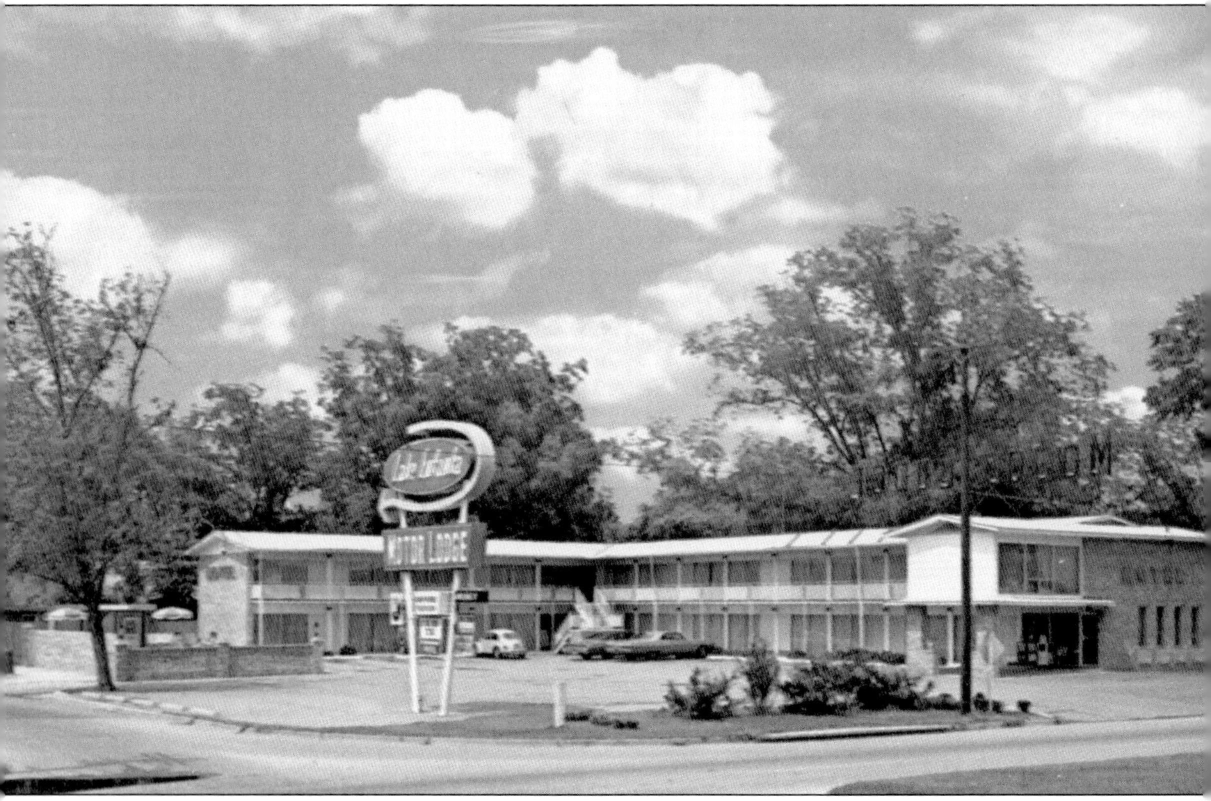

Built in the 1960s, Lake Eufaula Motor Lodge is located on East Barbour Street near the Georgia state line and Lake Eufaula. (Courtesy of Rob Schaffeld.)

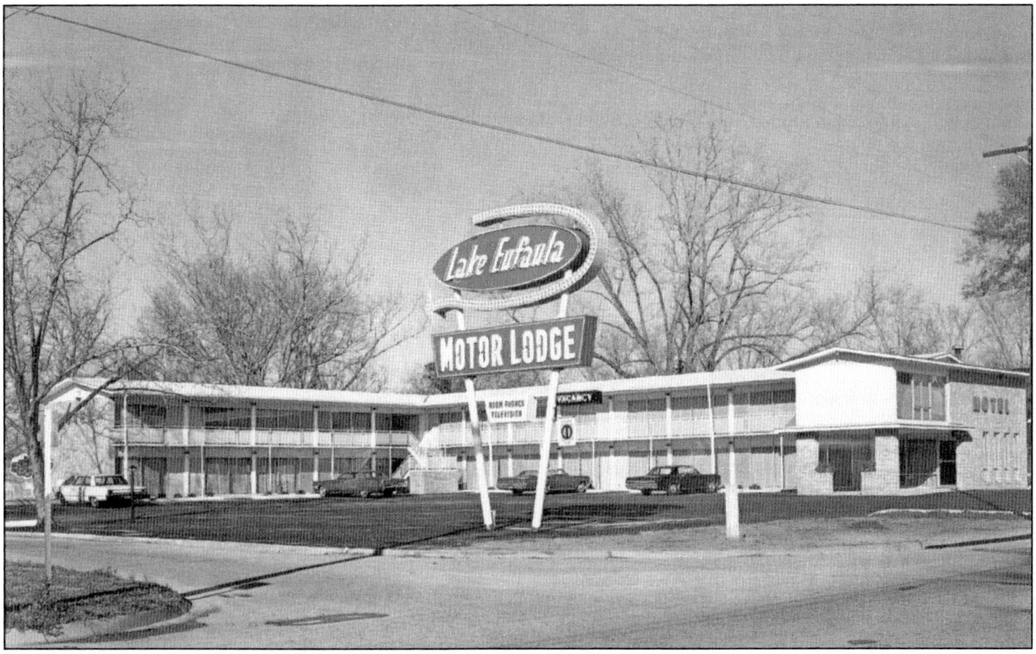

Thirty-eight rooms welcome visitors to the Lake Eufaula Motor Lodge. Fishermen and hunters in the area often make Lake Eufaula Motor Lodge their home away from home. (Courtesy of Rob Schaffeld.)

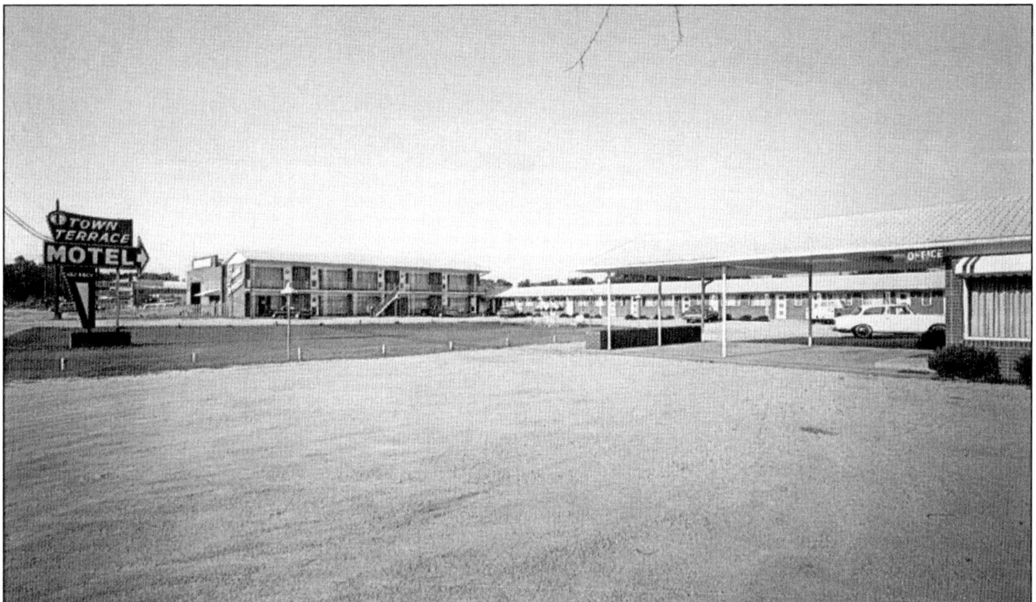

The Town Terrace Motel opened on Highway 431 in Eufaula in the 1960s as travel became one of America's favorite past times. (Courtesy of Rob Schaffeld.)

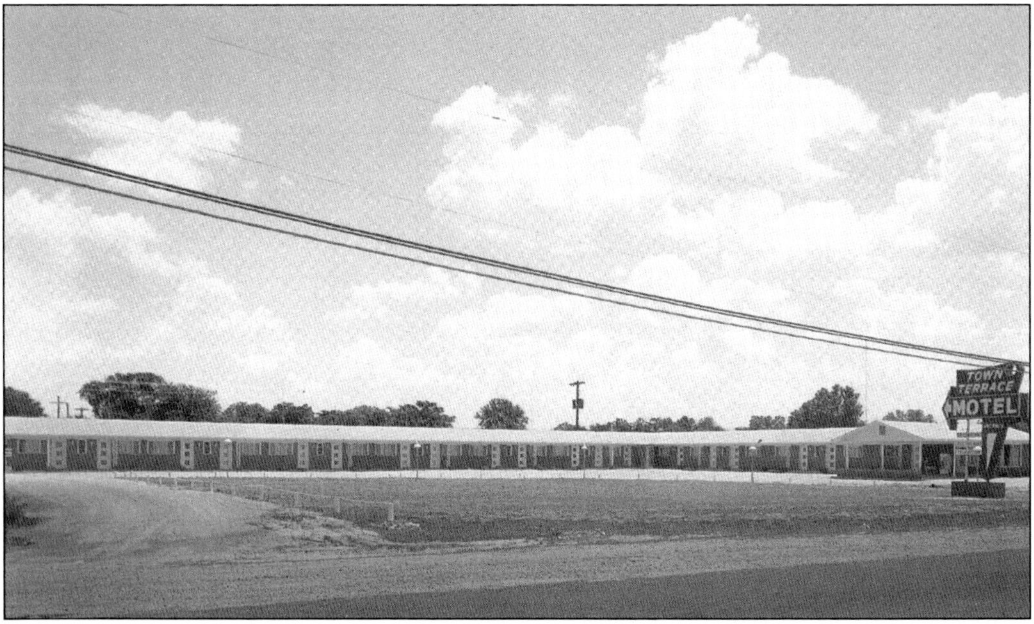

Thirty rooms still welcome visitors to the Town Terrace Motel. (Courtesy of Rob Schaffeld.)

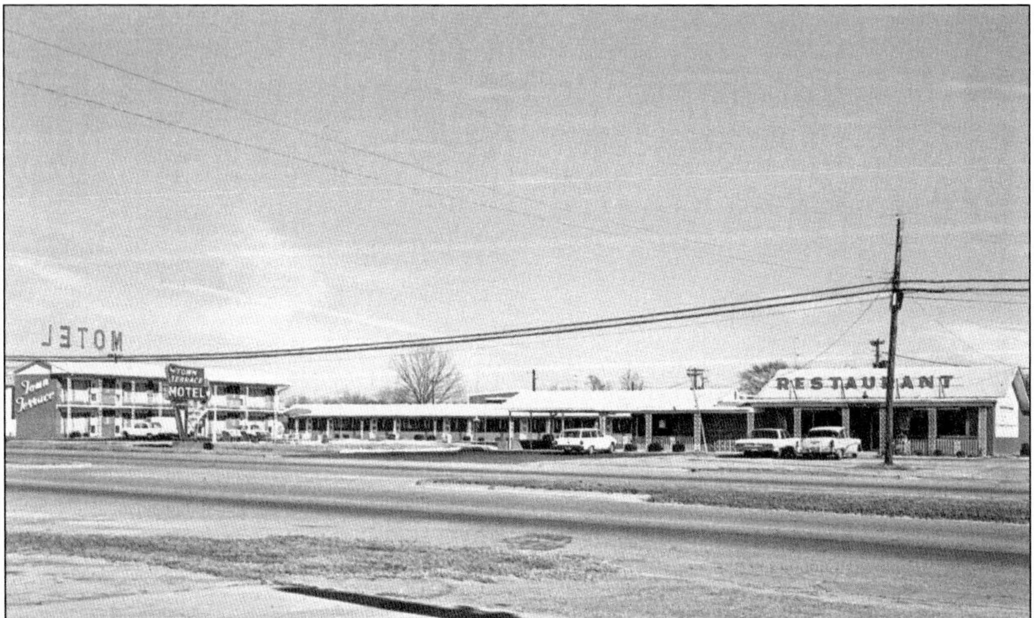

Town Terrace grew as the city of Eufaula grew. A few years after its completion a swimming pool was added and a restaurant opened next door. (Courtesy of Rob Schaffeld.)

Nine

Government and Community Life

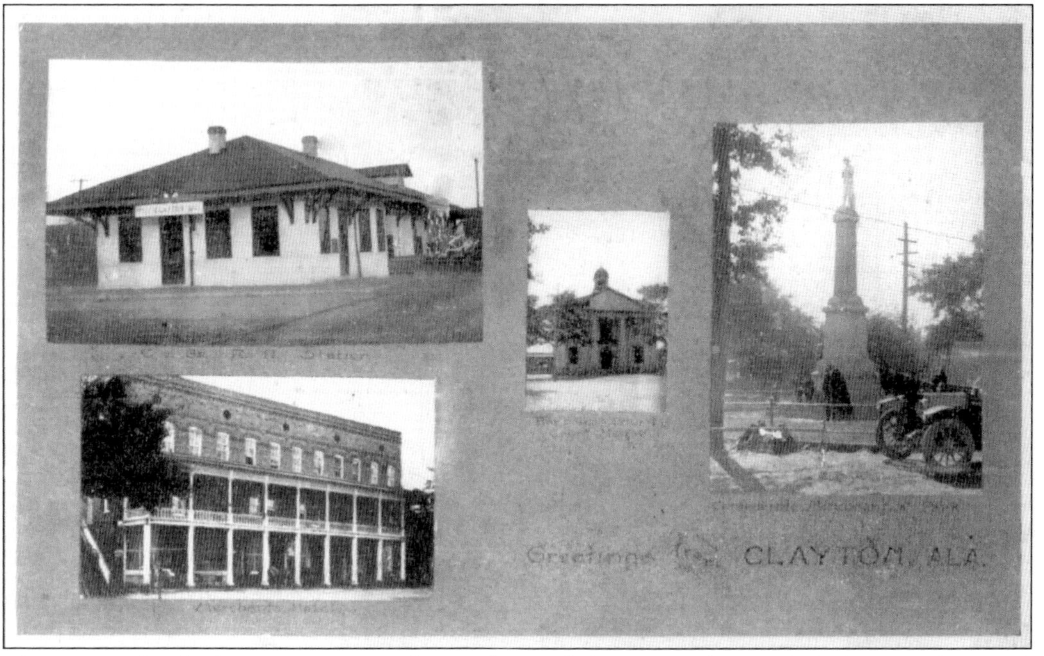

This postcard, which says "Greetings from Clayton," depicts, at the top, left, the Vicksburg and Brunswick Railroad, built *c.* 1889 and operated until the 1980s. The depot was renovated in 1999 and presently serves as the Clayton Municipal Complex. At the bottom, left, is the Enterprise Hotel, also known as the Merchant's Hotel and built around 1888 by local people who owned stock in the company. It operated until about 1910 or 1911. In the center is the Barbour County Courthouse, *c.* 1854. Clayton serves as the county seat of Barbour County. At the far right is the Confederate Monument in Clayton, which was erected in 1909. by the United Daughters of the Confederacy. The monument alone cost $2,000. (Courtesy of Rebecca Beasley.)

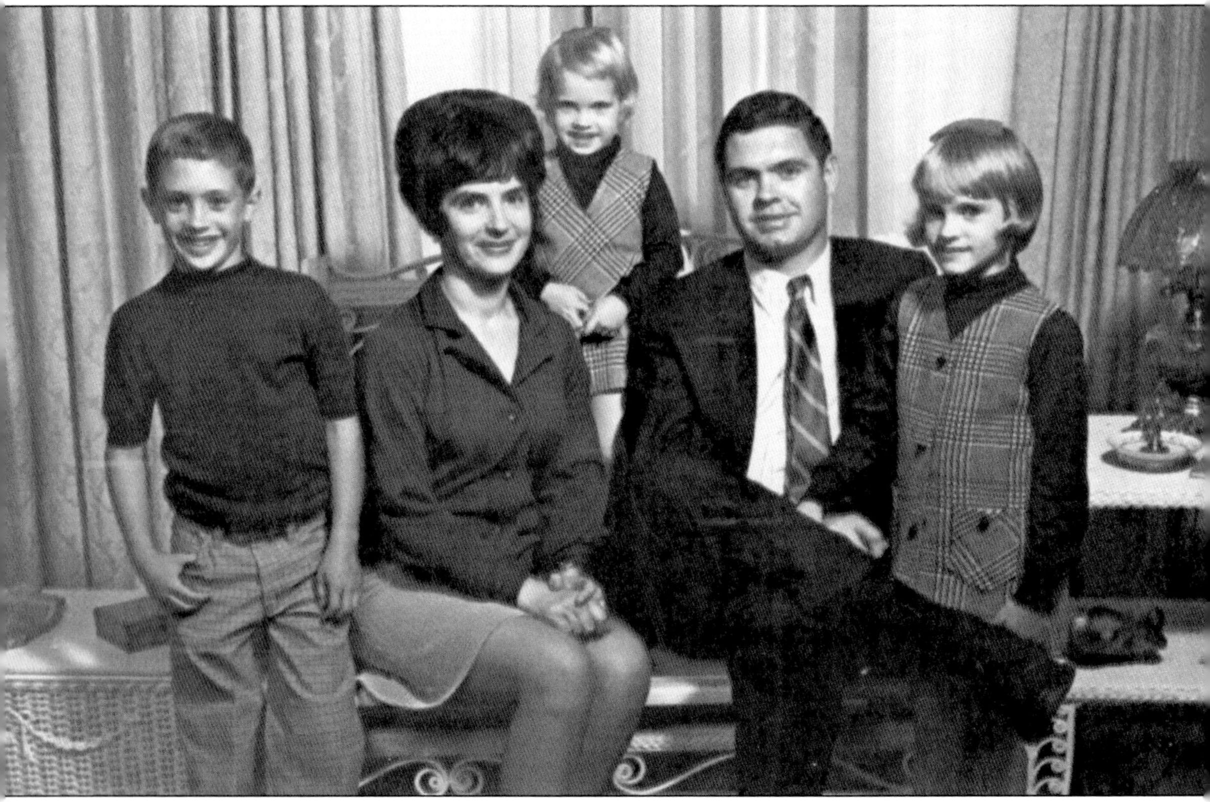

Jere Beasley served the State of Alabama as lieutenant governor from 1970 until 1978. During that time, Gov. George C. Wallace was shot and hospitalized in Maryland. Beasley served in Governor Wallace's absence for approximately 30 days. This campaign photo of the Jere Beasley family was taken in the early 1970s. (Courtesy of Betty Greene.)

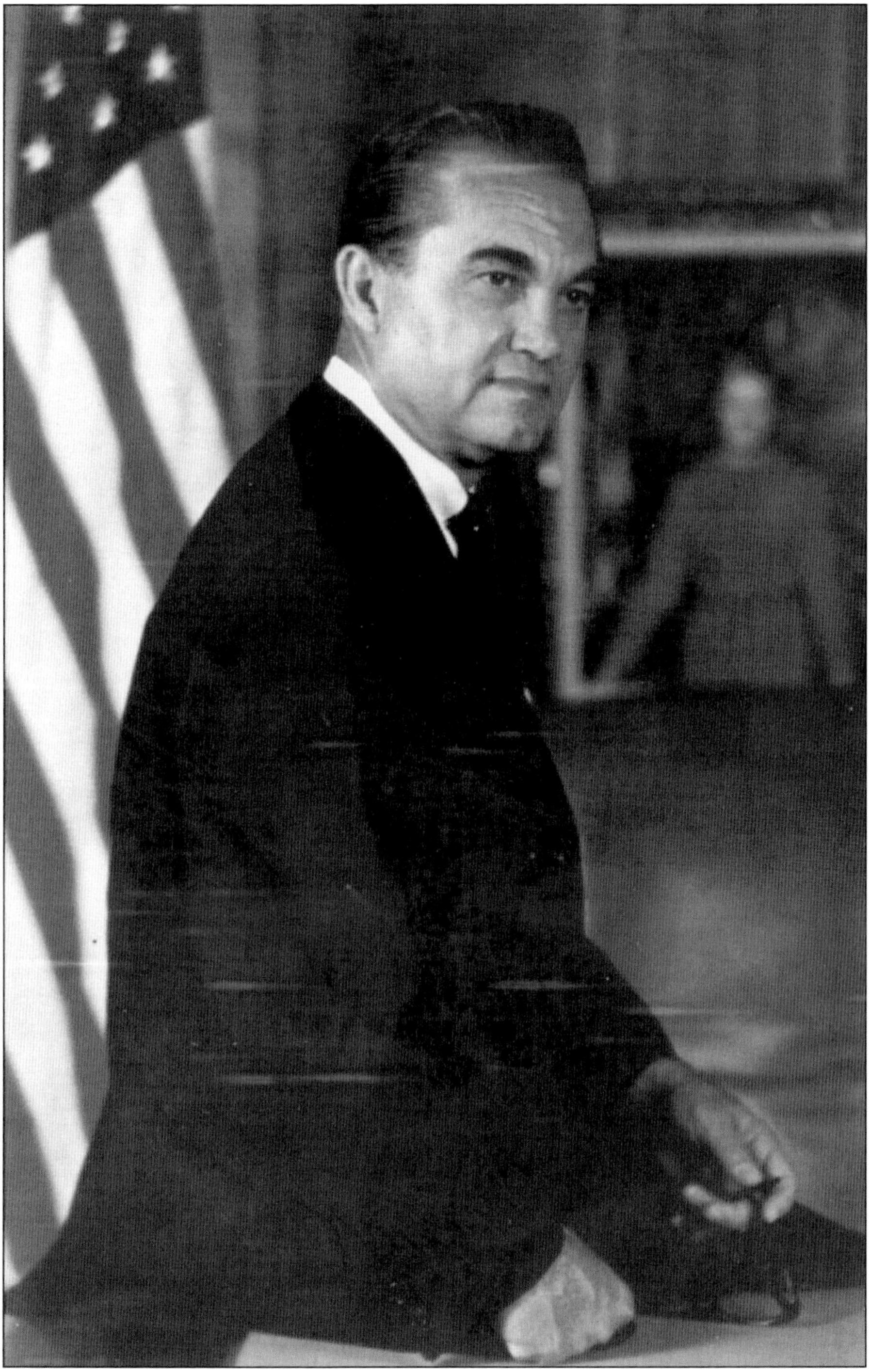

George Corley Wallace served four terms as governor of the State of Alabama. Wallace made two unsuccessful runs, in 1964 and 1972, for President of the United States. It was while campaigning for President that Wallace was paralyzed in an assassination attempt. Born in Clio, Wallace resided in Clayton and Montgomery, where he died in 1998.

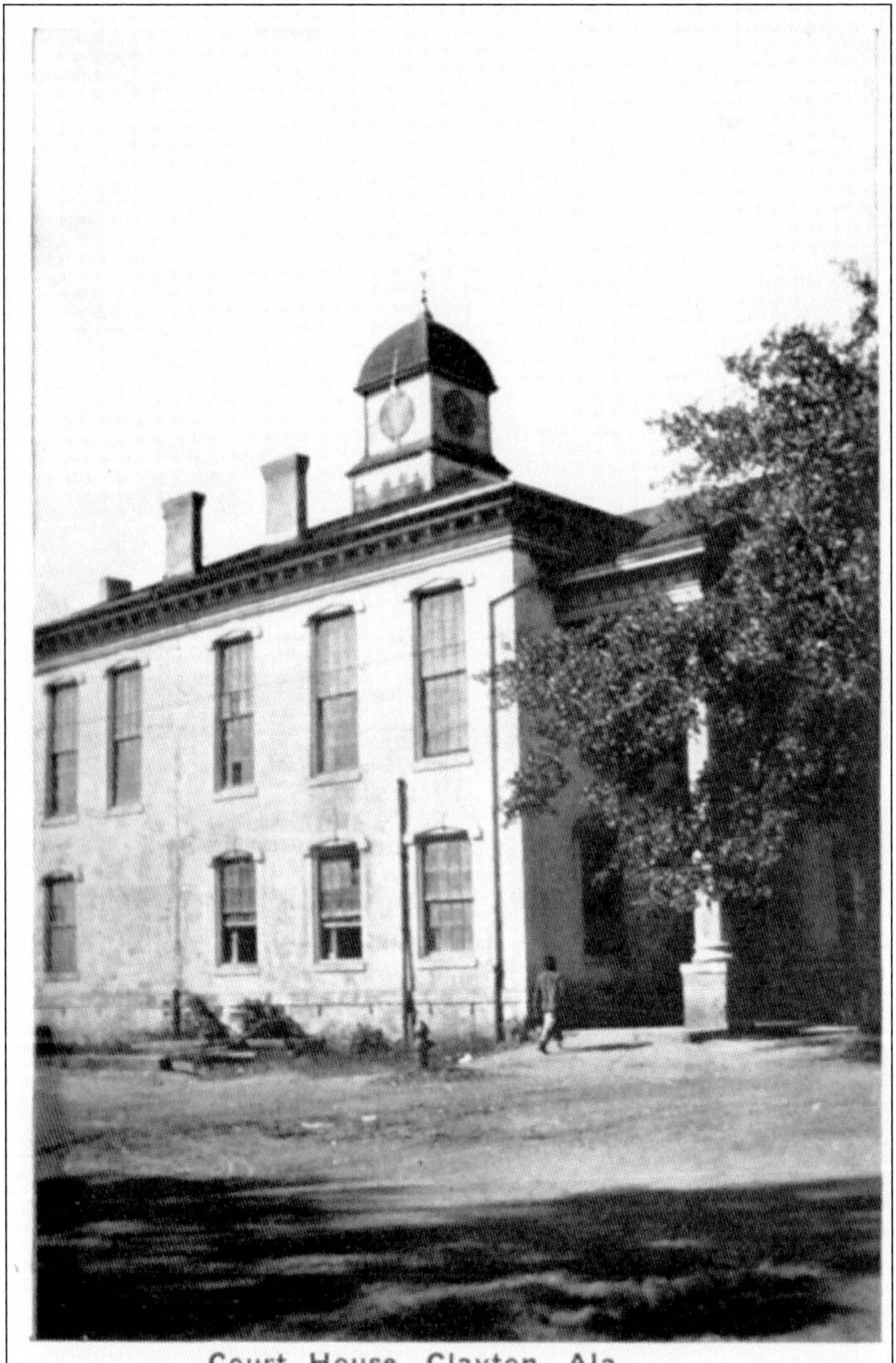

On December 18, 1832, Barbour County was created from Pike County and Creek Indian land. The legislature allowed the county's organization on January 11, 1833. The county's first court resided in Louisville. In March 1834, the circuit court moved to a 20-foot-square log building in Clayton. The log building was replaced in 1854 when a new courthouse was constructed for $9,695. This building was remodeled in 1924. (Courtesy of Betty Greene.)

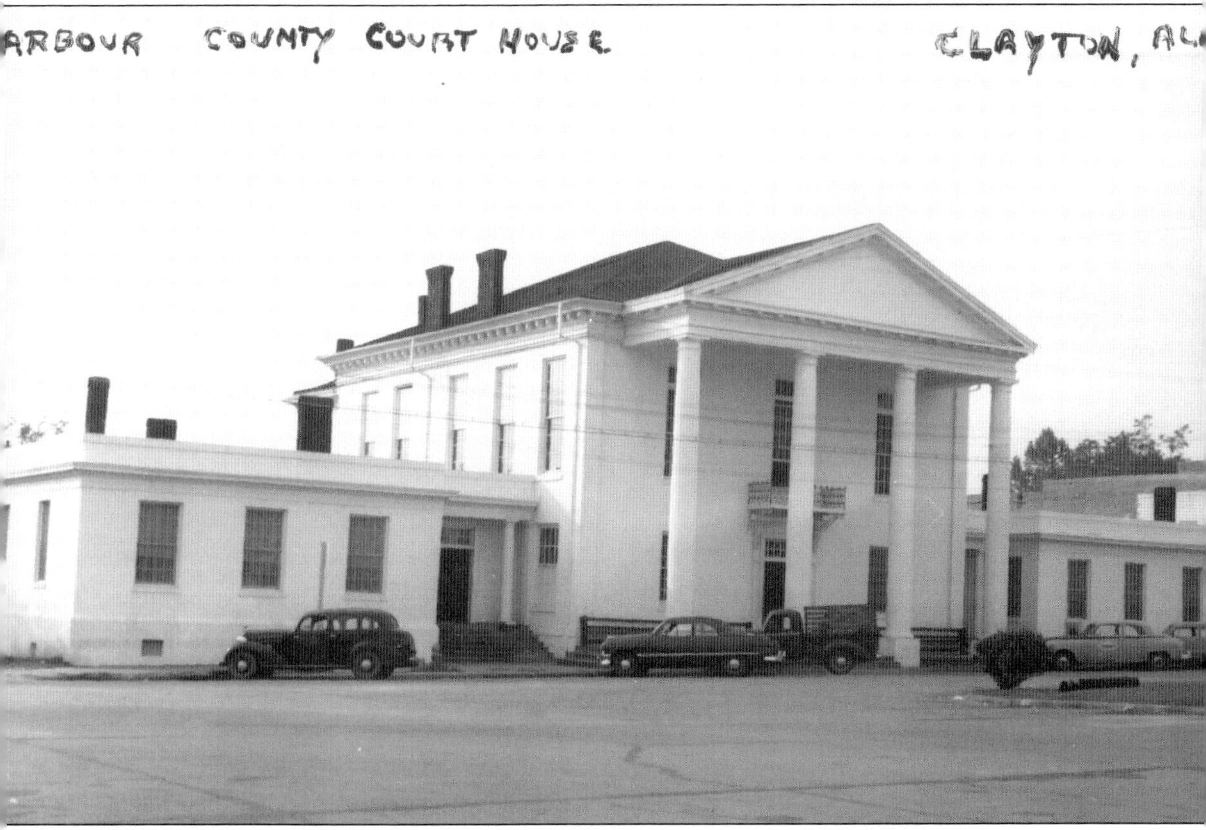

The Barbour County Courthouse was remodeled and expanded in 1924. This postcard shows the renovated courthouse with its added wings. (Courtesy of Ben Spurlock.)

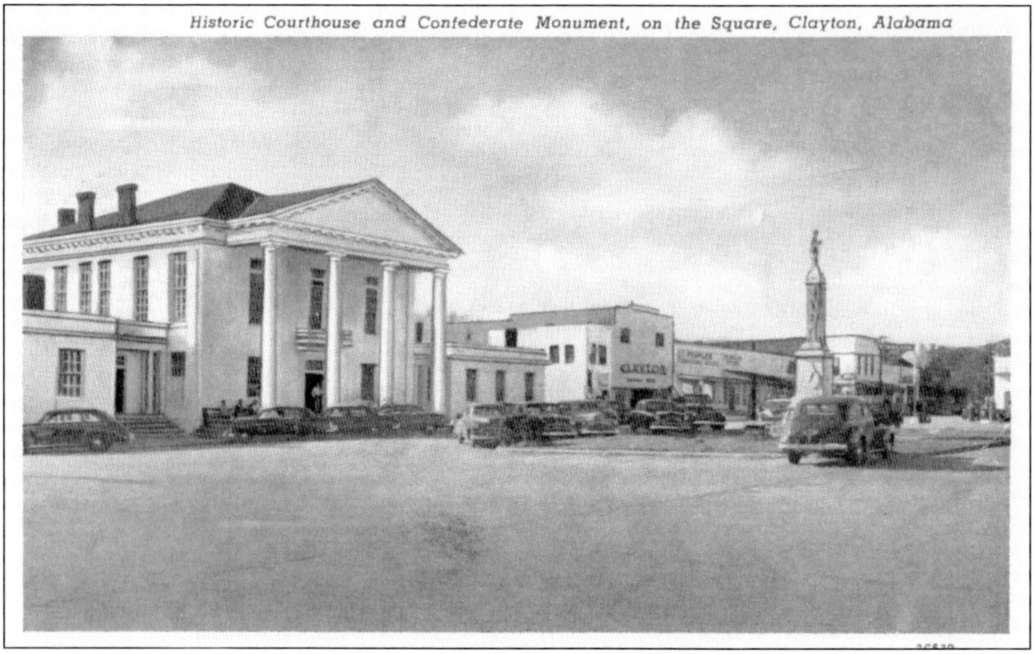

In 1924, the remodeled Clayton Courthouse allowed the addition of wings. The new look not only created more office space but also the total removal of the rooftop clock. (Courtesy of Ben and Lillian Hulen.)

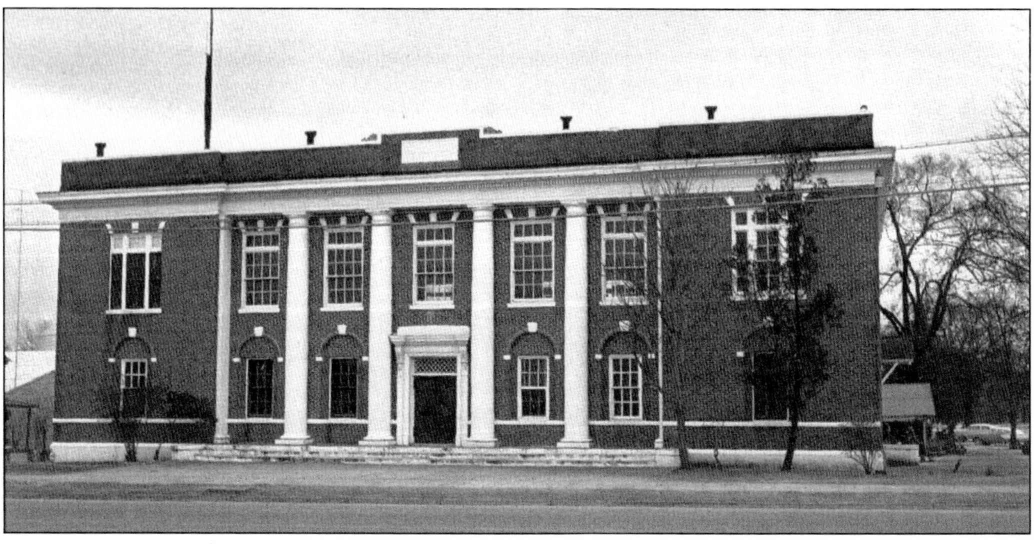

By the 1870s, Eufaula's population had grown significantly and moving Barbour County's courthouse from Clayton to Eufaula was a heavily debated topic. Instead, another courthouse was built in 1877 on East Broad Street for the convenience of the citizens of Eufaula. The land for the courthouse was provided by the City of Eufaula and the county constructed the building. The building served as both courthouse and City Hall for Eufaula. By 1922, the facility was declared unsafe by the state fire marshal and had to be replaced. This new courthouse was being built simultaneously with the renovation of the Clayton Courthouse. Construction of the Eufaula facility was completed in October of 1924. (Courtesy of Doug Purcell.)

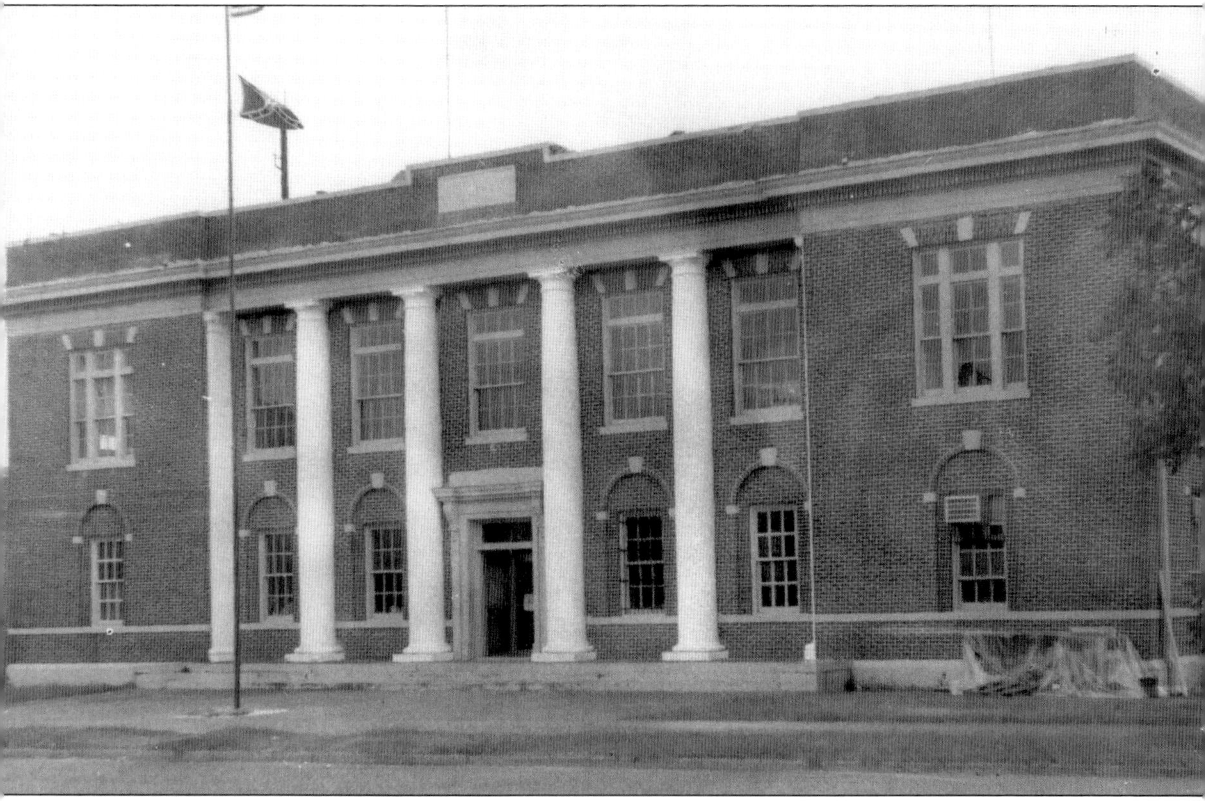

In 1923, $15,000 was appropriated by the City of Eufaula towards the building of a new courthouse on the same site as the original. A contract to build was awarded by the Barbour County Board of Revenue for $34,958.52. Both the city and county retained use of the new courthouse upon its completion in 1924. By 1975, the facility provided inadequate space for both county and city offices. An agreement was reached allowing the county to pay the city $100,000 for its half-interest in the building. (Courtesy of Rob Schaffeld.)

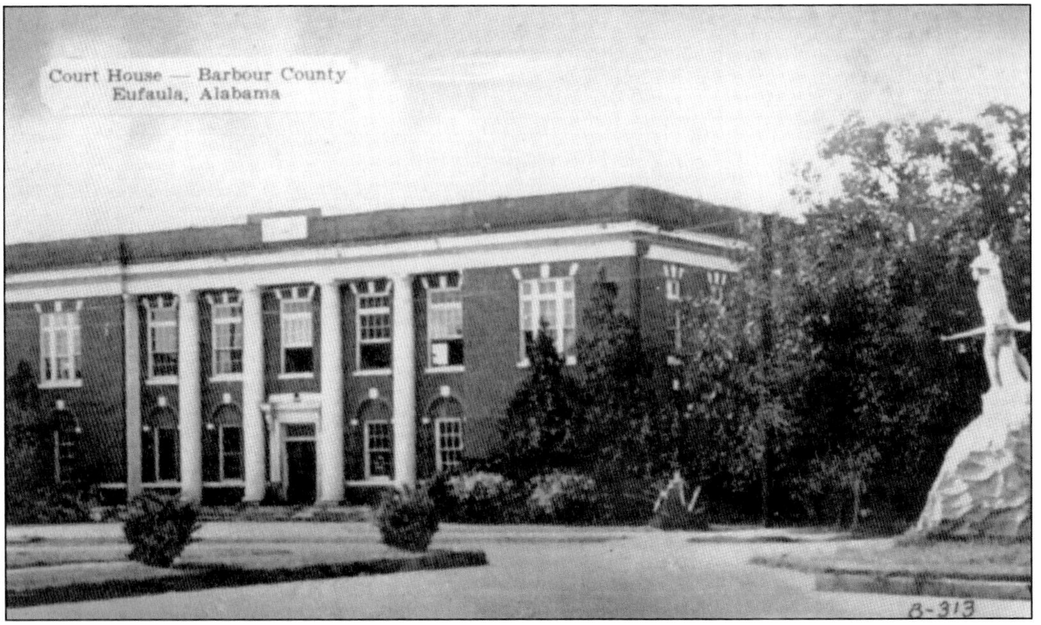

Completed in 1924, the Eufaula Courthouse was in need of expansion by 1984. In 1986, renovations modernized and expanded the building. (Courtesy of Eufaula Heritage Association.)

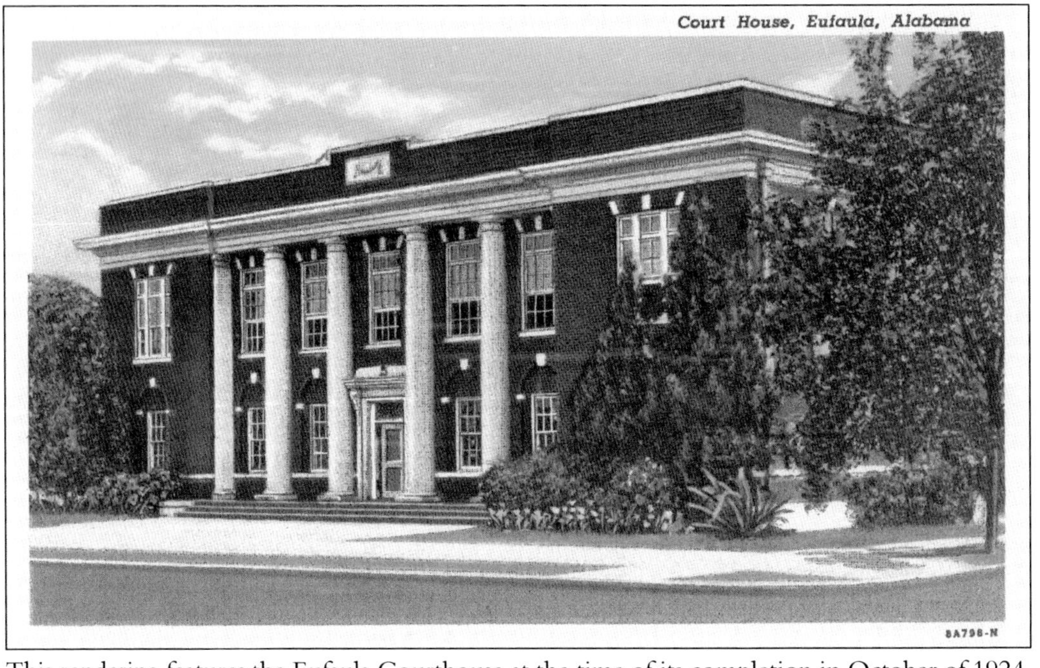

This rendering features the Eufaula Courthouse at the time of its completion in October of 1924. Shiels-Guice Lumber Company was awarded the contract for $34,958.52 for the construction of the building. (Courtesy of Rob Schaffeld.)

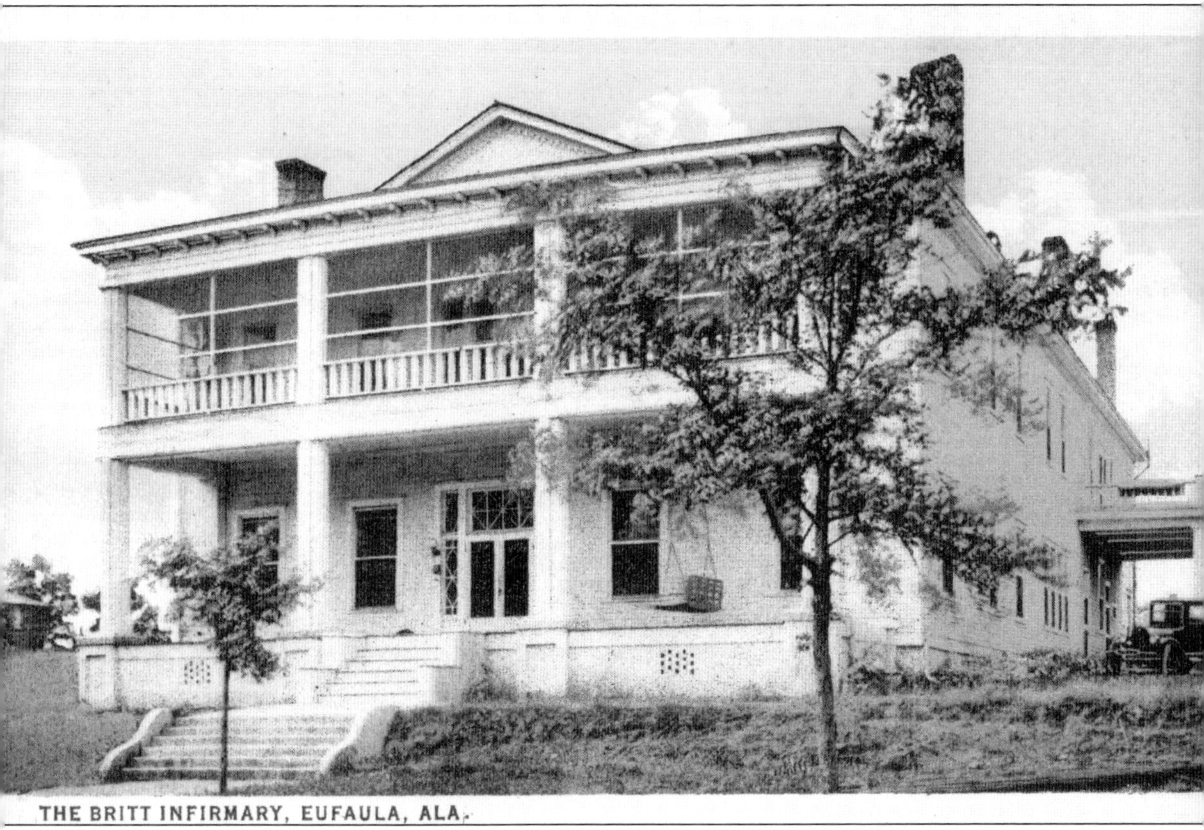

Britt Infirmary was founded in May 1920 by Dr. Walter Stratton Britt on College Hill in Eufaula. It served the community for 18 years. Dr. Britt was a leading business and civic leader. He was president of the Commercial Club for seven years, president of the Country Club, president of the Rotary Club, and a Mason. (Courtesy of Rob Schaffeld.)

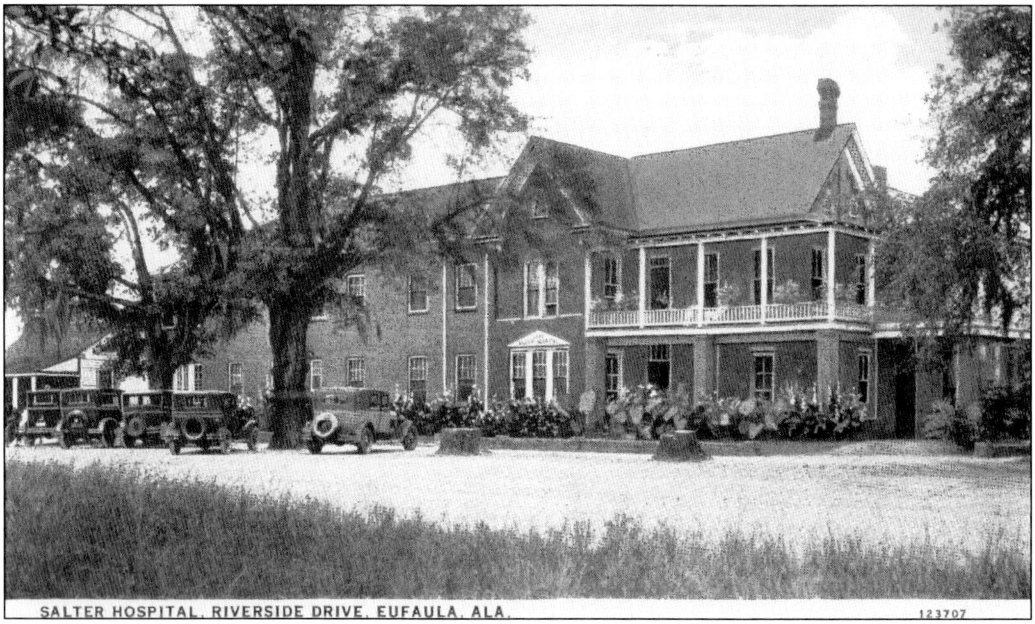

Salter Hospital opened in 1923 at a former residence on Riverside Drive in Eufaula. It served the Barbour County community through the mid-1950s. This card is dated 1928. (Courtesy of Frank Mixon.)

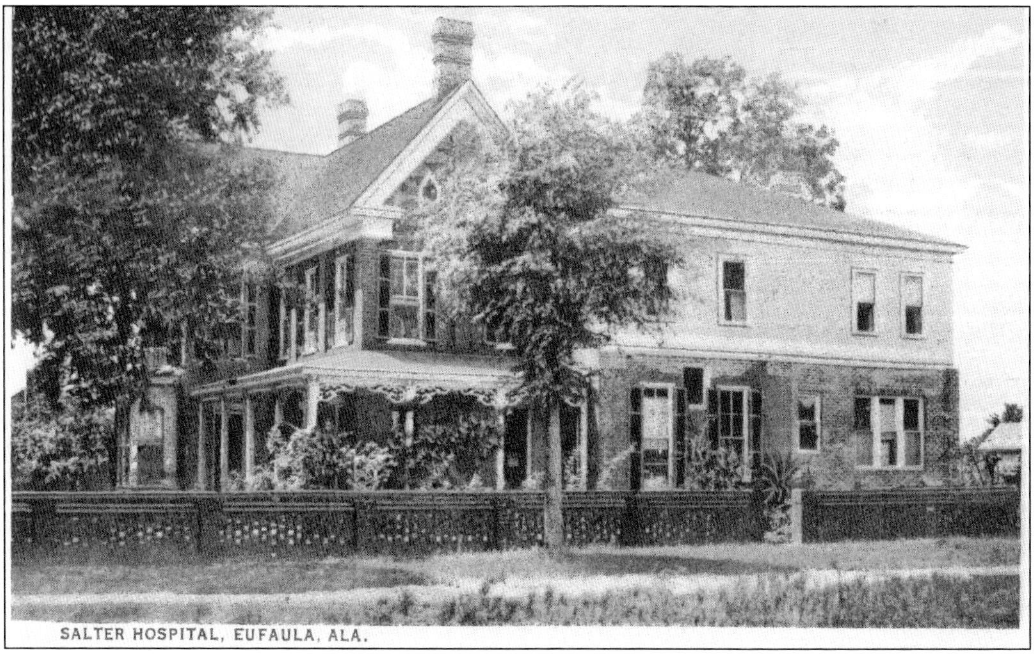

Opened in 1923 by Paul P. Salter, M.D., Salter Hospital was at one time the only hospital in Barbour County. There were two separate wards, one for whites and one for blacks. Four doctors served patients during World War II, including Dr. T.V. McCoo, who was black. Dr. Salter was a surgeon and was believed to be one of the first doctors in Alabama to use sodium pentothal as an anesthetic. (Courtesy of Frank Mixon.)

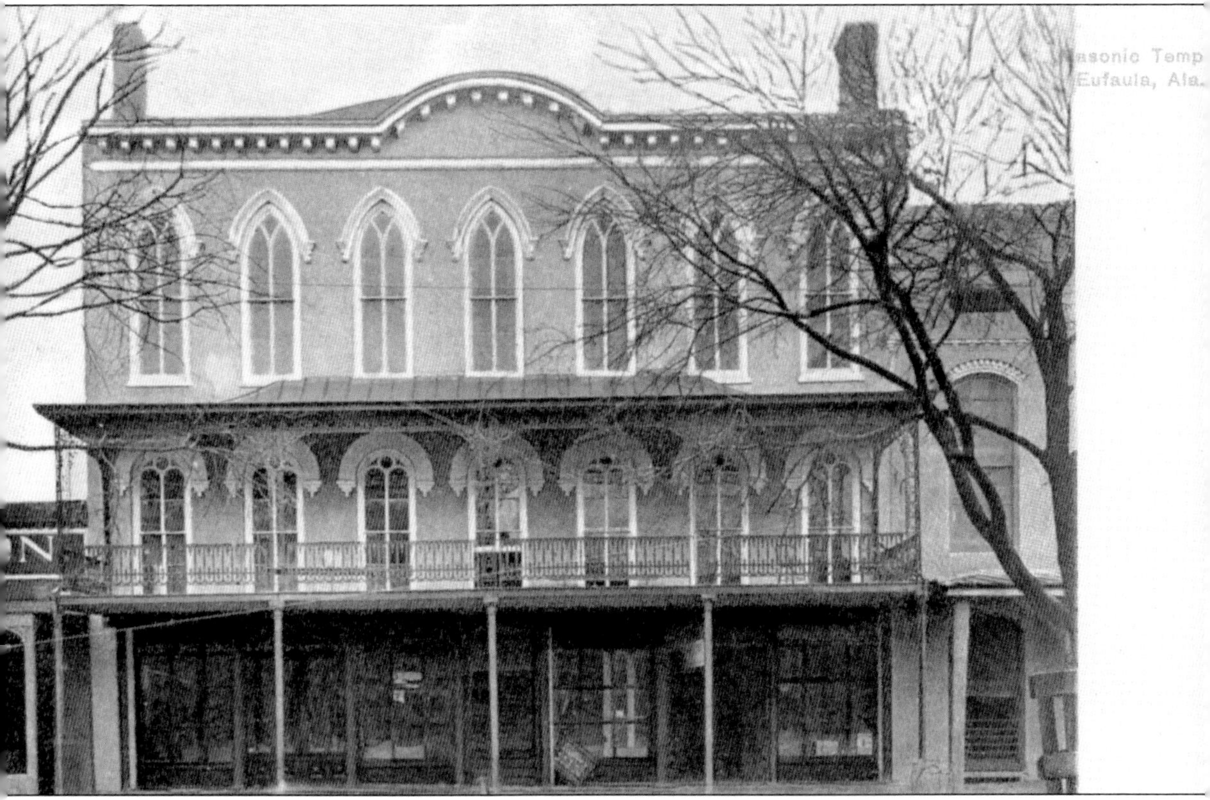

The Masonic Temple was built in 1871 on East Broad Street, Eufaula. The Harmony Lodge has occupied the building since 1890 and owned it since 1905. This card pre-dates 1952 when the grille was removed and placed on the Eufaula Carnegie Library. The La-Z-Boy Gallery currently occupies the building with the storefront altered only by the removal of the balcony and columns. The windows are still a major architectural feature of the building. (Courtesy of Eufaula Heritage Association.)

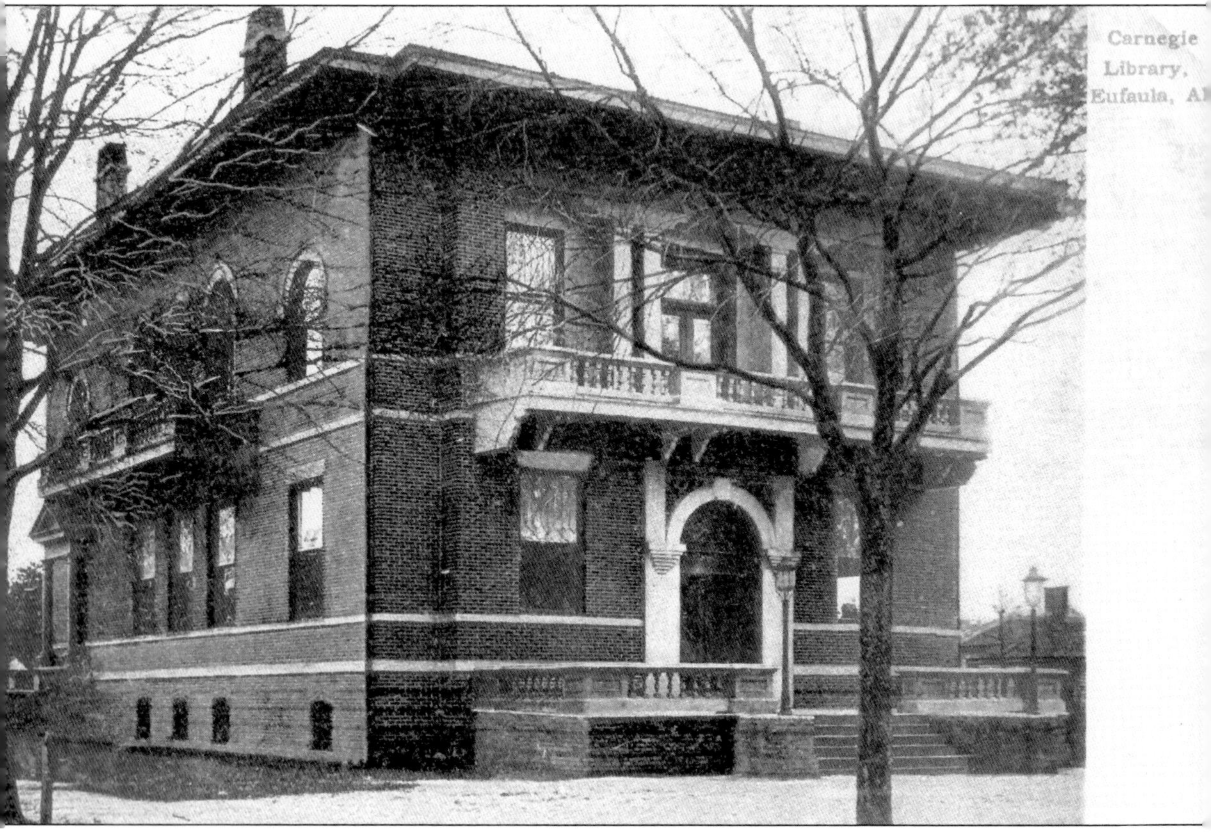

The Carnegie Library was funded by a $10,000, matching funds grant from the Andrew Carnegie Foundation. The original building is red brick with pressed, yellow brick trim and has Italianate features of large, over-hanging eves. Constructed in 1904, the library celebrates its 100th anniversary of service to the community in 2004. It is still in the same location. (Courtesy of Rob Schaffeld.)

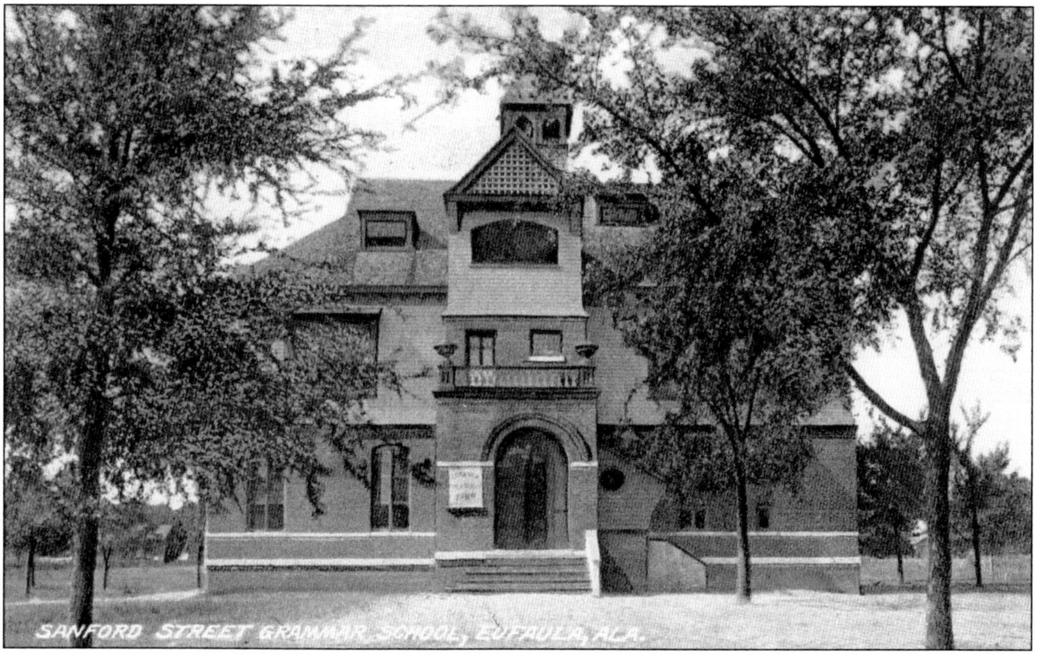

The Eufaula City School system, established in 1872, is Alabama's oldest city system. Sanford Street Grammar School has existed at this site since 1888. Grades one through twelve attended school at this location throughout most of the 1900s. In 1957 a new elementary school was built on Pump Station Road. In the 1970s a new junior high and high school were built, moving all but one elementary school from Sanford Avenue. (Courtesy of Rob Schaffeld.)

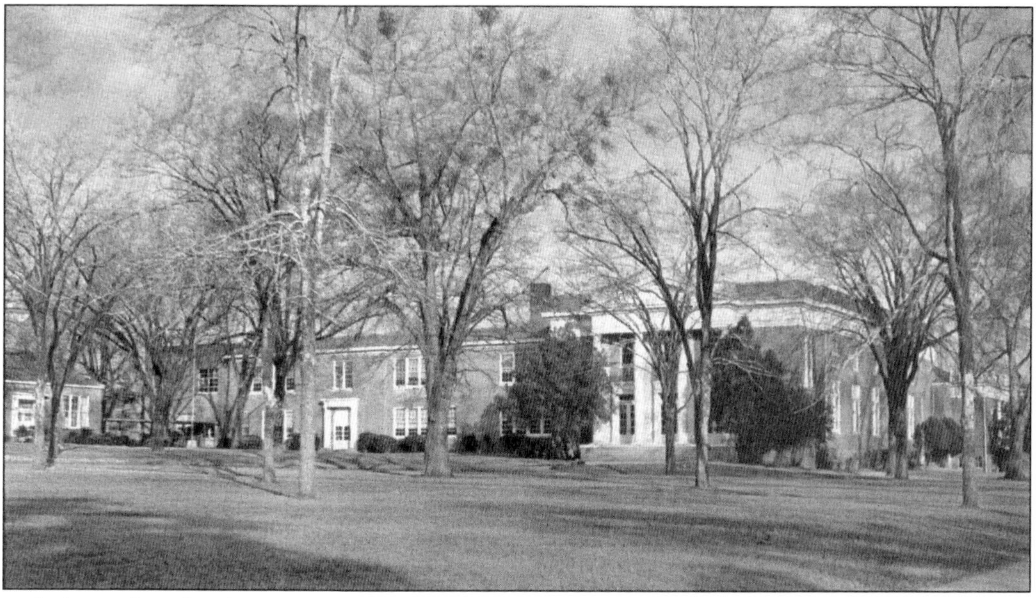

Eufaula High School started on Highland Avenue in a two-room house. In 1880 the school moved to Sanford Street. In the late 1920s, a brick two-story building with an auditorium and a gymnasium was constructed. The auditorium today serves as the city auditorium; the high school was relocated in 1978. (Courtesy of Doug Purcell.)

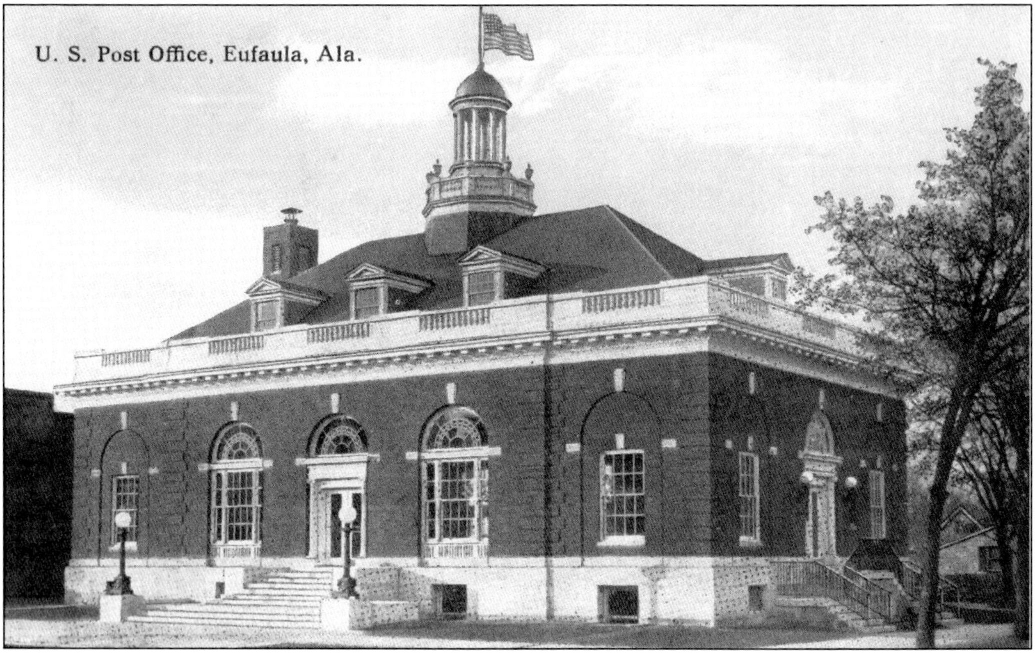

Congressman Henry D. Clayton Jr. was instrumental in getting a bill passed in 1908 "providing for a pubic building in the City of Eufaula costing $50,000 . . . . [T]he building will be an ornament to the city." This building was constructed from those funds and served as the post office from 1913 to the 1980s. It was built on the site of the old St. Julian Hotel where Jefferson Davis and his daughter stayed on a visit to Eufaula in 1881. The building is a one-story brick with dormer windows and a cupola. (Courtesy of Tade Lampley.)

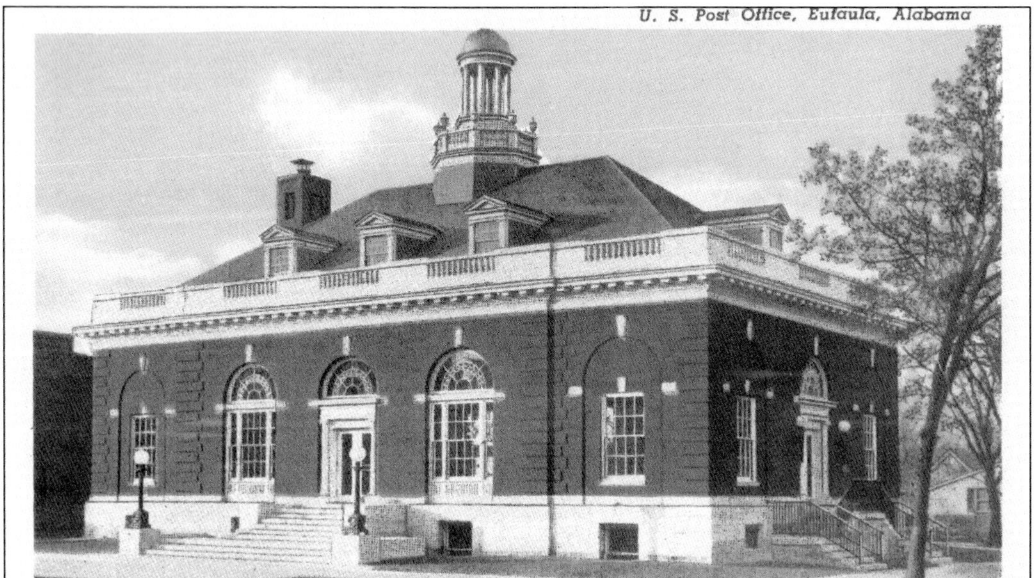

A new post office was constructed in the 1980s east of this location on Broad Street. Today the building is occupied by Blondheim and Mixon Architectural firm and Tommy Gaither, attorney at law. (Courtesy of Rob Schaffeld.)

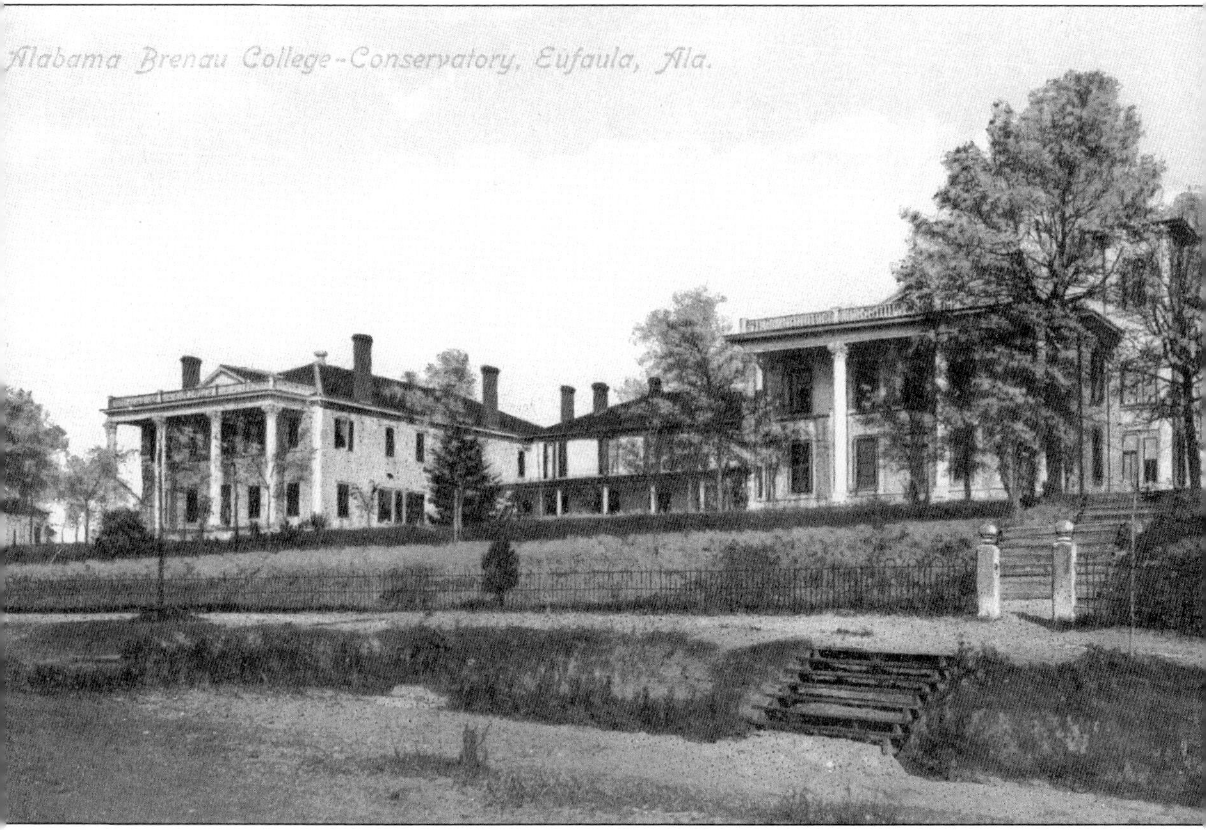

Originally known as the Union Female College, Alabama Brenau was an interest of E.B. Young. He served on its board of trustees as its first president along with John McNab and E.C.Bulloch. Plans were made for the placement of the cornerstone and its dedication by September 1854. Atop the roof stood a wooden statue of Minerva, the Goddess of Wisdom. The college belfry housed a large bell, and a covered corridor joined the main building and kitchen. (Courtesy of Eufaula Heritage Association.)

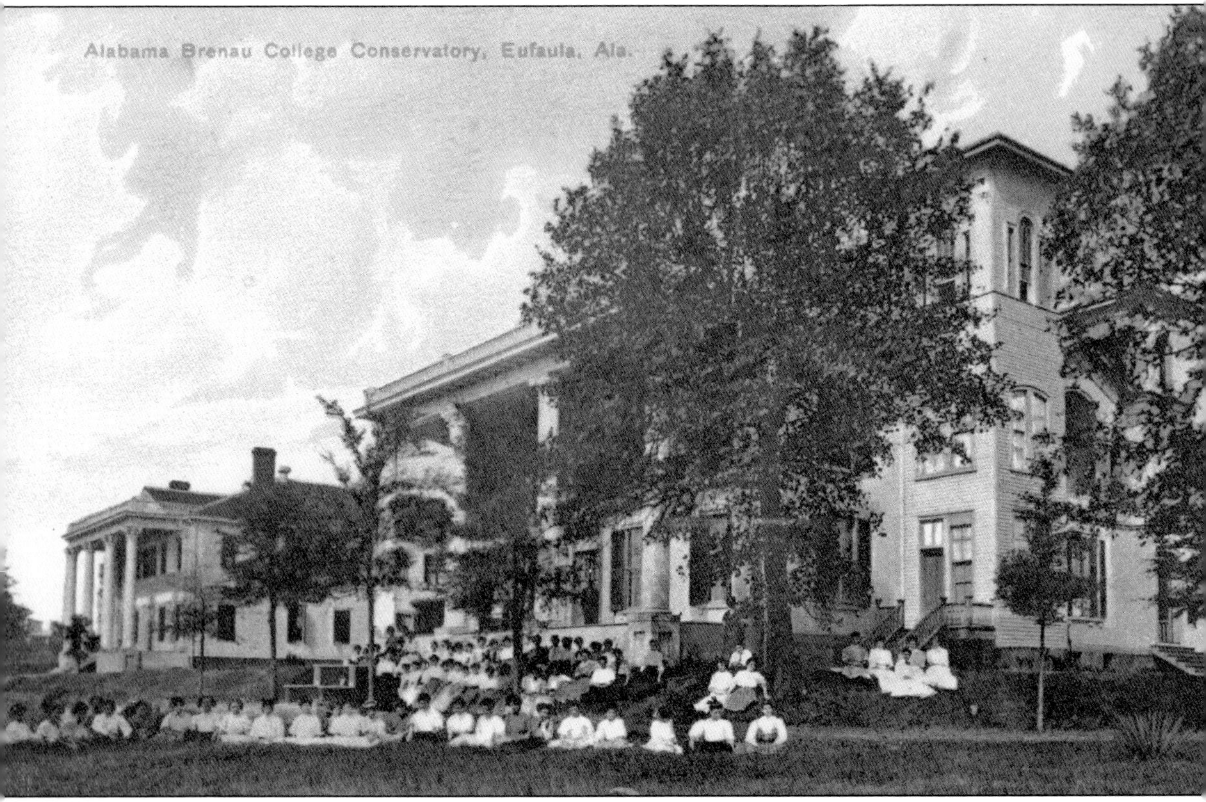

Seated on the lawn are students of the Alabama Brenau College Conservatory. Their uniforms were considered in style for that time, and a month's tuition and board was $15. The entire term cost $250. (Courtesy of Rob Schaffeld.)

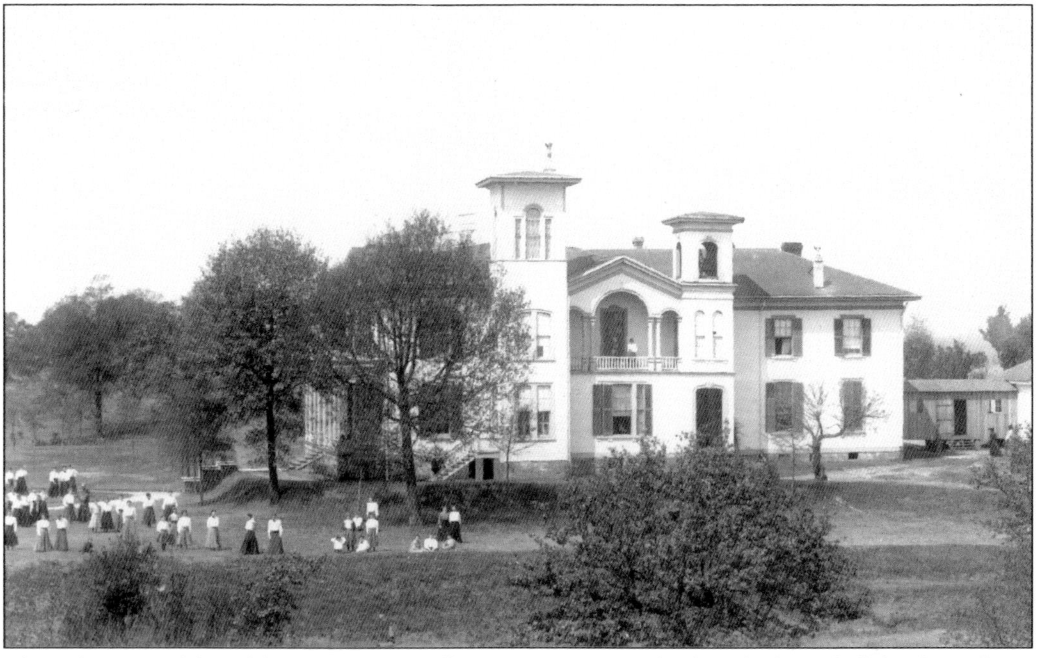

This side view of the Alabama Brenau College Conservatory displays the huge bell for the college, as well as the passageway leading to the kitchen. The college was located at the top of West Broad Street. The area is to this day known as College Hill. (Courtesy of Mary Gray.)

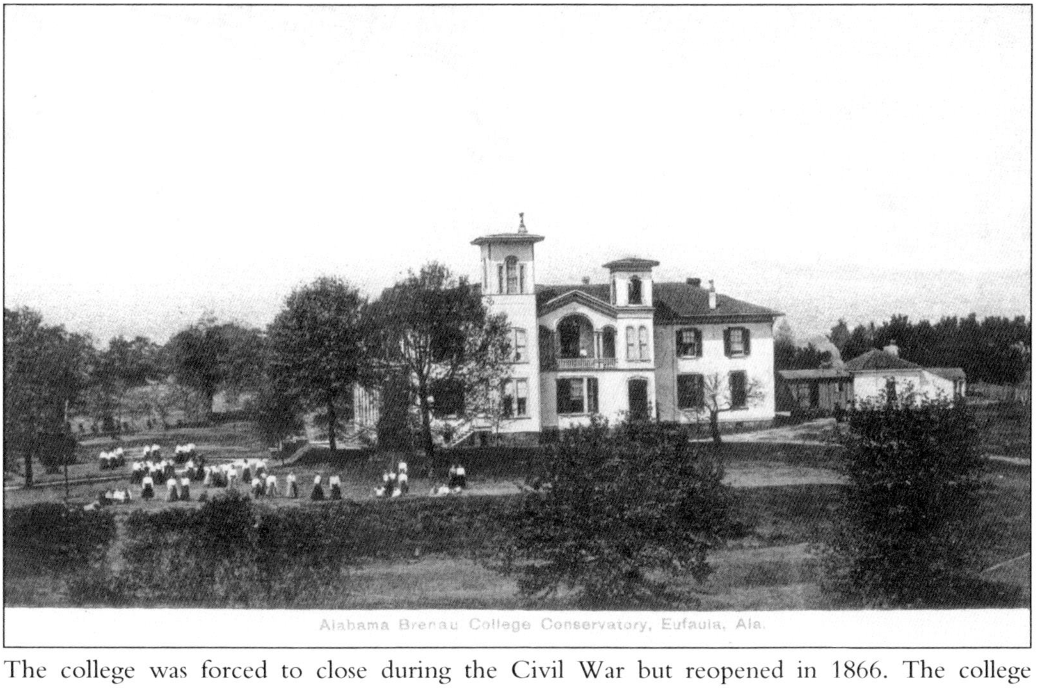

The college was forced to close during the Civil War but reopened in 1866. The college flourished until 1872 when the wife of president Hiram Hawkins died, and he resigned the position. (Courtesy of Rob Schaffeld)

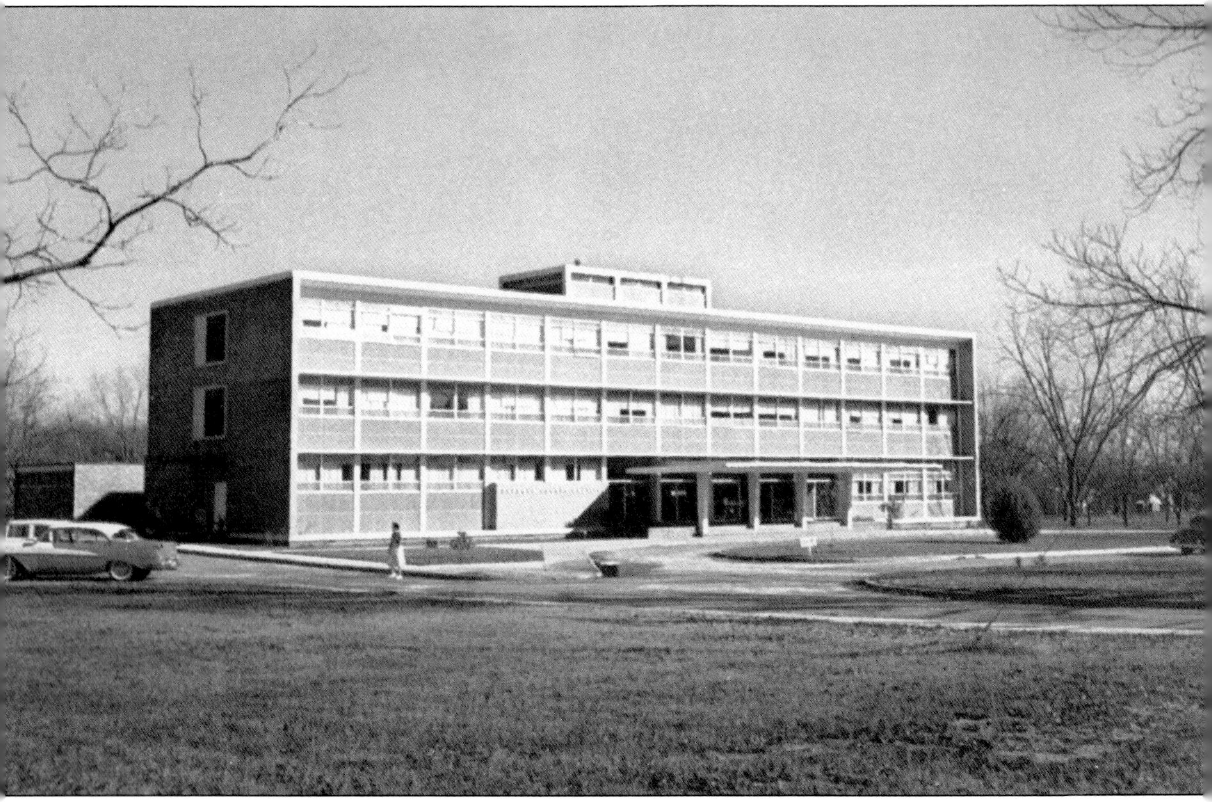

Barbour County Hospital has served the area since its opening in 1954. The land was donated by Cowikee Mills. Today the hospital is known as Lakeview Community Hospital and is in the same location. Though additions have been made and renovations have been done, the exterior remains virtually unchanged. (Courtesy of Doug Purcell.)

Ten

COMMERCE

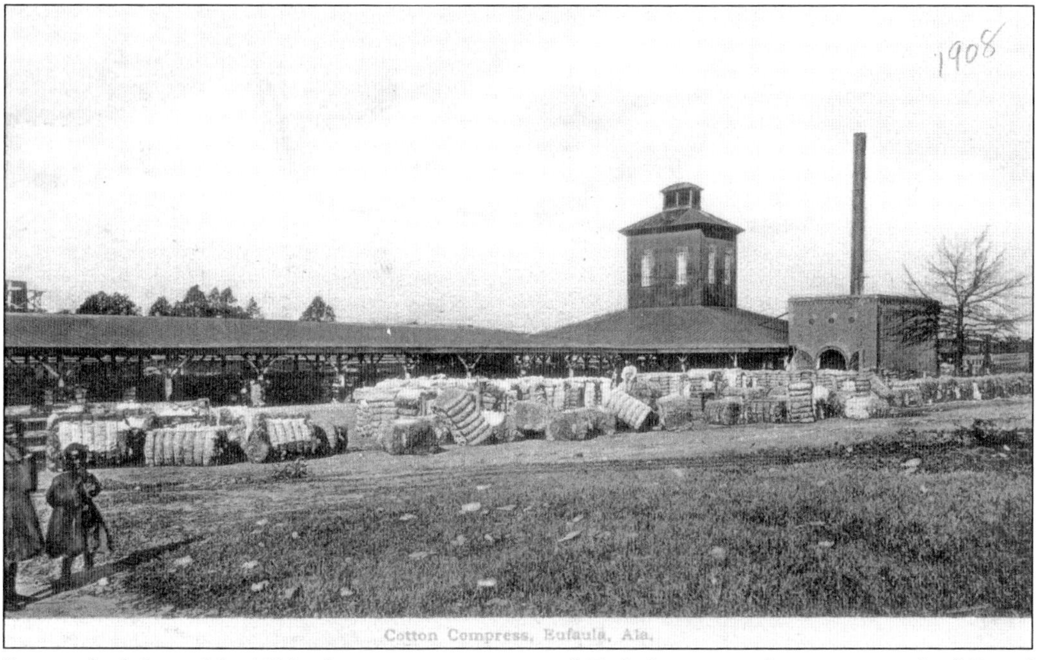

Postmarked June 23, 1908, the cotton compress of Eufaula sat on the eastern end of Broad Street. Cotton was a major economic force throughout the region, but especially in Eufaula where cotton mills dominated the job market. Cotton was shipped out of Eufaula via steamboat and later by rail. Eufaula Farm Center is in operation at this location today. (Courtesy of Doug Purcell.)

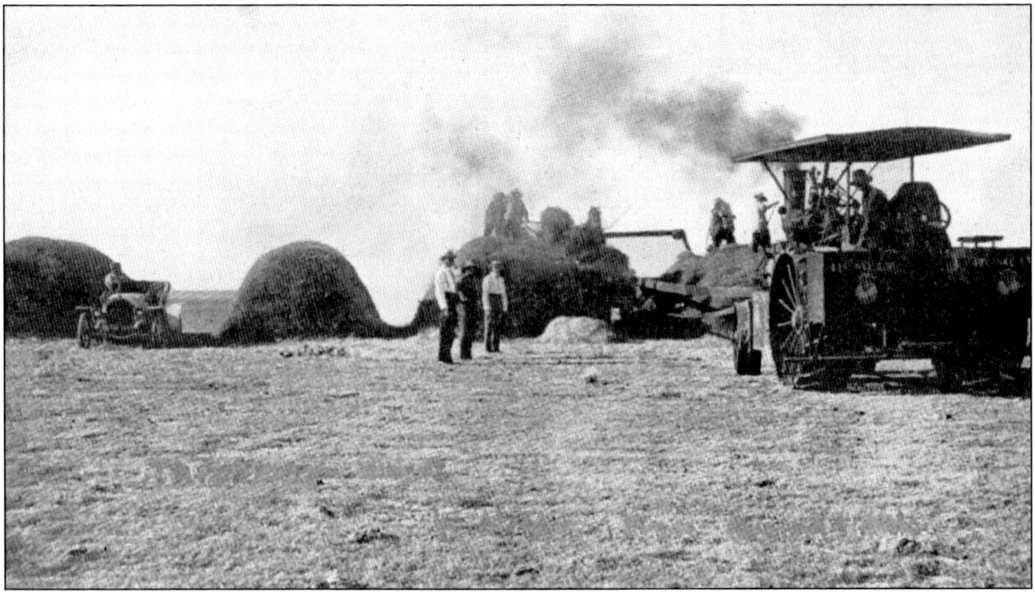

Peanuts have long been a staple agricultural commodity in Southeast Alabama. This early Depression-era postcard shows peanuts being harvested. (Courtesy of Tade Lampley.)

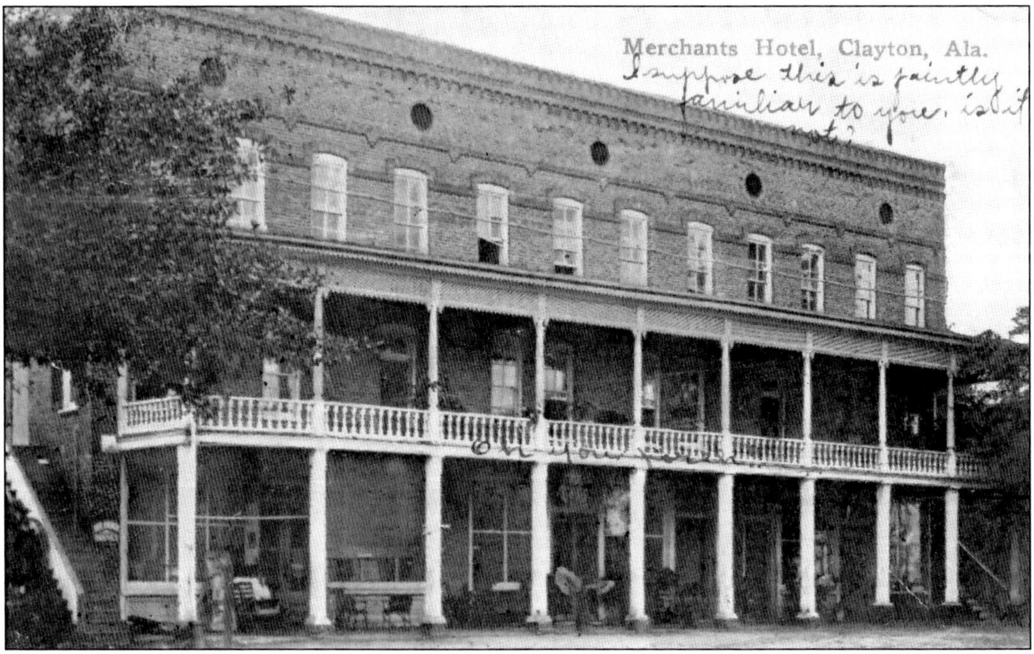

Built around 1888 on South Midway Street in Clayton, this hotel also housed a number of business firms including The Citizens Bank, two local doctor's offices, and an opera house. It operated until the mid-1940s when it burned with *The Clayton Record* newspaper office on the first floor. Postmarked 1912, this postcard was sent to Miss Mary Ventress of Meridian, Mississippi, with the note "I suppose this is faintly familiar to you isn't it?" (Courtesy of Betty Greene.)

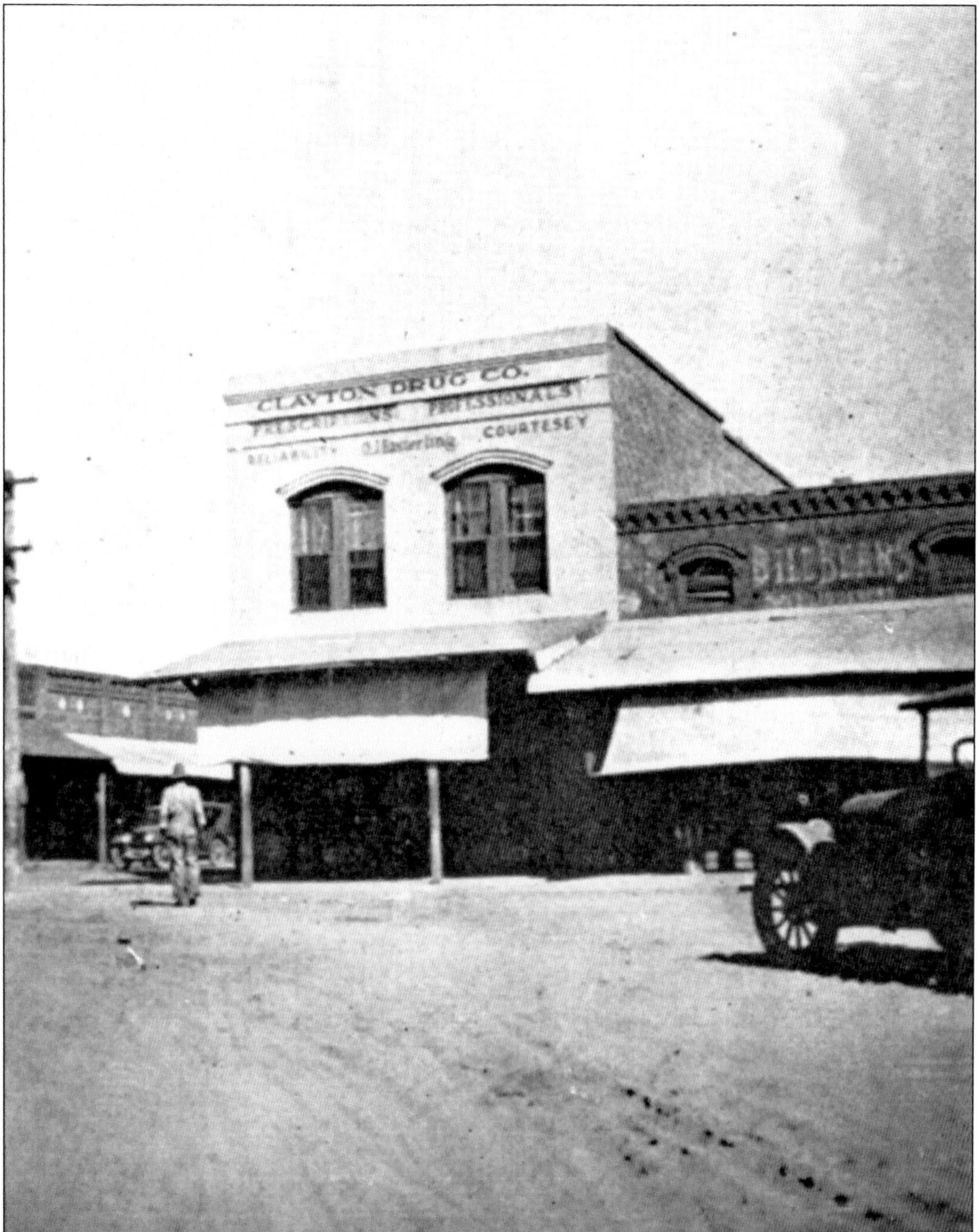

Clayton Drug Co., Clayton, Ala.

Built before 1903, this photo dates from 1923–1933 when Oscar Easterling owned the building. The Clayton Drug Company occupied the building for the better part of the past century and continuously since 1962. In 2003, Clayton Drug Company was moved next door by its present owner, District 84 representative William "Billy" Beasley, who has operated the drug store since 1996. (Courtesy of Betty Greene.)

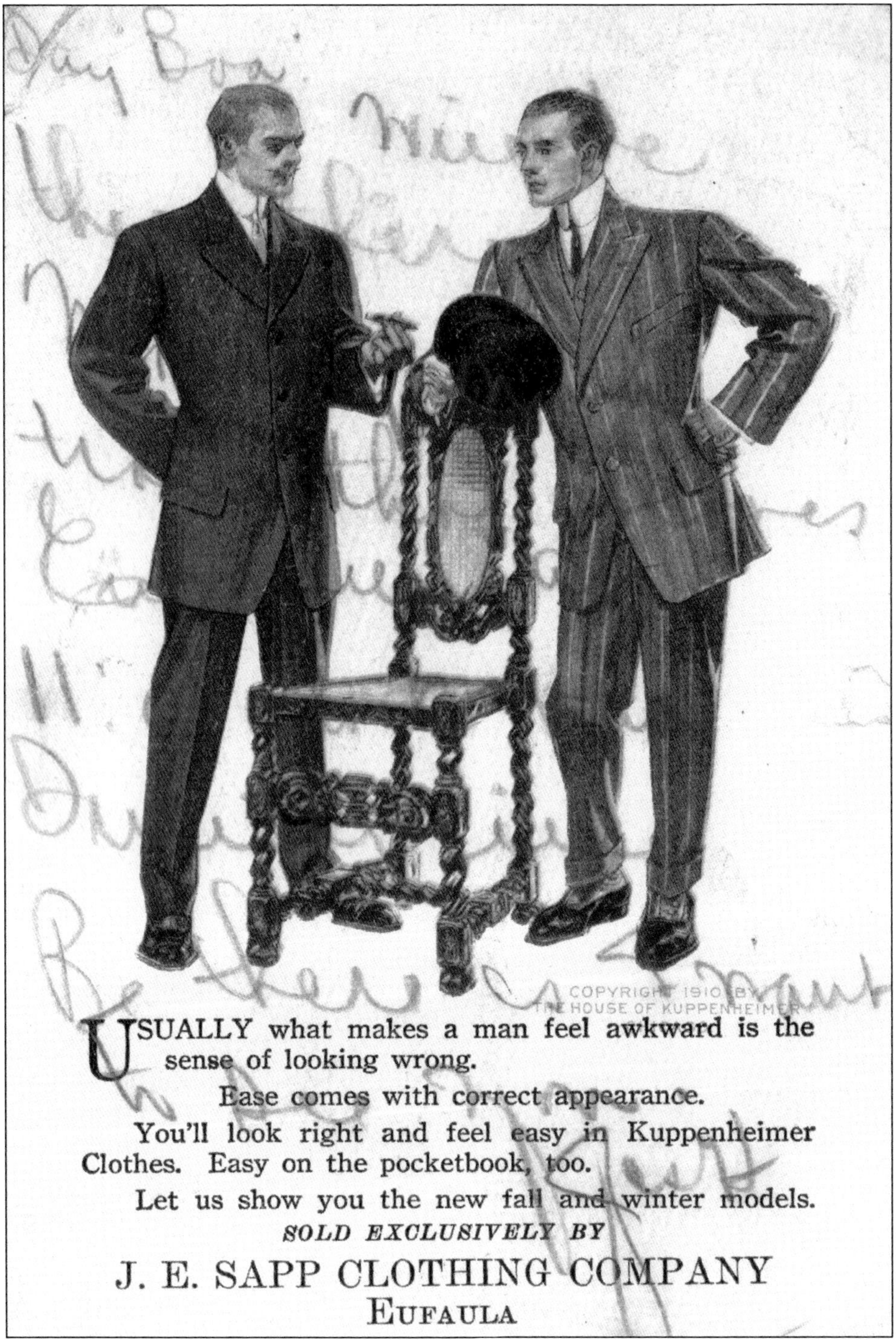

J.E. Sapp Clothing Company was operated on Broad Street by Mr. Sapp and his son Phil Allen from 1904 to 1929, when it closed. The store advertised the "finest men's clothing in the state." This card was postmarked February 26, 1911, to Mr. W.B. Smith of Albany, Georgia, and the writing across the front is illegible. (Courtesy of Doug Purcell.)

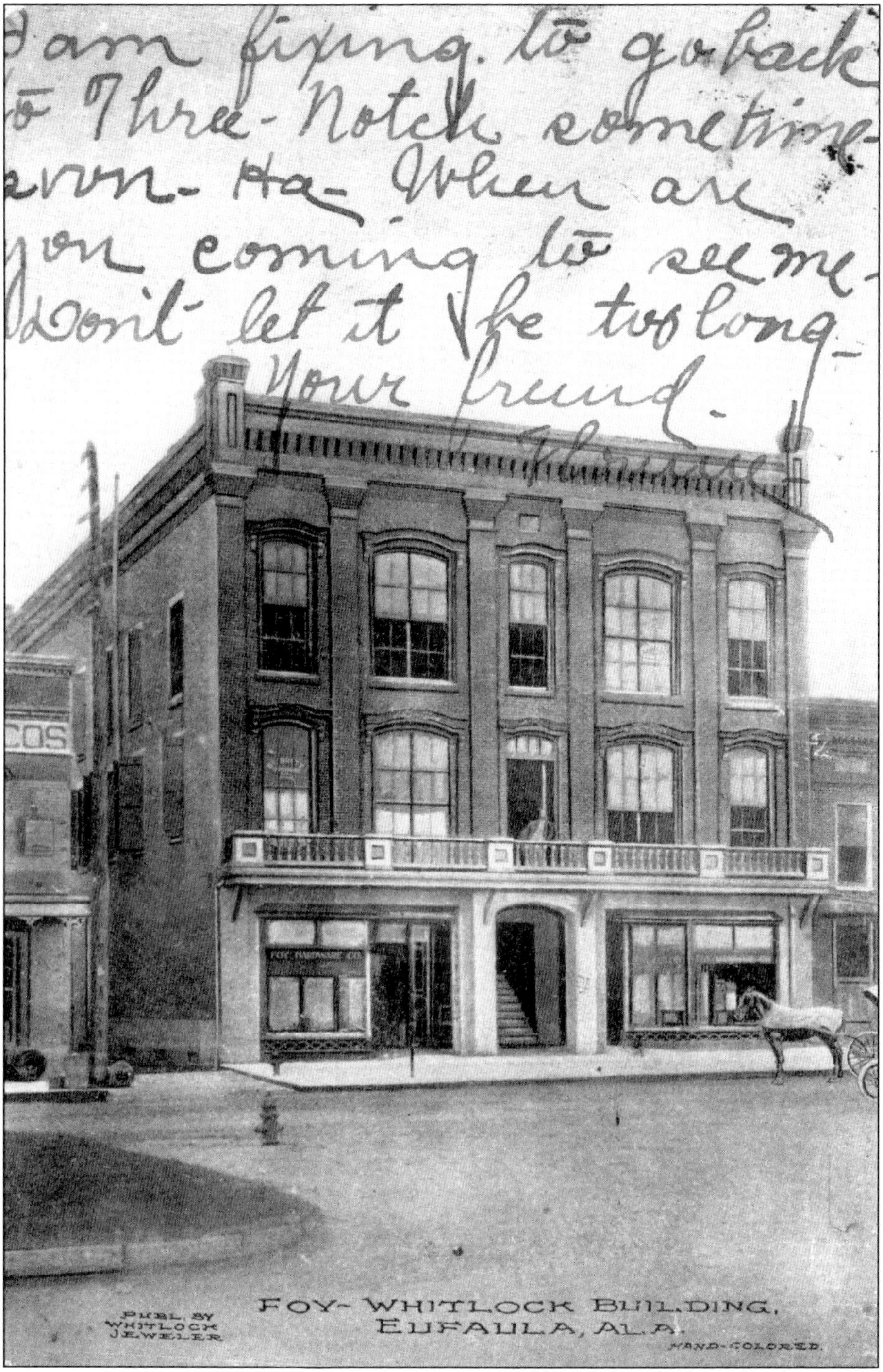

This turn-of-the-century, hand-colored rendering showcases the Foy-Whitlock building in downtown Eufaula. There is some debate on whether this building was ever constructed exactly as drawn. Miss Vera Bush of Belcher, Alabama, received this note from a friend in Eufaula. Unfortunately, the name of the sender is illegible. (Courtesy of Doug Purcell.)

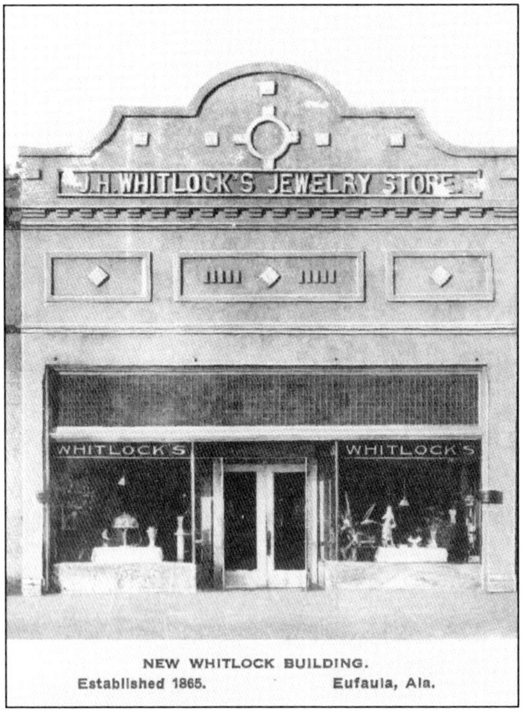

Opened in 1865 by John H. Whitlock, Whitlock's Jewelry Store has served the Eufaula community continuously since then. Mr. Whitlock was a leading Eufaula citizen beloved and trusted by all. His jewelry business has been a staple on Broad Street, having weathered the March 1919 tornado that devastated much of the heart of Eufaula. Shown here is the rebuilt storefront that still exists today, though the jewelry store has since relocated. (Courtesy of Tade Lampley.)

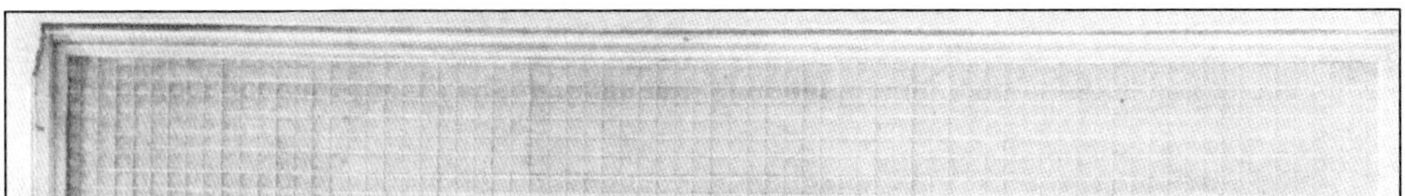

Purchased by E.P. Clark in 1930 from the Whitlock family, the store was operated by Mr. W.V. Neville Sr. Mr. Neville purchased the business in 1940 and operated it for over three decades. In 1970 the business was moved next door to this location. In 1974, Richard and Irene Harrison purchased the jewelry store and operate it to this day. (Courtesy of Rob Schaffeld.)

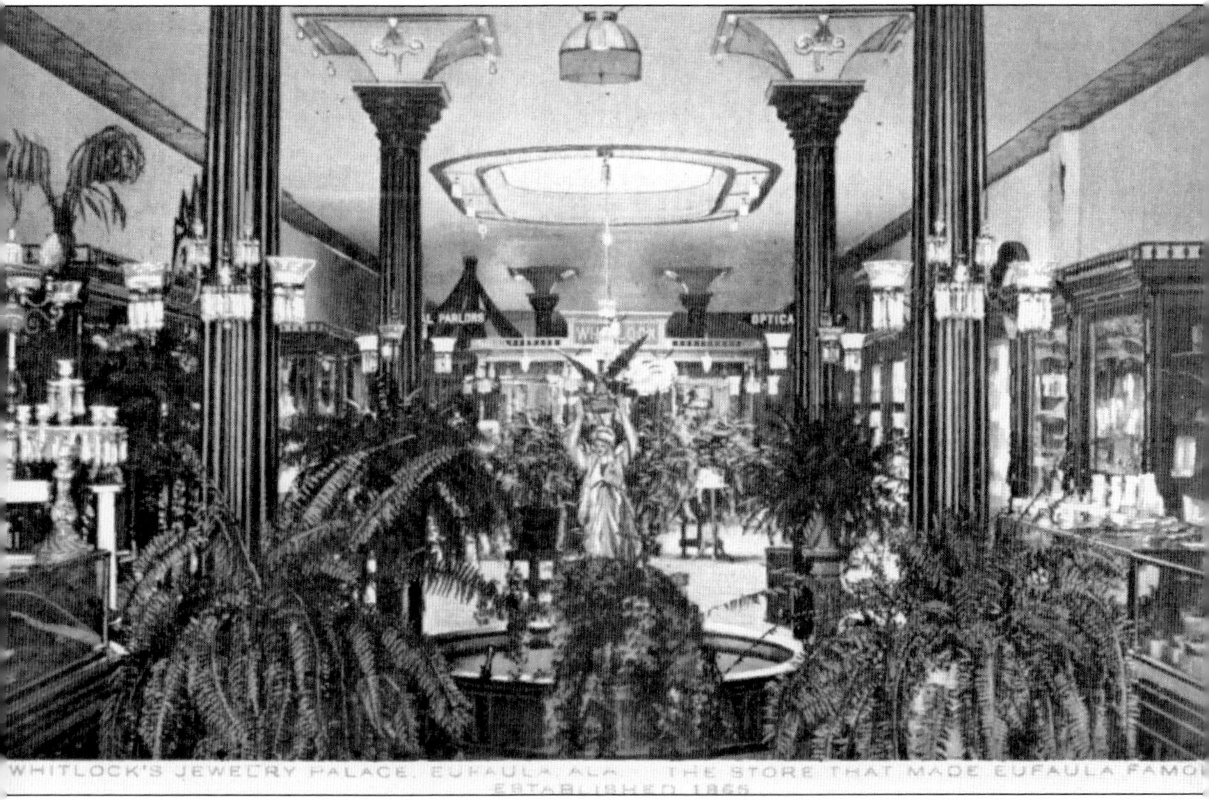

The opulence of the J.H. Whitlock Jewelry Store is evident in this 1920s postcard. The inscription on the bottom states, "J.H. Whitlock's Jewelry Palace Eufaula, Ala. The Store that made Eufaula famous. Established 1865." The jewelry store was instrumental in publishing postcards throughout the 1900s, many of which were used in the making of this book. (Courtesy of Eufaula Heritage Association.)

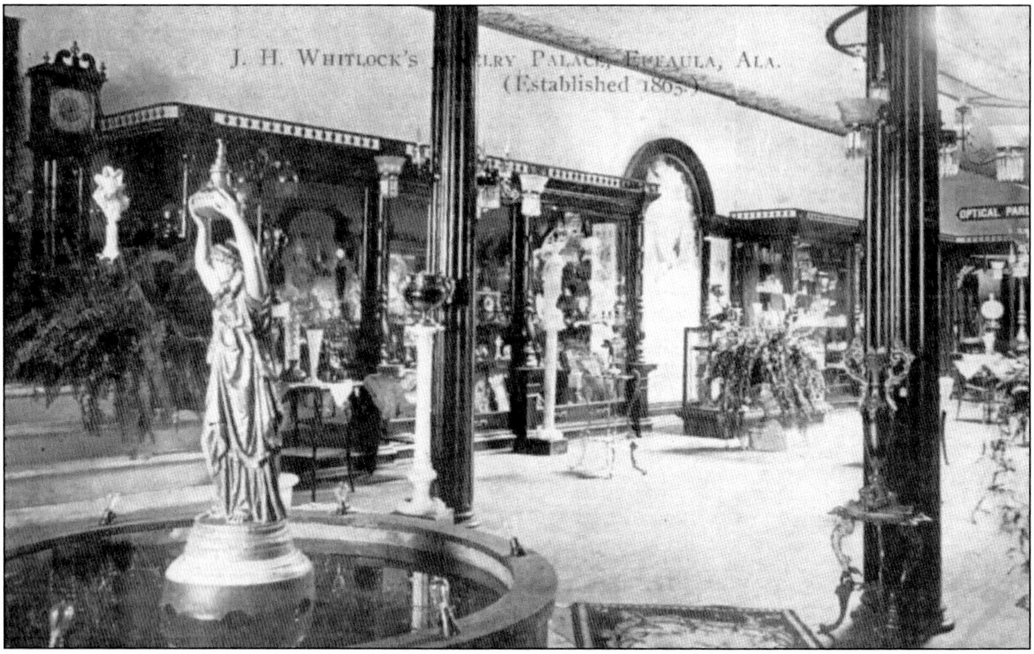

A closer look at the interior shows the magnificent fountain and wooden cases throughout Whitlock's Jewelry Palace that helped make Whitlock's famous. Towards the rear of the store, note the "Optical Parlors" sign-reminiscent of Dr. J.B. Whitlock, son of the business founder and a leading optometrist of his day. (Courtesy of Rob Schaffeld.)

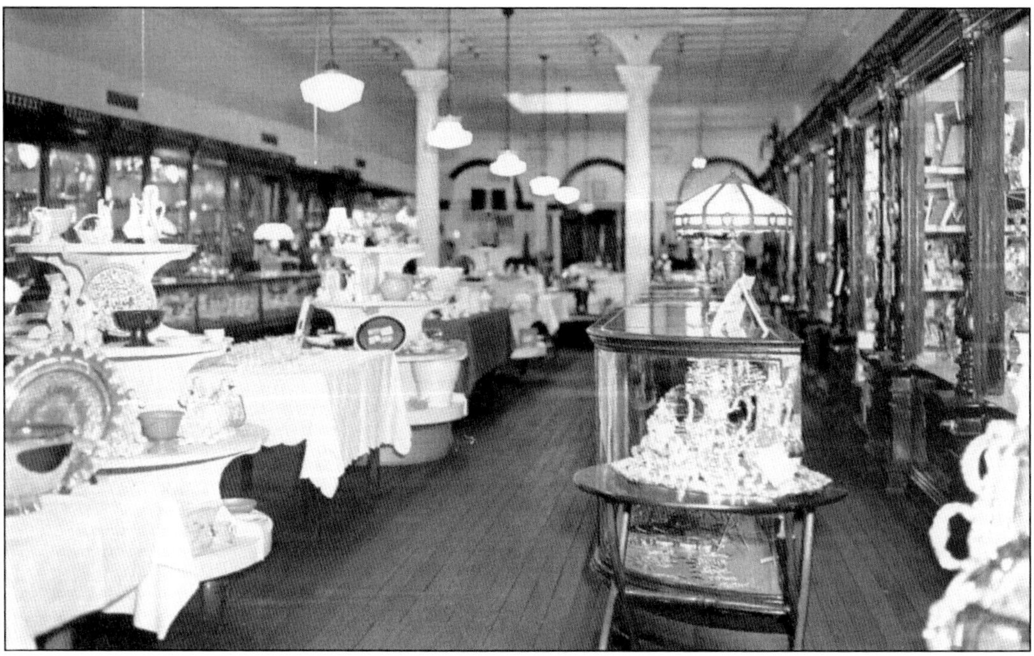

This 1960s postcard shows the inside of Whitlock Jewelry Store at its 1920–1970 location. The store was moved in 1970 to a building next door. Still in operation today, Whitlock's is Alabama's oldest jewelry store. (Courtesy of Doug Purzell.)

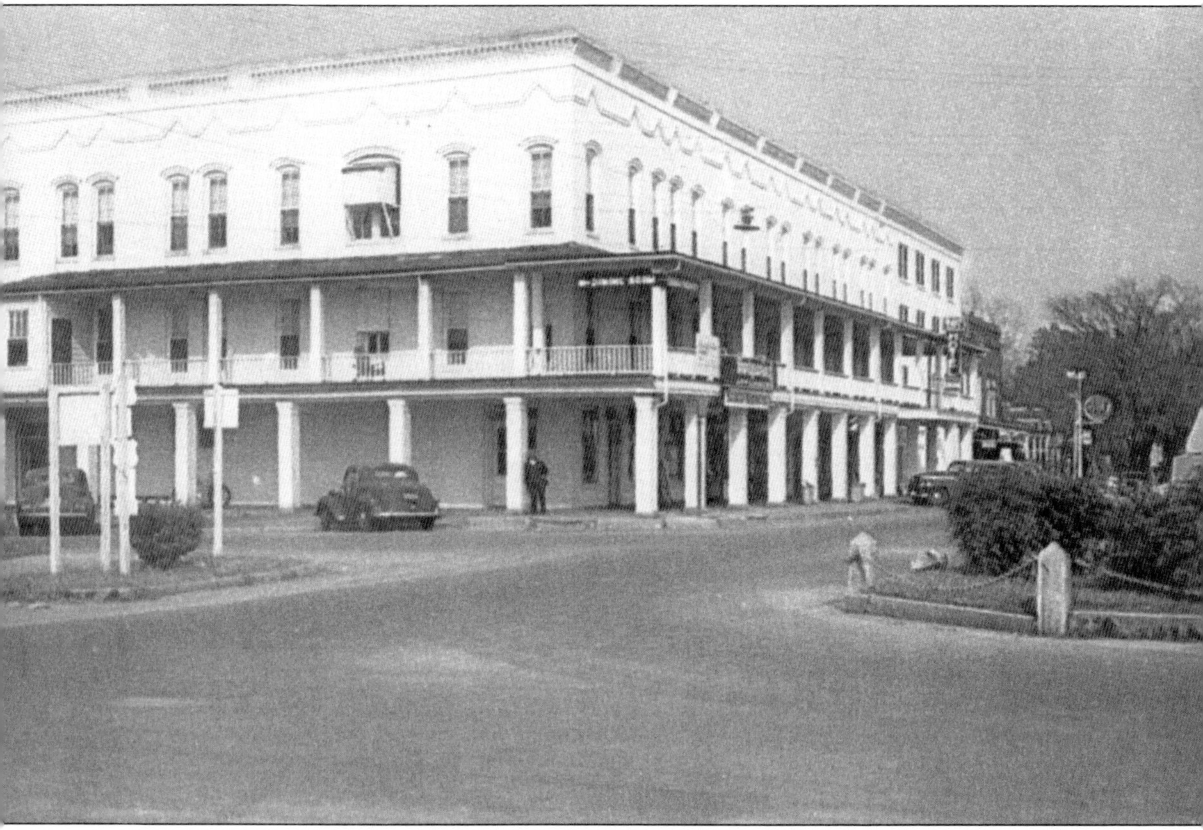

Built in 1885 on the site of the Old Central Hotel, the Bluff City Inn is shown here in the 1940s when it was painted white. It has since been restored to its original red brick. The back inscription reads "A Howard Dayton Hotel. Bluff City Inn-Eufaula AL. Located U.S. 41 and AL 82. A comfortable home away from home. Excellent dining room with reasonable prices. Informal—come as you are. Julius McCarroll, Manager. Phone No. 467" (Courtesy of James and Nan Palmer.)

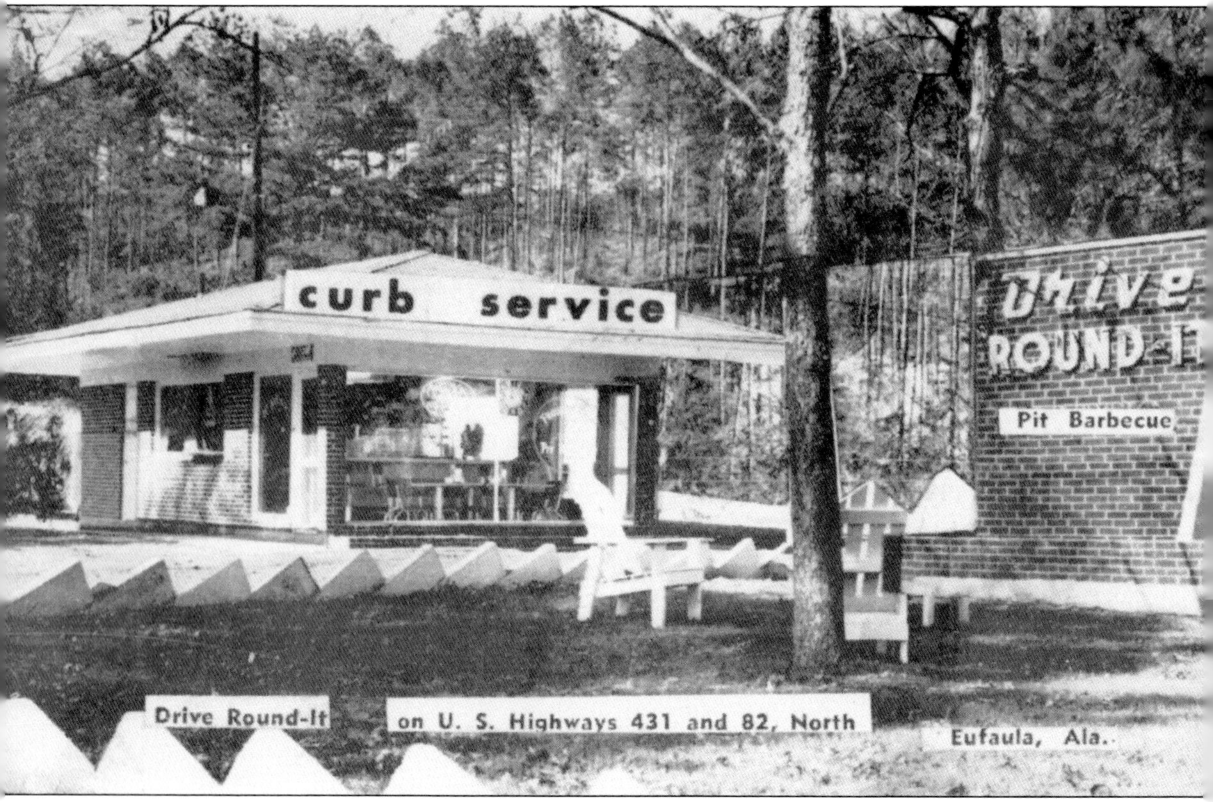

Located at the present-day site of Chewalla Restaurant, the Drive Round-It was a popular teenage hangout in the mid-1900s. Offering curb service, the Drive Round-It specialized in pit barbecue and served American classics such as hamburgers, hot dogs, and ice cream. Mr. Robert Hornsby Sr. was the proprietor. (Courtesy of Frank Mixon.)

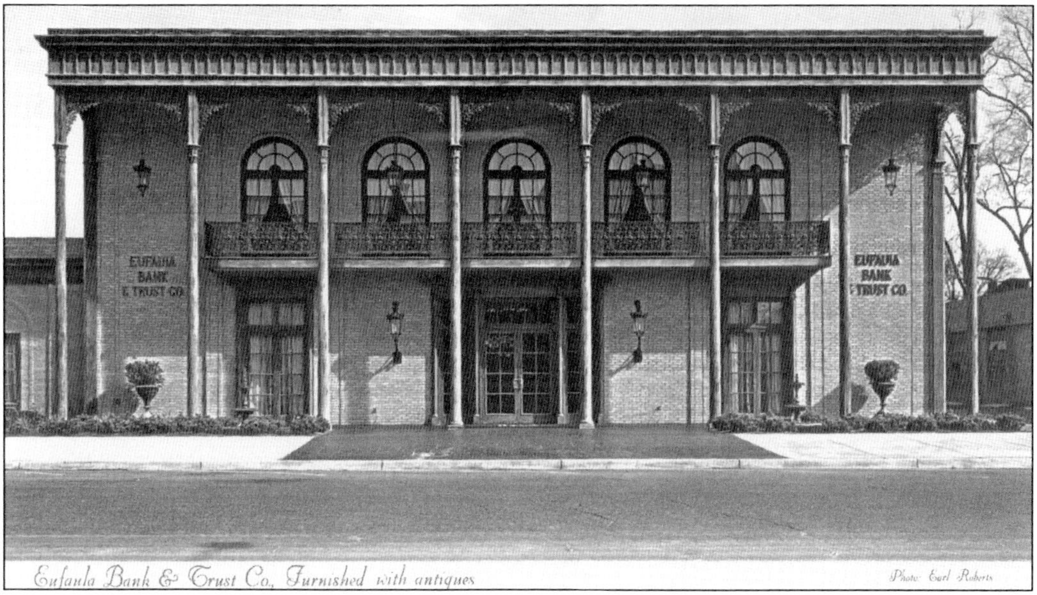

Opened in the summer of 1926, the Eufaula Bank & Trust Company has served the citizens of the area continually through present day. In 1969, this New Orleans–style building was constructed at a cost of $400,000 under the leadership of bank president L.Y. Dean III. Commerce South Bank, formerly Eufaula Bank & Trust, still operates at this location. (Courtesy of Historic Chattahoochee Commission.)

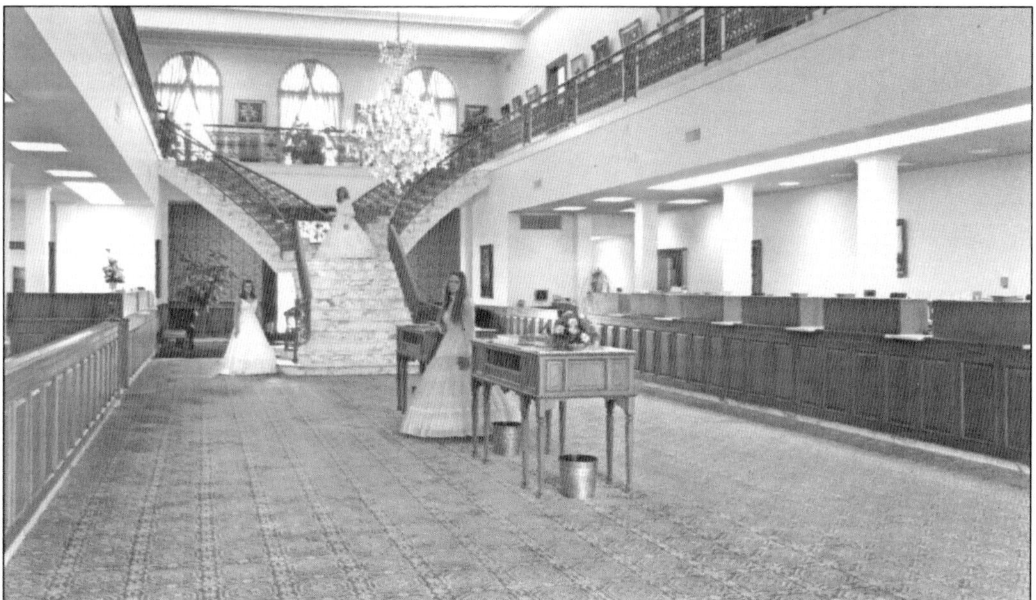

This Earl Roberts photo showcases the lobby of Eufaula Bank & Trust Company in the 1970s. The lobby features a Baccarat Crystal chandelier that originally hung in a French chateau near Paris, *c.* 1800. The staircase is made of Italian marble. (Courtesy of Historic Chattahoochee Commission.)

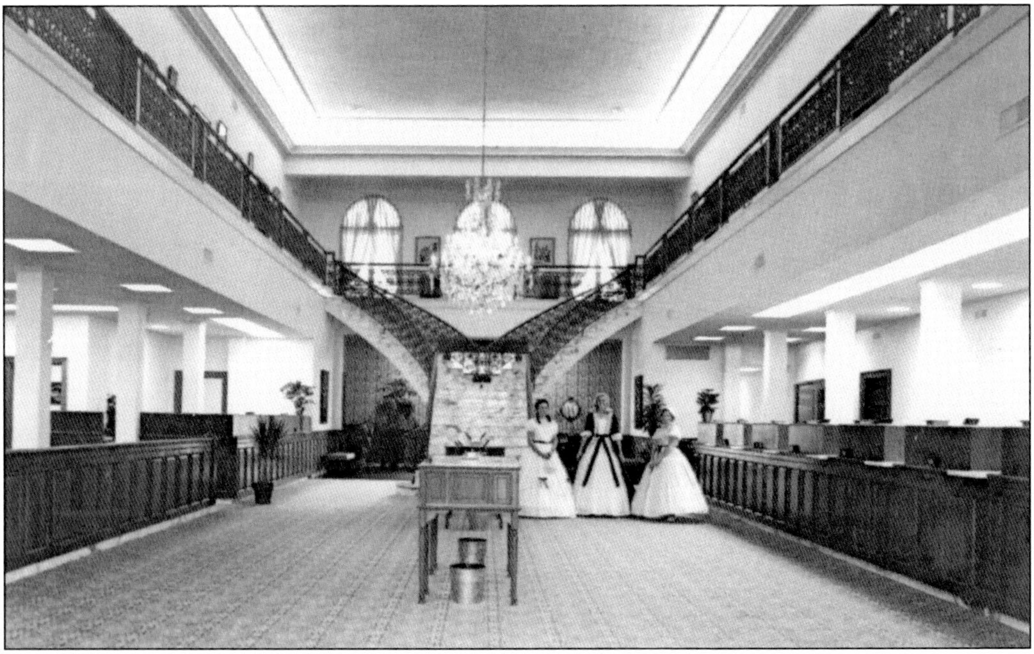

The exquisite lobby of the Eufaula Bank & Trust building is the setting for three lovely ladies dressed for the Eufaula Pilgrimage Tour of Homes. (Courtesy of Doug Purcell.)

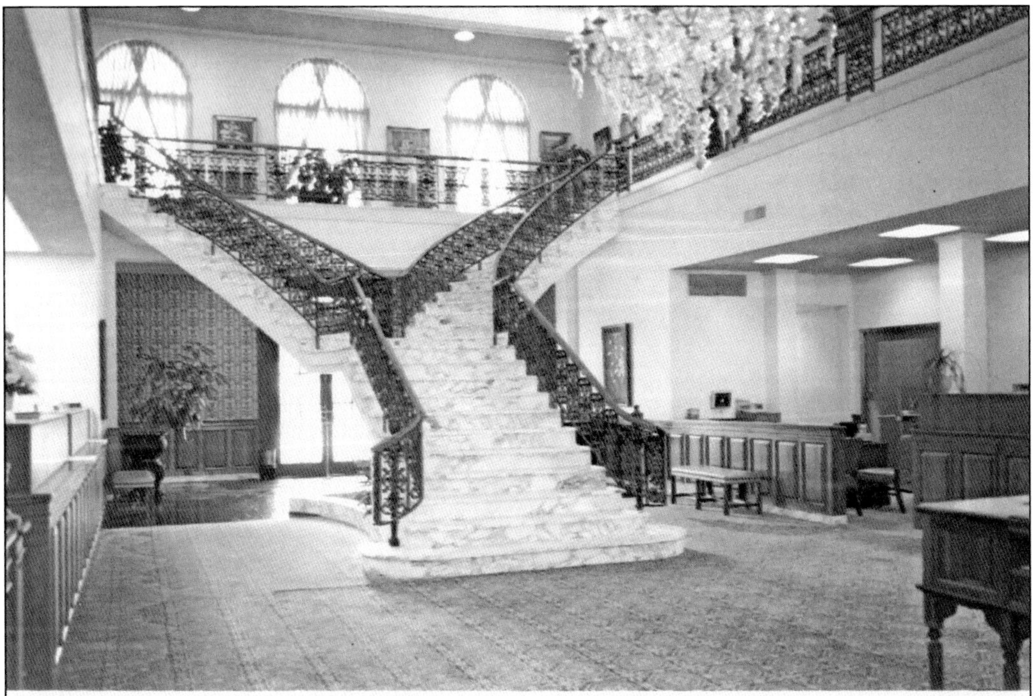

Completed in 1969, the Eufaula Bank & Trust Company houses many beautiful antiques and is a center of activity in downtown Eufaula. (Courtesy of Historic Chattahoochee Commission.)

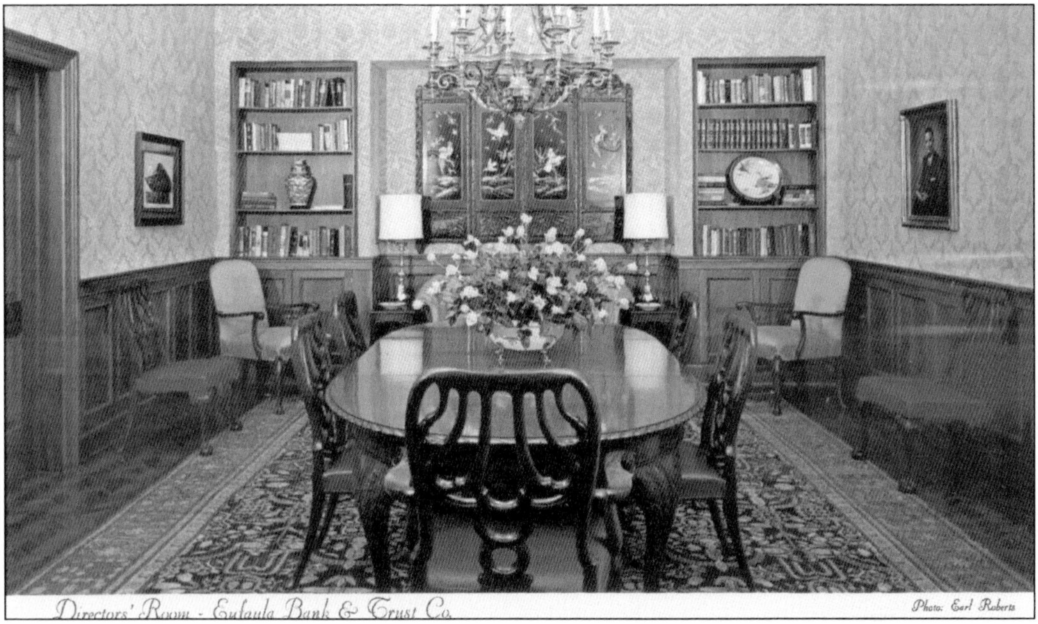

The Eufaula Bank & Trust Company director's room is furnished exclusively with antiques. Former bank president L.Y. Dean III's portrait hangs in the corner. This is one of several cards in a series showcasing the exquisite furnishings and architecture of the bank building. The series, along with several other cards in this book, was published by Earl Roberts Studio of Eufaula. (Courtesy of Historic Chattahoochee Commission.)

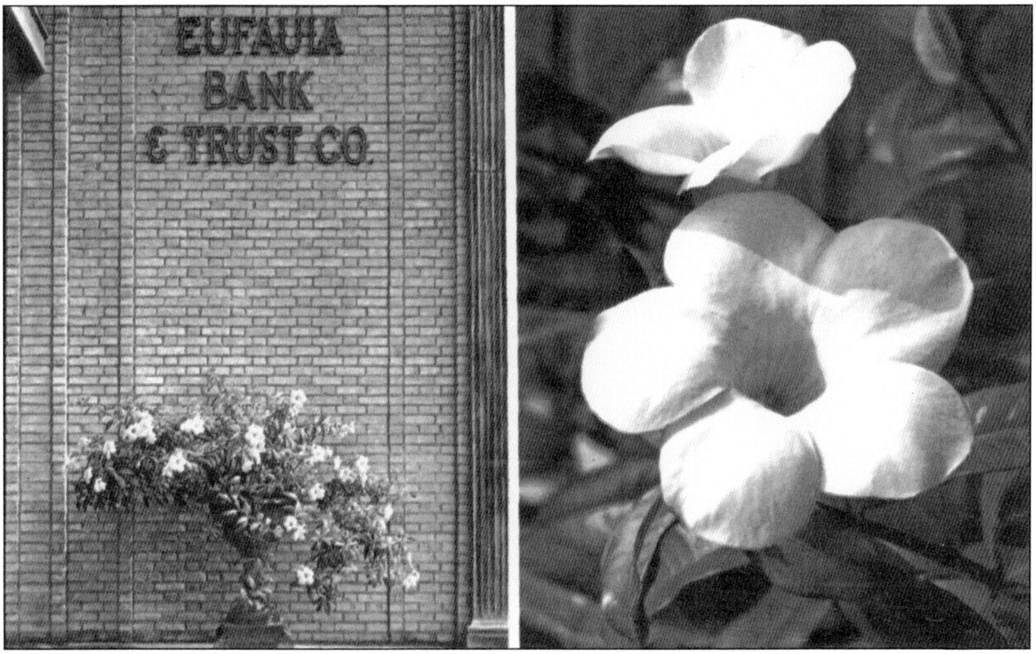

Another postcard published by Earl Roberts Studio shows allamanda blooming on the veranda of the Eufaula Bank & Trust building on East Broad Street. (Courtesy of Historic Chattahoochee Commission.)

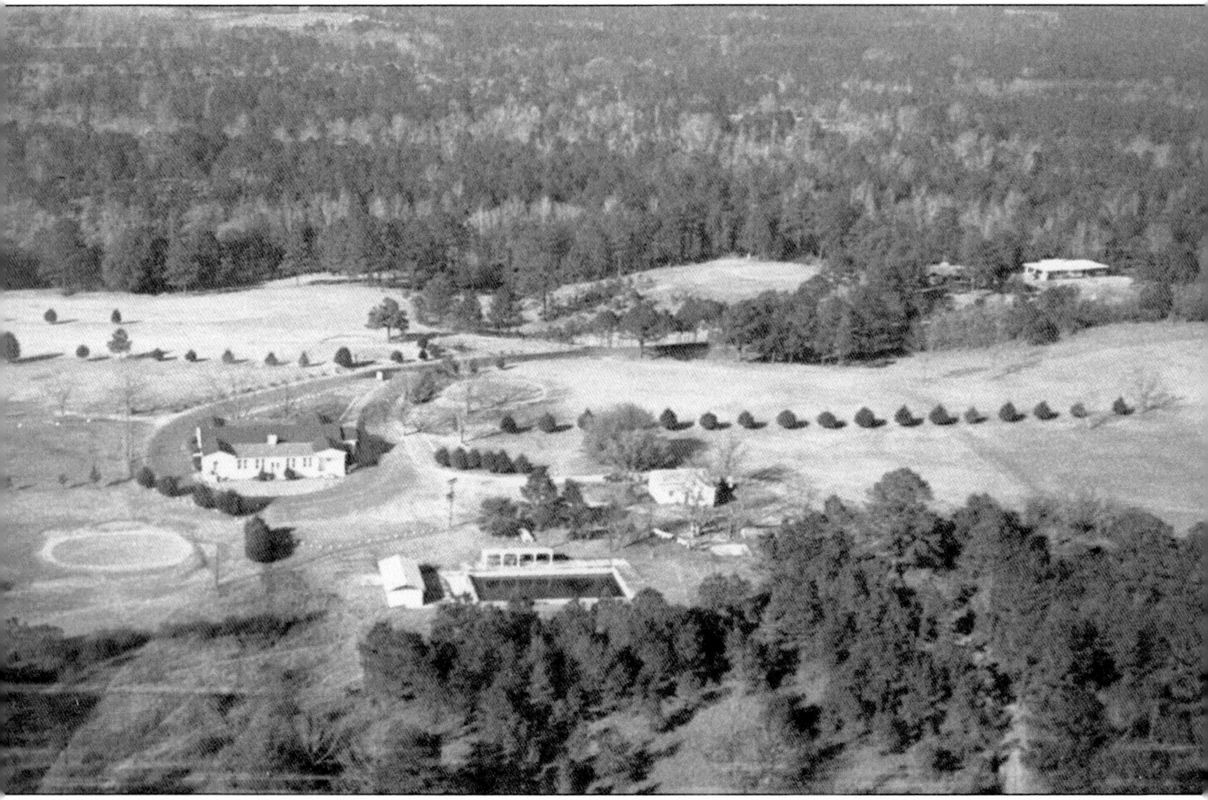

Chartered May 20, 1915, the Eufaula Country Club was originally built on land donated by Harmon Lampley. The original clubhouse was destroyed by fire and rebuilt in 1917. The club underwent major renovations and expansion in 1970. (Courtesy of Rob Schaffeld.)